Heartfelt ·

Andy, for all your unshakeable support, wisdom and unfailing love. Thank you for sharing this journey called life with me.

Mum, for all your courage, inspiration and unfailing faithfulness. Thank you for who you are.

My family and friends, for all your prayers, encouragement and unfailing loyalty. Thank you for being there.

Jacob, for all your heart, laughter and unfailing spark. Thank you for simply being my precious little boy.

Published in Scotland.

Unless otherwise noted, Scripture quotations are taken from HOLY BIBLE:NEW INTERNATIONAL VERSIONS ©1973, 1978, 1984, 2011 By International bible Society. Scripture verses marked NLT are taken from Holy Bible, New Living Translation © 1996, 2004, 2007. Scripture verses marked MSG are taken from The Message Bible in contemporary language, © 2004 Eugene H.Peterson. Scripture verses marked NKJV are taken from the New King James Version of the Bible © 1979, 1980, 1982. Scripture verses marked AMP are taken from the American Standard Version of the Amplified Bible © 1965, 1987, 2015

Printed in Airdrie, Scotland.

ISBN 978: - 1-9996309-0-4

For more information see www.fruitministries.com

Contents

Foreword

Dear Friend,

Thank you for opening the book now in your hands. It is a privilege to share even a window of life with you.

Many times, the pages you now see have been written then re written, crafted, then honed. All to refine the specific message placed deep within through the past eighteen years of life. With something so precious, it is not for me to casually scribe. Nor is it up to me to persuade you of its merits. My role is simply to steward the gift and to honour the giver. The rest, only He can do.

What is this precious gift? The precious gift is life. The *alive* sort of life. An exceptional life of absolute fullness - the sort of life only God could imagine.

Taking God at His word, this comes from my heart – I found every word is true. In return, I've been shown how to live the life He always promised – an amazing life of more colour, wonder and fulfilment than I could ever dream of. A life spent with Him, in Him, through Him and for Him.

Who is the giver of such an extravagant, meaningful, rewarding existence?

He is the Great I am. And He is my King.

God *is* life – and creator of The Promise.

1

Introduction

*'But you shall **receive power** when the Holy Spirit has come upon you;
and you shall be witnesses to Me in Jerusalem, and in all Judea and
Samaria, and to the end of the earth.'*

Acts 1:8 NKJV

It was 8am on the First of January 2017. As the new year dawned,
my eyes were awakened, stirred into consciousness from a vividly
clear dream. In it, the fingers of God wrote one simple name on a
large white stone. The name was Zoe. Replaying the image, a
conviction arose in my spirit. I was soon to find out why. Nine days
later came the unexpected diagnosis of an aggressive form of stage
3 cancer. In juxtaposition with this devastating news, I found Zoe in
the Greek means life; life in its fullest; abundant, eternal, filled with
vitality and flowing over. Zoe is life as God has in Himself. The God
kind of life. He'd sent me a message. *This* was the promise.

The ink was still wet. The ink from the initial manuscript of the very
book you now read. Would the contents survive the fire to be walked
through? Knowing and believing everything my Bible said, I took a
deep breathe. God was there. He brought stillness, He brought
peace, He brought certainty. He brought a reaction within I could
never have predicted. Not fear or trembling; what He brought
instead was an expectant anticipation – what would my God do?

Was the Zoe kind of life He promised really possible, even when
looking down the lens of a terminal disease? I'd written it, but now
was the time to see if every promise was actually true. In 2017, *this*
was my assignment.

Allow me to alleviate any fears this may elicit right away. This is not some sensationalist story of 'one woman's fight for survival', or a 'what I did and so should you' type of book. Nor is it a cathartic form of expressing a personal response to such news. It was written way before diagnosis. This book is about the truth of a simple promise. We can live a Zoe life, regardless of our circumstances. This book is about how to make it a reality.

The power is in who He is.

*'For if, by the trespass of the one man, death reigned through that one man, how much more will those who **receive** God's abundant provision of grace and of the gift of righteousness **reign in life** through the one man, Jesus Christ!'*
Romans 5:17 NIV

In many respects you could replace the word cancer for any challenging circumstance in life, be they big or small. In God's eyes, they are all equal anyway.

Whether we're travelling smoothly on the road, or whether we face a mountain before us, His word tells us there is a wonderful way to live life – every day. Not from anything we conjure up ourselves. Diligent pursuit, optimistic bravado and fierce determination will only ever get us so far. Sooner or later, there's always something we encounter that's bigger than us. Instead, the strength available to all of us is the power of God Himself. Our power is who Jesus is.

It is enticing to hear we are not at the mercy of our circumstances, our character, our upbringing or our world. A life lived this way could be our biggest witness. But can we truly reign in life – all the time? Are you reigning in yours right now? - consistently?

Whenever Jesus spoke of life, He was referring to the Zoe kind of life. A life so complete, exceptional and unlimited, we probably can't grasp the immensity of it. Abundant life, as God has in Himself. (John 5:26) Re-reading His voice through this lens brings a whole new dimension to how we could be living – everyday. What a prospect to get our heads around. *This* is the glorious life He always intended us to live. *This* is the promise.

The power is God within.

'His divine power has given us everything we need for life and godliness through our knowledge of him who called us by his own glory and goodness'.
2 Peter 1: 3-4 NIV

Time and again, we're promised all we need: the fullness of God (Eph 3:19. John 1:16) and fullness of life. (John 10:10) - whether relating to our nitty gritty day-to-day's, our life missions calling, or anywhere in between. So how often do our lives consistently manifest such a bold claim?

If you are anything like me, you may have spent a lifetime doing, reacting, controlling and trying. But when we were saved, Christ came to live in us. (Rom 8:10) In that moment, all the fullness of who He is was made available to us. Yet with all of heaven on our side, somehow our lives don't always seem to reflect such promises.

For years I believed in God, considered myself a committed Christian and thought I knew what all of this meant. And yet, in my life I was always wrestling with something... disappointments, the busyness of life, worry. Whether focussed on me, on others or on the world at large, my reactions to life varied greatly. Even when life seemed good, my character would often lead to challenges; being compulsive meant I pursued things – relentlessly. Being so driven meant I would strive to the point of burnout. Being feisty meant I could be impatient. Being impatient meant I lived in stress. Fill in the gaps. You'll know your own default settings and what triggers the shadow in you. So even though as a believer I knew what my Bible said, life didn't always seem to manifest all the promises God's Word contained.

I'd experienced seasons of His power. But they were just that. They were glimpses of what God had really put inside me. They were moments.

If you think about your own daily life for a second, how many of these responses do you find you recognise? As you reflect on your own tendencies, do any of the following resonate with your life today?

- Do habits, busyness and emotion prevent you from consistently connecting to the Holy Spirit first in all things? How often do you inadvertently (or consciously) find good intentions, the desired outcomes or your own resolve don't last?

- Do you convince others or yourself you have it all sorted, whilst inside you wrestle with things? (For example: stress or fears that shake you, worry you or make you feel over your head) How often do you doubt yourself, doubt God or that His promises belong to you?

- Do you find yourself self-absorbed or caught up by life, so you miss, don't seek or run away from God's steer? (For example: yo-yoing between what He says and striving to figure things out yourself) How often do you become lost/confused about what to do, heavily burdened, or locked inside your own hamster wheel of thinking?

- Do you struggle with the same things over and over? (For example: over committing, jealousy, being offended, impulsiveness, making sound decisions, certain people, temptations) How often do you make headway, only to find you wobble under pressure, crisis or in circumstances that trigger the very things you don't want to do?

- Do you ache to be more than ordinary, seek spiritual gifts, or simply lack the confidence, capacity or capability to be the best you can be? (For example: insecurity, weariness, or personal limitations interfere) How often does your existing skill miss the impact needed, or your future potential become blocked?

- Do you long for more of God, intensely desire His Kingdom come, or crave His sovereign power? (For example: healing, salvations, positive resolution of an issue) How often do you experience mighty moves of God or find yourself negating their possibility?

- Do you need a change, a break-through or deliverance in your life, that seems illusive or out of your reach? Do you feel you are trapped by your circumstances or your reaction to them?

These are the very challenges Jesus came to set us free from. (John 8:37) Setting us free enables the 'more' God always envisaged for us.

'It is for freedom that Christ has set us free. Stand firm, then, and do not let yourselves be burdened again by a yoke of slavery.'
Galatians 5:1 NIV

The power is exponential

*'And the disciples were **continually** filled [throughout their hearts and souls] with joy and with the Holy Spirit'.*
Acts 13:52 AMP

Over the years, it has taken the unfolding of life and all it has thrown at my feet, for God to teach me how those moments of His power can turn into hours, those hours into days and those days into a way of being. It has taken intentional focus, determination and obedience to go beyond. It can be hard to press into God when our flesh is dictating the show. And maybe that's the point. Because we cannot do it alone. Thankfully, in His grace, we don't have to!

Despite how at times I have denied, dismissed, disregarded and disobeyed God, He has never left my side. Through the power of His Spirit, He's gradually led me into a life of ever-increasing richness. If it's available for me, it's available for you too. Through the pages of this book, maybe how I learned the hard way means that you don't have to.

The power is His Spirit

'And now I will send the Holy Spirit, just as my Father promised. But stay here in the city until the Holy Spirit comes and fills you with power from heaven.'
                                                    Luke 24:49 NIV

When we walk closely, hand in hand with the mighty Holy Spirit, the good news is, we can receive all the help we will ever need. And He is a genius at what He does! Through Him, God's grace, perseverance and love teach us the life-long journey to fullness of life. The Zoe kind of life.

But mention the Spirit and many misconceptions can spring to mind. Let's start by saying what this is not: This is not some mystical, contrived, forced, or psychologically induced state of mind. And it's not only available to the elite, enlightened or exclusive few. It's available to everyone. Life in the Spirit is not weird and doesn't somehow make us involuntarily do strange things; it's actually the most natural, authentic way of living. Neither is it about us learning how to 'do'. It's simply about learning how to receive; regardless of what our circumstances, our soul or the enemy tries to throw at us. All we need to do is learn how to receive the most unforced, practical and powerful support we can ever find. The lifeblood help of Holy Spirit Himself. This, the very Spirit of Jesus, is what powers us to become all of who Jesus actually is.

The Holy Spirit was sent to live with our spirit and when we learn to be led by Him, (Gal 5:25) we receive perspective, character, knowledge, ability and impact that alone, we could never create.

Think about the times you have rushed to church, or that prayer meeting when your head is full of 'stuff' from the busy, stressful day you have just had. You arrive still thinking about what you need to do and probably don't quite feel in the mood for what lies ahead. You re-run conversations and may start to feel agitated about something that's happened. Or maybe you just feel distracted, tired and unresponsive. But as you start to pray and praise, something starts to lift inside. Before you know it, all your inner attention is focussed on something completely different. You've been elevated into consciousness of spirit, which by-passes all earthly logic and reason. It connects you to your Father in heaven. Suddenly, the mind-set you walked in with has totally shifted. You now see things from a totally different perspective. You are in tune with what your spirit is reflecting - through the whispers of the Holy Spirit within you. It's in this space that we often feel most complete.

The Zoe kind of life is possible when we think, feel and do what the Holy Spirit guides us into. To do this we have to learn to step beyond ourselves, to hear and then honour what our spirit is being shown – a divine relationship where almighty God partners with human-kind.

The power is in the partnering

*'You did not choose me, but I Chose you and **appointed** you to go and bear fruit – fruit that will last.'*
John 15:16 NIV

It blows my mind to think God chose me for this. He chose you too, and the beauty of our commission is the relational partnership it actually requires. Whilst God is sovereign, He also requires our engagement. Fulfilling this partnership requires all of God to be combined with all of who we have been made to be. Through the truth in His word, by His direct leading and by learning from my plentiful mistakes, over the years He has revealed how to step out from my own grasp. But it has meant taking accountability to follow that gentle, skilful guidance. Something tells me I am not alone.

Allow me to expand with a short story.

In my secular business I coach executives. Here I was on assignment, but on this occasion, I didn't quite know why I was there. Until I met Mark. The Global Marketing Director of a growing International company, he was part of a Board I'd been asked to support. It was an entrepreneurial, fast-paced environment. Mark was quiet and seemed hesitant of his place. His stature on the team didn't quite reflect the seniority of the position he held and he was yet to make his impact. He was overshadowed and overlooked. Then I got a surprise. In a one to one conversation, Mark revealed he was a practising Christian. Somehow, I just didn't see it.

The theme of his feedback centred around his confidence and underneath this, his sense of identity. His peers could see glimmers of potential, but were not yet experiencing the contribution they wanted to see. As we sat there together, I could sense Holy Spirit spurring me on to challenge this.

'Mark, you've said you're a practising Christian. That means you have all the power of Jesus himself living right there inside you. You have all the authority, all the ability, all the character and all the strength you are ever going to need. Inside you, there is an advantage that everyone else on this Board could only ever dream about. But that's just not shining. Why is that? What's holding you back?' *'If anyone is in Christ, he is a new creation; old things have passed away, all things have become new'.* (2 Corinthians 5:17)

Momentarily, Mark seemed stunned. In such a secular environment, the words had been unexpected. They had been direct. We both held the moment. After what seemed the longest pause, Mark finally replied: 'I needed to hear that. I really needed to hear that. It's true. I've been a Christian for ten years now. I know my Bible. I know what Jesus did for me. And I believe it. But I don't know how to live it. When I'm in church, everything seems to make sense. But out here, in this reality, somehow, I always seem to stumble. I doubt myself. I hold back. And I compromise. I know there's so much more in me; I know there is so much more to all of this. It's time I stopped accepting second best. I want to make an impact. But how do I do that? How do I actually live it all out?'

He was talking about the Zoe kind of life.

For a second, put yourself in Mark's shoes. Just imagine your own life: your home life, your work, your family, friends and your social environments. Think about the rough and the smooth, the mundane and the complicated. What would happen if every day, in every situation, you experienced every promise The Word holds - even in the trickiest days, circumstances and relationships you have in your life? What if you were able to operate in Christ; with all His characteristics, qualities, inheritance and power? What impact would that have on you and on those around you? What difference would it make to outcomes, to atmospheres and to the influence you could have? How would it change your life? How could it change the world around you? How different would it look to the life you have now?

The power is in His grace

*'Now to Him who is able to [carry out His purpose and] do superabundantly more than all that we dare ask or think [infinitely beyond our greatest prayers, hopes, or dreams], according to His power **that is at work** within us'.*
Ephesians 3:20 AMP

God loves you too much to leave you where you are. Your circumstances may change, get worse, get better, get harder, get easier, feel good, feel bad, feel challenging, feel rewarding and on it goes. This is the cycle of real life. You may say, but what of my circumstances? – I still need answer to prayer in so many areas. God knows all that – even before you ask Him.

But when you learn to be *in Him* in your circumstances, your circumstances will lose their hold, their power and their relevance to your level of victory. All hold from the enemy simply disappears. What if I told you that *whatever* your circumstances are, there is a way to live that keeps your joy, your peace, your emotional stability and your hope totally constant? With no fear in the night, with no dread in the morning, with no foggy confusion through the day, with no stress in all the margins. He is the good news - and the good news is, there is a way to live this way. How is that possible? When we allow Him to, through the grace He lavishes upon us. (Eph 1:7-8)...

...2017 proved it. A year further on, the tumour, accounting for two thirds of the breast tissue it once occupied has gone. But perhaps more incredible than what was taken, is what was given through the journey. With His empowering grace, God enabled me to live every day in freedom, devoid of the fear, uncertainty and the trauma often associated with this dreadful disease. Instead, He poured unshakeable resolve and peaceful stillness. Joy replaced anxiety, peace stilled the turmoil and His presence was the lamp that navigated me through the many twists and turns that unfolded. When chemotherapy failed, God never faltered. When Doctors couldn't agree, God always knew. When un-needed surgery was booked, God always blocked its path.

Friends, His grace is the empowering force that covers everything; what we need, what the situation needs and what the outcome needs. Whatever your circumstances are, whether big challenges or simply the day-to-day-ness of life, He's already walked before you. He is utterly perfect and in everything you ever experience, He is more than able. In Him, is all the provision you will ever need. (Psa 16:5)

The promise is our hope

'But thanks be to God, who gives us the victory [as conquerors] through our Lord Jesus Christ.'
1 Corinthians 15:57 AMP

Eighteen years ago, I finally embraced the God who through those years taught me the contents of this book – how to live it – how to make it real.

Was the Zoe kind of life really possible, even when looking down the lens of a terminal illness? Before diagnosis I hoped so. Now, with faith that has passed through the furnace, I *know* so. And maybe this was the point. In the most unexpected way, I found myself living the book I wrote. Under the intensity of the biggest fight of my life, every word in it was tried and tested. And in the process, was proved to stand the heat. God knew it would. He needed me to know it too.

Who did I find this merciful, sovereign and faithful God to be? He is the God of hope.

Routed in His word, under the covering of His spirit and through prayers to heaven itself, we can live life to the full, regardless of our circumstances. *This* is His promise. A rich, vivid, glorious life, freely available to all of us.

If God can show someone like me how to live it, He can show anyone. Devoid of formal theological schooling, who am I to even share such a thing? Perhaps that is the point. The kind of Zoe life God always intended is for all of us. No qualification is needed. Whatever your circumstances, background or view of yourself, this promise is also for you.

My prayer is that in the pages of this book, you will gain the insight, encouragement and empowerment, to learn how to live what you believe. This is God's intended design. To live the abundant Zoe kind of life. All you need to do is make that choice - this book in your hands could show you how.

'May the God of hope fill you with all joy and peace in believing [through the experience of your faith] that by the power of the Holy Spirit you will abound in hope and overflow with confidence in His promises.'
Romans 15:13 AMP

What comes next?

'If we [claim to] live by the [Holy] Spirit, we must also walk by the Spirit [with personal integrity, godly character, and moral courage — our conduct empowered by the Holy Spirit].'
Galatians 5:25 AMP

We live in an age that is awash with instructions. We have the knowledge and a wealth of teaching at our fingertips. But there is a big difference between intellectually understanding our bible and practically being able to apply it. So, this book does not intend to set out the doctrines of The Book we follow. Those principles are for you to love and explore. That's *what* you believe. Instead of being heavy on theory, this is not a book of biblical teaching; it's a book of biblical application. Designed to help you learn how to apply the truth, it's a practical handbook you can return to over and over again. The Promise is about *how* to live it.

God's word is His blueprint and our guide in The Promise. Accrued from years of study, personal experience and God's leading, the pattern we will follow is based entirely on The Word. Designed as a handbook to work through, this is something you can read and master. Or it's something you can dip in and out of, using the approach to address specific challenges in your life over time. Whether reading it alone, or using it with 2 or 3 others, it combines biblical activities with coaching best practice, so you can learn how to habitually live the Zoe kind of life. This book is about making *what* we believe a reality – by showing us *how* to live it.

Using practical steps, we will look at how to cultivate the heart, the discipline and the spiritual maturity to consistently develop the Zoe kind of life. By working with the Holy Spirit as the ultimate coach, He takes us, guides us and creates the changes within. We need to commit the decision, discipline and dedication to the process. Holy Spirit does the rest.

In part one we will see what the Zoe kind of life actually looks like. In this we will unpack the promises that can transform our lives. By looking at what's actually available, you can then decide what you would love to see more of. These promises will encourage, challenge and propel you into action.

In part two we make it all real, focussing on how to develop the Zoe kind of life. In this, we explore the biblical blueprint of how to receive, nurture and live this way. With practical step-by-step activities, this will help you put it all into practice.

In part three we consider the impact this will have, both on your life and on the world around you. As we discover the deeper benefits, we explore why it's all worth it. This helps us understand the 'more' God always intended for us. This will help you cement the commitment needed to embed the Zoe kind of life. So, if like me, you often want to skip to the end of the book, the overview at the start of part three may satisfy that curiosity.

You can experience the freedom and wonder that comes from living this way. Step fully into Him and step out into the world. May ever-increasing consistency, power, fulfilment and impact be yours – in abundance. Amen.

Reflections

'God made the earth by his power; he founded the world by his wisdom and stretched out the heavens by his understanding'.
Jeremiah 10:12 NIV

When I stop to consider the magnitude of this, it makes me realise that I'd sure rather have Him in charge of me, than me in charge of me!

Pause for a moment to stop and think about your own life.

- What difference would a rich, vivid, glorious life of abundance mean to you? A life where you live in all of Jesus, with all His provision and all His promises, all of the time – a quality of life that is unrattled by external circumstances, how you feel or what season you find yourself in.

- What would the Zoe kind of life mean to you?

This is the *more* that Jesus came to offer us.

As you ponder these questions, spend some time praying about what is stirred. Allow this to organically merge into a conversation with your Father. Allow time for silence and consciously allow the Holy Spirit to flow.

Is there anything else He says?

When you are ready, let's begin.

Part one

The promises of Zoe life

*'The one who keeps God's commands **lives in Him**, and He in them. And this is how we know that He lives in us: We know it by the Spirit He gave us.'*

1 John 3:24 NIV

2

The promises revealed

'The thief comes only in order to steal and kill and destroy. I came that they may have and enjoy life, and have it in abundance [to the full, till it overflows].
John 10:10 AMP

How often do we read a verse and skip over the depths of its meaning? What does overflowing fullness of life mean to you? Pause for thought. What could that practically look like in your life today? Now take that and multiply it by infinity and you may just catch a glimpse of what God wants to give you - in this life, not just in the next.

Now if that differs from your current reality, what is the enemy taking that really belongs to you? What could you be experiencing?

Our Bibles are full of incredible promises and these promises become real when we develop the Zoe kind of life...

... After ten years of miss-carriages and Doctors left scratching their heads, on the second of May 2011, along came our one and only child. A trophy of God's faithfulness, Jacob is the wonderful little boy my husband and I were gifted with. At night, as his head hits the comfy pillow, he whispers the Lord's prayer, before dropping peacefully into slumber. 'Thy Kingdom come' is a well-known phrase, with a profound meaning. All of heaven brought here, to earth. It all sounds wonderful, but how is that even possible when we are trapped in the demands of a busy, fallen, complicated world?

*'For in Christ all the fullness of the Deity lives in bodily form, and **in Christ you have been brought to fullness.** He is the head over every power and authority'.*
Colossians 2:9-10 NIV

It's possible by living in Christ. Romans 8 tells us we live in Christ by the power of the Holy Spirit in us. Taking just seven key components from the treasure of what this means, we will now explore how living in Him has the power to transform our lives. In Him we are promised:

1. His presence (v35)
2. His significance (v17)
3. His perspective (v27)
4. His nature (v29)
5. His empowerment (v31)
6. His sovereignty (v33)
7. His strength (v37)

'Remain in me, as I also remain in you. No branch can bear fruit by itself; it must remain in the vine. Neither can you bear fruit unless you remain in me.'
John 15:4 NIV

Try as we might to do life in our own steam, the Zoe kind of life is only possible by abiding in Jesus – consistently. He is our provision.

Living **in** Christ, these seven key promises lead us into the heart of the Zoe life.

1. Through *His presence*, we receive *spiritual intimacy*. The glow from this love stills us and replaces our empty independence with blissful inner communion with God. This becomes our peace. (Exo 33:14. 3:17. John 14:27)

2. Through *His significance*, we learn our inheritance and from it, our *renewed identity*. This confidence brings certainty from

knowing we are a child of the King. This becomes our authority. (Gal 4:7. Luke 10:19)

3. With *His perspective*, we gain the clearance needed *to Hear God*. This clarity replaces our limited thoughts with insight that comes through the ascended lens of heaven's view. This becomes our joy. (Col 3:1. Psalm 16:11)

4. With *His nature*, we gain the virtue needed to *accelerate our ability to change.* This character creates a hunger to be transformed into all God made us to be. This becomes our motivation. (Psalm 41:12, 2 Cor 3:18)

5. With *His empowerment*, we receive *heightened ability*. This anointing replaces grinding effort with natural flow. This becomes our confidence. (Acts 1:8. 2 Cor 3:5)

6. Through *His sovereignty*, we build the trust to stake everything on God's *supernatural might*. Our belief in such supremacy replaces all earthly limitation with the impossible. This deepens our faith. (1 Chron 29:11-12. 2 Cor 5:7)

7. With *His strength*, we build the conquering spirit that enables us to deal with anything. This brings us *victory*. More of Him is exchanged for less of us. This becomes our wholeness. (Phil 4:13. Josh 1:9)

When we live in Christ in this way, it is His grace that provides all the virtue we need. **His power in us is the provision that enables the very promises He makes.**

The chances are you may well recognise many of these glorious signs in your life already. As you read, just imagine what the impact would be if you experienced all these things all the time! These are the components that enable us to reign in life, consistently, in all circumstances.

Taking one key promise at a time, let's now explore the potential that God has placed within us; the potential that comes with the Zoe kind of life.

'It's in Christ that you, once you heard the truth and believed it (this Message of your salvation), found yourselves home free—signed, sealed, and delivered by the Holy Spirit. This signet from God is the first instalment on what's coming, a reminder that we'll get everything God has planned for us, a praising and glorious life.'
Ephesians 1:13-14 MSG

3

Promise 1
His presence – our spiritual intimacy

The loving peace of inner communion with God.

'Then [with a deep longing] you will seek Me and require Me
[as a vital necessity] and [you will] find Me when you search
for Me with all your heart'.
Jeremiah 29:13 AMP

'Cast your cares on the Lord and He will sustain you; He will
never let the righteous be shaken'
Psalm 55:22 NIV

...'The heartbeat is slowing again, it's gone right down this time'. Silence... More silence... Then action: 'There's no time for an emergency C section, we have to get this baby out. Now'.

To avoid the fear and panic setting into the room, I'd not looked into the consultant's face. It was life or death. When our baby came, he was in trouble. Placed immediately in an incubator and whisked straight to intensive care, we had no idea what was happening, how he was or whether he would live.

How I'd longed to hold that baby in my arms, but he was gone. Hours later, we were still none the wiser. He was breathing, but his condition was critical. With no idea what to expect, in the days to come, if he made it, warnings about brain damage were amongst the conversations. Hours turned into days, as we stared through the small holes of the incubator, watching the rise and fall of his tiny chest. Tubes fed through his nose, on limbs so small they were unable to retain the catheter wires. So fragile, so vulnerable, so unaware. Nervously glancing at the beeping noises of the machines he was wired to, we wondered with every alarm, what was going to happen next?

I was exhausted, stunned and confused. But despite the horror and uncertainty of the situation, I was also being held. Held by a source far greater than the circumstances themselves. Held by the presence of God within...

What is spiritual intimacy?

Spiritual intimacy is the gift that comes from God's presence, when we experience the weight of His being descending upon us. This is the deepest connection with Him - the loving inner communion with God.

It's not about a feeling, although incredible feelings can emerge from it. With an immeasurable tangibility that defies such an intangible grace, when His presence immerses us, we just *know* it.

Think for a moment of the times when you've been caught in such a way. Perhaps during worship, when sitting with a steaming mug of coffee, or when feeling the sand between your toes on the beach. It can happen anytime in any way. I've even known people who don't know God to have experienced this heavenly consciousness.

When does this happen with you? Just dwell for a moment in the memory of the times His powerful presence has washed over you like floods of living water. (John 4:4) Can anything compare to the indescribable, majestic beauty of His touch?

Contrast this with the times you're wrapped up in life, busy inside your own head or operating on auto-pilot. How empty, unfulfilling and lonely is this in comparison? The truth of life, is that disconnection from the God who lives in us is more frequent than we'd like.

Possible for anyone, anywhere, connection with His presence isn't limited to the one-off experiences when we intentionally draw close. As a friend of mine once said, 'it's easy on a Sunday. It's Monday through Saturday I need help with'.

If we engage, this can be a way of living. In airports, on buses, out running, at the hairdressers, in the boardroom, at the kitchen sink, at the playground, through the day and in the middle of the night – it can be a constant, beautiful, vivid communion.

Our God is always in the mood and never says He doesn't have the time. This is a spirit bond that never hurts, disappoints or lets us down. It's ever faithful. With one breath He can instantaneously re fill us with His Spirit, as our awareness of His presence, His touch and

His light gradually become more and more prominent. Through it, He shows us His heart.

With this type of intimacy comes a sense of protection; we feel under His wing. This brings oneness. In the tranquillity of this stillness, we know we are not alone.

When we experience hurt, difficulty or pain we think is unbearable or impossible, it is our Lord who can stand in the gap and be our strength and comfort. Even when utterly bereft, the love and embrace we receive eases all sorrow, as His presence carries us into healing waters. Whether instantly or over time, He gently and sensitively restores our brokenness. In contrast, when we experience joy, it is our King who applauds and dances alongside us. And in the calmness of life going steady, He tenderly watches and waits for our attention. This is the nature of the God we serve. Present with us in every breathe – whether we know it or not.

Sometimes we encounter such presence through His Word. Sometimes as we pray and worship. Maybe it's when we are serving. Sometimes it's even in the silence; just knowing He is right there without anything needing to be said.

As we draw nearer and nearer in this way, we really get to know who God is. God is love. He is the ever-present Father, who brings us unconditional, perfect, pure, matchless love. And as this happens, we can't help but pass it onto others.

When you learn how to live the Zoe kind of life, you will experience this connection all the time - not just when you remember to engage with Him, when you have a crisis or when you have room in your day.

What spiritual intimacy can bring

'I love those who love me, and those who seek me find me'

Proverbs 8:17 NIV

Living the Zoe kind of life, there is a way for you to operate from a place of being loved, knowing your protection. When you embrace His presence, you activate your spiritual intimacy. This becomes your peace.

Imagine your own life for a moment and consider what the impact of this could practically mean to you. The more you develop this, the more you will:

- Often have the sense you are being held and never feel alone. Instead you feel known, valued, and unconditionally loved.

- Find there is no contentment like just being in His presence. The love this brings will be above anything else in life.

- Sense God just knows what you are thinking, feeling, or needing, without uttering a word.

- Sometimes find things on earth to be an inconvenient distraction, for you will be so preoccupied by thinking about Him. The importance of things in the natural, will somehow seem to fade in comparison.

- Increasingly encounter what's actually going on in the heavenlies, as you sense what God is impressing upon you. (for example: you may suddenly feel what He feels; times when you suddenly become aware of an emotion that in the natural, you were not experiencing until that point.)

- Seem to see people as God does. When you are with others, (even those that in the natural you cannot like), you will actually love them.

- Always know you carry truth; like a weight of certainty regardless of your circumstances. This will rise in the face of opposition. Even if you can't tangibly feel God's presence; you will just know He is there.

- Find that just being with Him is when you feel most alive.

- Automatically just talk to him about everything, anywhere, any time. It's not about when you remember to; it turns into a constant flow of conversation.

- Want to prioritise time with Him above everything else. He becomes the most exclusive relationship in your life.

The power of His presence

'Or what do you think the Scripture means when it says that the Holy Spirit, whom God has placed within us, watches over us with tender jealousy?'
James 4:5 TLB

No matter what life looks like, when we live in Him, the power of God's presence leaves us feeling loved, covered, supported, and captivated. In Him we are never empty, rejected, unheard or uncared for. Instead, we are adored as we experience God's nurturing embrace, constancy and tenderness. This brings a vibrancy to our heart, the deepest restfulness and a sense of protection that stabilises us. As we become the love God gives us, this permeates to all our relationships, regardless of what we do or don't receive in return. This safety equips us with the confidence to face anything in the world. We are never alone – we face it together with God.

Are there situations in your life where more of this would help you right now?

In the Zoe life, the constant, loving inner communion with God is a key promise we can experience every day, regardless of our circumstances...

... On 2nd May 2011, Jacob Zachary Simpson came into the world. His arrival was not what we had expected. Life became a blur of Doctors, hospital corridors and fitful intermittent sleep. But in those days, I would awake to God singing 'great is my faithfulness', key verses were impressed upon my mind and despite the uncertainty, the whispers kept coming – 'eyes up. Don't look to the left or to the right; just look at me'. I was held.

At times, the fear became indescribable and I poured out the pain, the loss, the grief, the anger, the disappointment, the anguish, the confusion, the sadness. But God was within, covering it all. Despite some further bumps along the way, as I write this now, Jacob is a thriving little boy. He is happy, outgoing and we enjoy every day with him to the full. Traumatic as those days were, the constancy of God's presence, the understanding of His amazing love and the certainty of specific promises were the anchor to my soul.

God wants to be your anchor too. In the rough and the smooth, the mundane and the extreme, the happy and the sad, the busy and the calm, He is there - just waiting to be encountered – continually.

'Therefore we will not fear, though the earth give way and the mountains fall into the heart of the sea, though its waters roar and foam and the mountains quake with their surging. There is a river whose streams make glad the city of God, the holy place where the Most High dwells. God is within her, she will not fall; God will help her at break of day.'
Psalm 46:2-5 NIV

Reflections

'Who shall separate us from the love of Christ? Shall trouble or hardship or persecution or famine or nakedness or danger or sword?'
Romans 8:35 NIV

The blessing of such constant loving intimacy is available to all of us. Thinking of your own life;

- Where do you experience God's presence and recognise this type of spiritual intimacy the most?

- Where do you experience or recognise it the least?

- Is there anything you would like to change about this?

- How would it help your life if you did?

In part two we will look at how this can become your reality.

4

Promise 2
His significance - our renewed identity

The authority that comes from knowing you are a child of The King.

"Before I formed you in the womb I knew you [and approved of you as My chosen instrument], And before you were born I consecrated you [to Myself as My own]; I have appointed you as a prophet to the nations."
Jeremiah 1:5 AMP

*'For all **who are allowing themselves** to be led by the Spirit of God are sons of God. For you have not received a spirit of slavery leading again to fear [of God's judgment], but you have received the Spirit of adoption as sons [the Spirit producing sonship] by which we [joyfully] cry, "Abba! Father!". The Spirit Himself testifies and confirms together with our spirit [assuring us] that we [believers] are children of God. And if [we are His] children, [then we are His] heirs also: heirs of God and fellow heirs with Christ [sharing His spiritual blessing and inheritance], if indeed we share in His suffering so that we may also share in His glory'.*
Romans 8:14-17 AMP

...'Mike will see you now'.

I was nervous. Our business had not long been established. This, our first piece of work with a major global company, had the makings of a long-standing, fruitful contract. But it all depended on how the CEO responded.

The business I share deals with other businesses. In it, we coach executives, collectively, as a Board and individually, as the human beings who make it all happen. We had conducted our research and knew what the challenges were. And a major one was now sat right in front of me. The CEO. In this I've called him Mike.

Amongst the great findings, there were some key difficulties; about the Board and about Mike. So here I was now, about to deliver some really tricky feedback. Waves of uncertainty hit my stomach. I was apprehensive. Walking to the plush and spacious office, I knew I had a choice. Should I duck it - after all, the fate of our contract rested with the decision of this guy? Should I dilute it, in the hope that a few key messages would land better? Or should I legitimise our integrity, by trusting and compassionately sharing the truth?

An impressive and powerful guy, the charming smile and warm handshake belied the steely glint he always carried in his eye. From experience I knew that with a certain trigger, in an instant, pleasantries could turn to passive, simmering anger. I sensed his own uncertainty, not quite masked before my own interrogating eyes. An awareness of both the consequences and the intensity of the moment held energy in the room. For a moment, we both danced the dance. Then taking a deep breathe, I began...

What is renewed identity?

This is about experiencing a confidence that is beyond relying on what you know, what your track record shows or what you can do. It's about when you have a sureness and authority that comes from knowing who you are in Christ. Through His identity, we learn our inheritance and from it, our significance. This confidence replaces our uncertainty with the authority that comes from knowing we are a child of God.

Life has a way of throwing us before all manner of circumstances that can challenge this certainty. Through situations, through people we encounter or through our own faulty thinking, there are times when we are unsure, intimidated or feel over our head.

Much of life comes down to two fundamental questions: Do we really know who our God is and do we really know who we are in Him?

Think about your own life for a second. Do you ever find yourself worrying about things or your place within them? When we know the real answer, we never adversely worry, feel intimidated or overwhelmed by what is before us. But the reality is that we live in a world that often seems to scream its authority, power and grip on our society. Our lives can sometimes feel at the mercy of a hold beyond our power to influence or change.

In many coaching sessions, the biggest fear even very senior executives often have is 'am I really good enough'? One day will I get found out?' This drives all manner of toxic self-preservation tactics. These tactics are mainly used for people to hide behind. But we don't need to hold such esteemed positions in life to experience such doubts.

The reality is we often struggle with insecurity – I know I did for two-thirds of my life. This means we can become preoccupied by what others would say, think or feel. We doubt whether or not we are good enough or liked enough. We worry about whether we can stand up to people, situations or we worry about our imagination of what may happen. That comes from our ego; our self-preservation; the way we look after ourselves. But when the Holy Spirit helps us to see, accept and value who we are in Christ, what He has given us, and what our inheritance really is, all those fears fall away. It takes us out of our own ego, so that no matter what the response is, no matter what the outcome is, no matter how well we do, we still feel the same level of confidence we started with. We are freed as we put our trust in God, not in ourselves.

I've likened this type of experience to the work of a sheepdog. Living in rural Scotland, we are surrounded by fields and roaming cattle. The sheepdog knows who he is. He knows who he belongs to. The shepherd instructs which sheep he wants moving to where. The sheepdog, quick as a flash, just gets on with the job. Whilst the sheepdog runs he feels alive and vibrant. Like it's the most natural feeling in the world. He follows the shepherd's instructions and even with the few rogue sheep who seem to go the wrong way, he diligently remains calm and assertive, until the job's done. At the end of the day, the sheepdog doesn't look for praises or rewards. He wants to get fed. He wants to get watered. He knows his master will do that. But really, all the sheepdog wants to do, is sit with his nose on his master's lap or curl up contentedly at his feet.

That's what it's like when we know who we are. The Holy Spirit seals within us a recognition, faith and trust in our identity. We know what we are meant to do and delight in doing it. We just long to be at one with our master, as we apply ourselves to His requests and guidance. This comes from a belief that we are the adopted sons and daughters of the One Most High. When we know who we are, we are at ease and surrendered to simply wanting to do what he asks. Not for us; just for Him. And as we obey, all we want is to keep being nourished by Him, with the constancy of His company. Through His grace, we get to inherit all the blessings that the Father wants to bestow upon us.

But we also know that Jesus has been given ALL authority. It is this truth in which we find our rest. (Matt 28:18) The Bible tells us that we are actually co-heirs with Jesus. (Rom 8:17) When we know this, we realise we can inherit the same providence, legacy, characteristics, favour, power, riches and qualities that Jesus himself has. It suddenly puts into perspective the faith we can have in who we are! God is the sovereign creator of all that exists. He trumps every power, principality and in Him is all authority.

When you learn how to live the Zoe kind of life, you can experience a confidence in this authority through all situations, regardless of who you are through an earthly lens. This is a position that's permanently assured, not just when your natural sense of comfort provides re-assurance, courage or poise within.

What His significance can bring

'See what an incredible quality of love the Father has shown to us, that we would [be permitted to] be named and called and counted the children of God! And so we are! For this reason the world does not know us, because it did not know Him.'
1 John 3:1 AMP

Living the Zoe kind of life, we become one hundred percent certain of who we are. No 'self-help', validation through promotion or reassurance through others can ever achieve this. No circumstance or person can take this confidence away. This changes our countenance, giving us an authentic gravitas that increases our impact. When you access His significance, you activate your renewed identity. This becomes your authority.

Imagine your own life for a moment and consider what the impact of this could practically mean to you. The more you develop this, the more you will:

- Know who God is and always carry total belief in His omnipotence, regardless of the situation.

- Know who you are in Him – an adopted royal heir. You will carry this position in your countenance and the presence you bring into any environment. You will feel certain of your Kingdom status in natural or spiritual situations.

- Eliminate insecurity or heaviness, because you aren't confident in you – you are confident of Him in you.

- Be confident to do anything God asks you to do. You will believe you have the capability to carry out what He's asked you to. Supernatural courage will flow, which will leave you feeling strong, calm and anointed in natural or spiritual conflict.

- Have total faith in all God's promises. You will believe they all apply to you. You will experience no security like it. You will permanently feel covered by Him. You will believe the enemy has no hold on your spirit.

- Have an authenticity that people seem drawn to – you will be comfortable in showing the real you; without mask. You will feel no need to hide behind being a certain way, as you will know, trust and value who you are.

- Not be concerned about yourself. It will no longer even be about you. You will simply feel you have nothing to prove to anyone. So, your soulish ego and self-protection mechanisms will become redundant.

- Not be affected by what other people think of you. Being liked, being right and being approved will seem un-important. Your knowledge of how God sees you will supersede any fear of man.

- Easily move past what others may say to offend, hurt or insult you. You are anchored regardless of the response you get.

- Believe you are an adopted son or daughter: so, you will make the same requests and expectations of the King that any other member of the royal household would. Your prayers will come from being favoured, not from being fearful. You will come to actually expect God's abundance: not because of who you are, but because you will know who you are in Him.

The power of His significance

'So in Christ Jesus you are all children of God through faith, for all of you who were baptized into Christ have clothed yourselves with Christ.'

Galatians 3:26-27 NIV

Regardless of what we come up against in life, the power of our adoption leaves us knowing who we are, feeling confident, courageous, humble, and assured. When we live in Him we are never low in self-worth, overcome, inadequate or belittled. Instead, we are promoted as we get to experience our position as royal heirs, bringing a stride to our step and greater conviction to be bold. Such security gives us an authentic comfort in our own skin and our countenance starts to actually carry God's presence into the world. This gives us a compelling impact wherever we go. As our gravitas increases our credibility, we are equipped to influence and assert ourselves more effectively.

Are there situations in your life where more of this would help you right now?

In the Zoe life, we are a somebody. With this comes the privilege of unshakeable confidence in authority that comes from knowing we are a child of God...

... As the conversation unfolded, a coldness fell over Mike's face. As he bristled through well-veneered responses, the feedback gave its sting. A familiar old feeling of uncertainty created a knot of tension in my stomach. But Holy Spirit gave the game away and encouraged me to hold the ground. 'Don't forget who you belong to. Trust me', came His comforting reassurance. In quiet confidence that held the moment, silence hovered, leaving the burden of the messages at Mike's feet. No needing to prove myself right, no heaviness of 'what's going to happen now?', no wishing the ground would swallow me up, no fear of what Mike now thought of me. There was just truth. The truth of the feedback.

Mike never did go on to fully embrace all of the feedback discussed that day. But despite the resistance, God gave me courage. I knew I was His. I knew who I was in Him. God knew what He was doing. All He needed was for me to believe that too!

What is it that you need to believe about yourself today? Maybe it's time to learn how to step into all of who you already are?

'But now you have arrived at your destination: By faith in Christ you are in direct relationship with God. Your baptism in Christ was not just washing you up for a fresh start. It also involved dressing you in an adult faith wardrobe—Christ's life, the fulfilment of God's original promise.'
                                        Galatians 3:27 MSG

Reflections

'But you are a chosen race, a Royal Priesthood, a consecrated nation, a (special) people for God's own possession, so that you may proclaim the excellencies [the wonderful deeds and virtues and perfections] of Him who called you out of darkness into His marvellous light.'
                                        1 Peter 2:9 AMP

In the Zoe life, the certainty of such an unshakeable strength in our identity is available to all of us. Thinking of your own life;

- Do you recognise the significance of who you are and stand securely in this?

- When and where do you not feel this unshakeable authority?

- Is there anything you would like to change about this?

- How would it help your life and this world if you did?

In part two we will look at how this can become your reality.

5

His perspective – our ability to hear God

The clarity of accurate, precise revelation through heaven's lens.

'Call to Me and I will answer you, and tell you [and even show you] great and mighty things, [things which have been confined and hidden], which you do not know and understand and cannot distinguish.'
Jeremiah 33:3 AMP

'These are the things God has revealed to us by his Spirit. The Spirit searches all things, even the deep things of God. For who knows a person's thoughts except their own spirit within them? In the same way no one knows the thoughts of God except the Spirit of God. What we have received is not the spirit of the world, but the Spirit who is from God, so that we may understand what God has freely given us. This is what we speak, not in words taught us by human wisdom but in words taught by the Spirit, explaining spiritual realities with Spirit-taught words.'
1 Corinthians 2:10-13 NIV

...The day we arrived at the new house, it was thick fog. A terrible headache had set in. The penetrating cold of the empty house hit me. Despite the gnaw of discomfort, it was time to re-make life in this new destination. This new life, that on paper should be far easier, was about to begin.

Living in a remote part of Scotland for the previous four years had taken its toll. Church and connected activity was anything up to a 3-hour round trip away, the nearest pint of milk was a 15-mile round trip and the nearest supermarket a 50-mile journey. With a fledgling business, money was tight, so every fee generating trip away counted. With a huge carbon footprint and exhaustion from the travel, for a long time we'd known something needed to change. After praying for months, there had still been no audible instruction about what we should do. What I'd received instead was a knowing sense. This knowing sense was saying patience!

Through impetuous self-fixing, today was the day of the move. Circumstances had prevented us from a permanent move, but for now, renting this new home in a different location seemed to make sense. After bargaining with God, I still didn't have peace. Having ignored the cues of turmoil, over the nine-month period we went onto stay for, a catalogue of evidence appeared. Evidence that quite clearly shouted its message - we were outside of God's will...

What is the ability to hear God?

This is about being open to hear from God, by stilling our soul. In this we clear away our own interferences, so our limited thoughts can be replaced with heaven's. The starting point for this is always through His word, then breathed on by the Spirit. It is the Holy Spirit that enables us to hear things in our spirit, that we often can't through our own mind, will or emotions. These are the times when God brings a knowing, a discernment, a direction or a word that is from heaven itself. Then He provides the wisdom so we know what to do with that insight. This clarity replaces our limited thoughts with accurate, precise revelation. In exchange, we receive certainty from the truth of hearing from God. This is what echoes the mind of Christ. (1 Cor 2:16)

Think about your own life for a minute. Are there ever times when you're struggling with how to resolve an issue, or times when you feel confused, foggy or even unsure about what is what? How many times have you made a decision and later regretted it? How many times have you prayed until you have no more words left, only to find you're still uncertain of what God says? How many times do you take action and then ask God to bless it afterwards? Conversely, how often do you have a sense of what God's saying and ignore it? God does not purposefully try to complicate our communication with Him. The problem is, that quite frequently, we are the ones who get in the way!

God speaks to us in so many different ways, from the faintest whisper, to the physical jab in the shoulder. Whether cues, senses or specific guidance, He wants to be heard. When we are close to His word and Spirit, He can always make a way. If we let Him.

What about the times you're reading your Bible, when a quickening seems to reveal or impress something specific of importance? It never fails to amaze me how the very passage I happen to be reading speaks straight into the heart of a current situation. Or what about the occasions when you can't explain with logic why you know what you do? How many times do you ignore the nudge, discounting it as a mere fleeting thought?

Alternatively, you may have experienced the times when you know God has spoken clearly. It may be to warn you of something, or it may be to encourage you. It may be to teach you, or it may be to remind you. It may be to reveal something, a word of knowledge or to deposit prophecy. It may be to show your purpose or to show you what to do in the here and now. When people describe this experience, they say they just knew that they heard or saw something from God. The Spirit understands things the mind cannot know. Often when in our most natural state, we usually experience these revelations when not forcing the answer; in the shower, exercising, drifting into sleep or simply spending time with God agenda free. He's even shown me scriptures I needed to re-read in my dreams!

This type of understanding is as infinite as heaven itself. God can and does speak to us in so many different ways. It may be through our circumstances, a film we are watching, something we happen to overhear, something we see in nature, our work situations or our children. The list is endless. And if we pay attention, He then provides the wisdom about how to handle what He has revealed. This is when the Holy Spirit teaches us how to honour, nurture and protect what's been placed in our hands.

In these moments, it's a bit like the shepherd and sheepdog analogy. The sheepdog is so tuned into the shepherd's every movement, that it knows precisely when the shepherd wants him to run, which direction to go in and when to return to his side. The raise of an eyebrow, the tone of the whistle, the pitch of a call are often the only signals needed.

To be honest, I have sometimes found that this direction is so subtle, that I don't know I am about to take the action or say what I am about to say. It's as if Holy Spirit just literally walks me into it. At other times, there can be a definitive 'do it now/say it now' moment. In contrast, there is sometimes a clear 'don't say this/don't go there with that person' instruction.

Whatever the approach, receiving this Kingdom insight is not something that just comes in quiet times or isolated moments. In most of our lives, getting that type of space is a far cry from the reality of busy lives in a busy world. I have found the Holy Spirit to be more robust than I ever knew was possible. He's diligent about getting through. He's spoken so clearly to me in the strangest of places; a noisy theatre, a swimming pool, a packed train, to name just a few. The question is not about how busy or quiet our lives are - it's about how 'tuned in' to hearing Him we are. Is there room for Him to talk, or do we constantly fill up the air waves?! Our ways often seem so right, but when our perspective comes from the ascended throne room itself, this is the real wisdom we need. (Prov 14:12)

When you learn how to live the Zoe kind of life, you can hear from God in all things. Not just when you fast for a week, when you intentionally press in or when you seek the council of trusted prophets! You will find He constantly communicates when you learn how to hear it.

What hearing God can bring

'Trust in the Lord with all your heart. And do not lean on your own understanding. In all your ways acknowledge Him, And He will make your paths straight'.
Proverbs 3:5-6 NIV

Living the Zoe kind of life, there is a way to receive clarity that brings inspired revelation and enables wise choices. When you access His perspective, you increasingly activate hearing from God. This becomes your joy.

Imagine your own life for a moment and consider what the impact of this could practically mean to you. The more you develop this, the more you will:

▪ Find when you read The Word, deeper meaning, relevance and insight will seem to spring from the pages. It will be beyond what your own intelligence could have noticed or conjured up.

- Consciously be able to dial down what your own mind, will and emotions are communicating to you, so that you create the space for the Holy Spirit to bring fresh revelation.

- Experience times when a knowing sense seems to carry information through something you experience, read, spiritually hear or see. There's no particular rationale you can attach to it. But the knowledge, insight or wisdom seems to come from within your spirit.

- Experience times when you receive clear messages. Rarely through an audible voice (although it can happen), this instruction will help you to instinctively know what to say, think, feel or do in a situation. It will be above and beyond the earthly wisdom your own logic would bring you.

- Find your senses often invisibly seem to tell you when something is wrong or when something is right, even if you are not initially tuned into this. Sometimes you will feel this physiologically in your body first. When something is wrong you will notice a spiritual 'jarring'. When something is right you will notice a spiritual 'flow'.

- Find when it comes, this type of knowledge and wisdom will leave you in a state of total sureness. You will feel no certainty like it.

- Experience a different dimension to your prayers. You will find yourself praying about things you never intended to. The Holy Spirit will spontaneously lead what and when you need to pray.

- Find when you pray, you know when something has been prayed out and will know when victory is confirmed in your spirit.

- Find that sometimes the knowledge or wisdom released is completely counter to what any worldly logic or rationale would suggest is right. In the natural, you will just know you need to trust what you have received.

- Naturally scan your spirit. You will be able to discern things of the Spirit. For example, when you walk into an atmosphere, when you meet someone or when you are simply doing life.

The power of His perspective

'He changes the times and the seasons; He removes kings and raises up kings; He gives wisdom to the wise, And knowledge to those who have understanding. He reveals deep and secret things; He knows what is in the darkness, And light dwells with Him.'
2 Daniel 21-22. NKJV

The world can be a confusing place. But the power of His mind leaves us knowing how God sees things. His messages give us a knowing when we have been directed by God. When we live in Him we are never lost, trapped, or going around in circles. Instead, we pioneer as we get to experience immeasurable insight and certainty. This brings clarity and an accuracy that helps us permeate to the heart of a matter. We get the privilege of experiencing this promise of Kingdom knowledge and wisdom, as we learn to tune into His mind and hear all His leadings. Our entire perspective is changed – changed to know, see and do things through heavens lens. This inspired revelation gives us a certainty about how to tackle the things in our lives, so we think and act with wisdom. Our choices then create the best possible outcome.

Are there situations in your life where more of this would help you right now?

When we develop the Zoe life, we are in tune with a relational God who guides us into His word, will and wisdom. He brings a clarity that replaces our limited thoughts with accurate, precise insight, knowledge and instruction...

...The situation had become dire. Constantly on my knees, in both prayer and exhaustion, we desperately needed to know what to do. For nine months following the move, everything that could go wrong in this new location did. The geographical hub of work ran dry. With Jacob (at eighteen months) old hospitalised twice, it was soon apparent that cold and damp in the rented house didn't help. As we battled the worst snowy winter in 30 years, a subsequent miscarriage, months of Jacob teething and sleep deprived nights only added to the picture.

Then one day, something shifted. When I had finally stopped trying to work it all out; when I had finally let go of what I wanted the answer to be; when I had finally accepted I had mucked up, came the divine direction we needed: 'Go back to where you came from'. In an instant, peace returned. My husband felt it too. Naturally, it made absolutely no sense - we were going right back to where we started. But the burden, the pressure, the fear I had carried was lifted. This way was the right way forward. This way was His way. And as we would all later come to understand, His way, as ever, was perfect.

He is the eternal, omniscient God who really does know all; past, present and future. In him is all the knowledge and wisdom we will ever need. Of course, the next important step is that we learn to listen and obey!

'God's wisdom is something mysterious that goes deep into the interior of his purposes. You don't find it lying around on the surface. But you've seen and heard it because God by his Spirit has brought it all out into the open before you.'
1 Corinthians 2:7-10 MSG

Reflections

'Then He said, "Go out, and stand on the mountain before the LORD." And behold, the LORD passed by, and a great and strong wind tore into the mountains and broke the rocks in pieces before the LORD, but the LORD was not in the wind; and after the wind an earthquake, but the LORD was not in the earthquake; after the earthquake a fire, but the LORD was not in the fire; and after the fire a still small voice'

1 Kings 19:11-12 NKJV

The certainty that comes from being in tune with the perspective of Christ is available to all of us. Thinking of your own life;

- When and where do you recognise this type of heavenly perspective and insight the most?

- Where do you recognise it the least?

- Is there anything you would like to change about this?

- How would it help your life and this world if you did?

In part two we will look at how this can become your reality.

6

His nature - our accelerated change

The servant-heart to propel your transformation into all God made you to be.

'Moreover, I will give you a new heart and put a new spirit within you, and I will remove the heart of stone from your flesh and give you a heart of flesh. I will put my Spirit within you and cause you to walk in My statutes, and you will keep My ordinances and do them'.
Ezekiel 36:26-27 AMP

'But whenever anyone turns to the Lord, the veil is taken away. Now the Lord is the Spirit, and where the Spirit of the Lord is, there is freedom. And we all, who with unveiled faces contemplate the Lord's glory, are being transformed into his image with ever-increasing glory, which comes from the Lord, who is the Spirit'.
2 Corinthians 3:16-18 NIV

...The knot inside my stomach felt like the size of a tennis ball. Those carnal emotions returned. They were fierce, gripping my soul. My whole body was filled with an intense drive. A drive to make it happen. Somehow.

After eight years of living in the Scottish wilderness and our return from the nine-month relocation a couple of years before, the time had come. It was our time to finally move. We'd heard with clarity and now knew the location, the house and the timing. Everything was perfect. There was only one problem; selling our existing house to fund the move. Through prime real estate seasons, it sat idly through months with not a single viewing. Despite the tension, the desire and the long distances we were travelling daily, God was moulding me - holding me in the fire of refinement. He was changing me - from impetuous, wilfully controlling and demanding, to restful, patient and contented. As days, weeks and months drifted, absent of any viewings, initial excitement and calmness gradually shifted into nervous frustration.

Right now, a momentary soulish meltdown had crept surreptitiously into my thinking. The price of the house we were buying had been dramatically slashed in price. The owners now needed to move quickly and could no longer wait. Would someone else now snap this away? Was there any way we could make it happen, somehow? Was there anything at all that we could do? Could we do a bridging loan? Could we, could we, could we...? My head exploded with ideas, driven by an intensive desire to fix this. 'Don't even go there,' my husband wisely said. But in the heat of this long awaited and much needed move - so tantalisingly out of reach, was the pull of how I always used to deal with such things just too strong?...

What is acceleration of change?

Our change is accelerated when we are motivated to pursue it. The nature of Jesus within us, is our enabler for this. Sometimes this can literally happen immediately. At other times, it can take the working of a longer process to break from our old out-of-date ways. It's in the big character issues, but it's also in the small day-by-day reactions. This is the power of God at work within us. It's how we die to self and how we are renewed. (Rom 6:11)

What's most amazing, is that we are being transformed into the image of how God already sees us.

'For by one sacrifice he has made perfect forever those who are being made holy.'
Hebrews 10:14 NIV

We've already been made perfect. But we need to walk through the process of being made holy. Our thoughts drive our feelings. Our feelings drive our behaviour. This is why we are instructed to be transformed by the renewal of our minds (Rom 12:2) God can change the parts of us that alone, we would never be able to achieve. This is the empowerment that transforms us into all God made us to be. It's the newness of life His resurrection promises. (Rom 6:4)

Think about your own character, patterns of behaviour and the cycles of how you think. Some will work for you. Others won't. Some will work until a certain trigger. Some will be part of an ongoing wrestle to change. How many times do you find yourself in the same sort of situations, experiencing the same challenging circumstances, inner reactions or outward responses? Could it be that such things arise over and over until we finally address them? What freedom comes when we finally do.

In the Zoe life, we gradually become increasingly aware of our own behaviour. Bit by bit, in His kindness, God does this so we have a choice. The choice of whether or not we want to change.

But it's not just about the things we need to improve. It's also about what needs to grow. God knows the potential He has put inside you - and longs for you to know it too.

As an adolescent I struggled with low self-esteem. I would literally blush to the top of my head if addressed directly by less-known people. Living in a hidden fear that one day I would make a total fool of myself, self-help and positive thinking only ever got me so far. What I portrayed on the outside belied what I felt on the inside. Over the years, God was able to reshape me. With His tender potter hands, He built up the authentic confidence He always knew was there. He knew it, because He designed me.

He's designed you too. Within you lay every aspect of the character you will ever need. This is where His gaze is fixed. So, whenever we fail or fall, He simply longs for us to get back up again – and press into what He is already looking at within us. In the process, He takes us back to who we were born to be - before the layers of conditioning were imprinted upon our souls. He takes us into who we really are, without the labels, the habits and the consequences of living in a fallen world.

The transformation He has in store may take discipline – there's an undeniable need to pro-actively engage with it. But the good news is, it doesn't take forced effort. We don't change ourselves. When we engage with Him, the Holy Spirit in us does. When I am tired, my perspective can be affected. So, if I feel agitated about something in that state, I consciously have to discipline myself not to listen to those feelings. As soon as I make that choice and ask Holy Spirit to carry me, gentleness comes. I don't have to strain to obtain it.

These personal changes will come in different ways. Sometimes this change comes from the quiet times you spend with God, as you read The Word and He ministers to you. Sometimes it comes gradually as you put things into practice. Sometimes it comes when you need it most, in the heat of a situation. I was recently in a crucial discussion.

The conversation was intense and in that moment, I knew I had come to the end of what I was able to do. It required a turnaround in my attitude. In that moment I prayed one word; the word was 'help'. In an instant, a meekness fell, enabling me to listen more humbly. This change in my demeanour enabled a resolution that would otherwise not have been possible. This was the fruit of the spirit in action.

The whole process of transformation is done with such compassion, step-by-step, over time. God doesn't expect us to change everything all at once. It's a lifetime's work - the learning never stops. So how do we know if we are changing? It's when the thoughts, feelings and behaviour we have look less and less like they used to, and more and more like the qualities of Jesus that at conversion, He gave us.

Now, when in circumstances that would have historically called on my old ways, instead of praying for the situation, my first prayer is for God to work on the character I need, to enable me to deal with the situation the right way – His way. My focus prioritises who He is making me, not what I want to happen. It's the most liberating place to live from.

'The Spirit produces love, joy, peace, patience, kindness, goodness, faithfulness, humility and self-control. There is no law against such things as these.'
Galatians 5:22-23 GNB

Friends, we already have all of Christ in us. We just need to put Him on. Instead of focussing on what we are not, we focus on the virtues of God's character that the Holy Spirit can activate within us. When we partner with Him and submit to this, He is able to mould us. As this happens, the world around us experiences something different. They experience a walking, talking example of the power of God at work. This is our biggest witness; the ability God has to transform our lives for the better. Through this, God shapes us into who we already are in Jesus, so we are equipped for what we are here to do.

When you learn how to live the Zoe kind of life, you will experience change that sets you free from the power of your old nature. Not just until the major trigger hits. This will become a gradual, but permanent sanctification into the beauty of how God sees you right now.

'You were taught, with regard to your former way of life, to put off your old self, which is being corrupted by deceitful desires; to be made new in the attitude of your minds; and to put on the new self, created to be like God in true righteousness and holiness.'
Ephesians 4:22-24 NIV

What His nature can bring

'And in Him you too are being built together to become a dwelling in which God lives by his Spirit.'
Ephesians 2:22 NIV

Living the Zoe kind of life, there is a way to operate in the fruits of the spirit, positively changing outcomes by behaving in the most appropriate way. It is His nature within that creates the hunger we need to pursue this. When you access His nature, you activate your accelerated ability to change. This becomes your motivation.

Imagine your own life for a moment and consider what the impact of this could practically mean to you. The more you develop this, the more you will:

- Gain a greater conscience around your own behaviour; of how it could be versus how it actually is. You will proactively feel challenged by God's word and this will leave you questioning how your own life stacks up against this. You will desire holiness. Conviction will arise that you find increasingly difficult to ignore.

- Gain an increasing awareness of something that's not working for you. This may be through a specific incident, through something you are gradually becoming more bothered by, or through the Holy Spirit revealing an area you need to address.

- Gain a stronger awareness of your strengths and what is actually holding you back. You will want to take accountability for addressing this and will become stirred by exploring your real potential.

- Experience the Holy Spirit literally breathing a different, more constructive response into you. You will naturally just become this and it will not be through the gritted teeth of self-determination. It will be a response that flows from connecting with what's already been put inside you.

- Find the nature of your thoughts will shift. They will move from being about what you see, to being about what God sees. Over time you will notice how the bar has constantly been raised. Your standards will constantly be coming up higher. As this happens you will notice the hand of God on your life. You will see the changes He is engineering. You will gain different perspective on the value of how the challenging circumstances have served to dismantle the old you and release the new you.

- Find you become ever more reliant on God's support. As you are changed, the realisation that it all comes from Him will make you ever more dependent on Him.

- Find that if you wrestle with certain changes or are tempted to revert to your old ways, the Holy Spirit increasingly brings the self-control to avoid this and the resilience to sustain the shifts made.

- Find that when these changes happen, you experience a freedom, lightness and ease coming with it.

- Recognise it's a lifelong process and avoid beating yourself up. Your mind-set will shift, moving from your old thinking ('I'll always be like this. A leopard can't change its spots - this is just the way I am'), to new man confidence ('I already have all of Christ in me. I am on my way to learning to become who I really am'.) As your mind-set shifts, the resulting changes in your behaviour will follow.

- Find it may not be easy, but your attitude will move from wrestling through the change that's needed, to submitting to it, valuing it and even enjoying the process.

The power of His nature

'But we must forever give thanks to God for you, our brothers loved by the Lord, because God chose from the very first to give you salvation, cleansing you by the work of the Holy Spirit and by your trusting in the Truth.'
2 Thessalonians 2:13 TLB

Our default ways can be powerful. In the past they may have served us well. But when we live in Christ, there is another realm of freedom possible. Freedom from the constraints and limitations of how we used to live. In the Zoe life, we experience accelerated ongoing personal change. It is His nature within us that enables this. In humility, we bow to embracing a different way of being. These changes leave us with different hearts, mind-sets and behaviours. In Christ we are never a lost cause, incapable of change or destined for mediocrity. Instead, we conquer as we get to experience being transformed into His image, accessing all His qualities, characteristics and power. Our maturity enables us to come up higher, as our behaviour aligns with the fruits of the spirit. These changes in our disposition bring better outcomes, greater harmony and enable us to be the salt and light of Matthew 5; authentically attracting people to God.

Are there situations in your life where more of this would help you right now?

In the Zoe life, we are privileged to be lovingly changed. With this comes the life-long transformation into all God has made us to be – His very image…

… Eventually, through some quite miraculous circumstances, the old house was sold. And whilst my soul occasionally tripped me into rollercoaster emotions, the old grip of wilful control was receding. But God was not quite done with me! For despite the shift in my behaviour, I had not quite yet stepped into total freedom from that old limiting habit - the habit of forcing things in my own strength. He wasn't going to leave me half way there.

For many complicated reasons, the conveyancing process was ridiculously complex. Legal stickiness presented a very real danger of the whole thing falling through. With it, a battle started to surface inside. Humanly, all of the difficulties, challenges and frustrations were tugging at the default settings of my old ways, as I wrestled with how to respond. But the Holy Spirit within me was stronger. Every time I felt that familiar almighty pull to step in, my spirit was calmed, my faith was strengthened, superseded by the fruit of patience and self-control. It was bliss. I was being freed from a drive that so often in the past had burned with fury. My mind played tricks, I would dream deeply uncomfortable dreams, but every day I renewed to break from its hold. When declaring this, a rest beyond the circumstances was re-filled. Ludicrous legal gymnastics, with impossible scenarios put the whole process in jeopardy on the very day the removal van arrived in the driveway. We were at stalemate…

With nothing left to do, reaching for my overnight bag, I dug out a well-worn pair of running shoes. The mountain trails were calling. This was where God often elevated me, virtually in the terrain and spiritually into His realm. Running hard without feeling my legs, the cool air was on my face as the last rays of sunshine penetrated the cloudy sky. This day, the day of the intended move was drawing to a close. Everything I said and felt came from deep within. There was literally no more we could do, yet despite the reality of what this stood for, in that moment, I worshipped. The grip of wilful striving had gone. I was totally and utterly free from its control. This liberation was like the dead limb of a tree that's almost been severed, suddenly breaking off, to allow the rest of the healthy branches to bounce back into full life. It had gone. The very last layer of burden, holding on and weighing down. The reality of 2 Corinthians 3:17 burst into life before me: 'Now the Lord is the Spirit, and where the Spirit of the Lord is, there is freedom'.

Arriving back home to a house full of packed boxes, unable to move either in or out, it no longer mattered. It was a Friday and five minutes before the solicitors closed for the long weekend break. My husband came off the phone, speechless. 'Well I don't know what on earth has happened, but it's all going through as planned'. It was not something on earth that had happened. It was something in the heavenlies that had been released. My Lord had done it. And in the process, he had changed me. Like the silversmith in Malachi 3:3, he held me in the fire just long enough to see His own reflection. And the second it was done, He got me straight out of the flames.

'And in Him you too are being built together to become a dwelling in which God lives by his Spirit.'
Ephesians 2:22 NIV

Reflections

'You have taken off your old self with its practices and have put on the new self, which is being renewed in knowledge in the image of its Creator.'
Colossians 3:9-10 NIV

The ability to accelerate our development into all God made us to be is available to all of us. These changes bless us with all the fruitfulness and freedom we are promised. Thinking of your own life;

- Where do you recognise this type of personal change the most?

- Where do you recognise it the least?

- Is there anything you would like to change about this?

- How would it help your life and this world if you did?

In part two we will look at how this can become your reality.

7

Promise 5
His empowerment - our heightened ability

Anointing that increases our effectiveness and impact.

'Have I not commanded you? Be strong and courageous! Do not be terrified or dismayed (intimidated), for the LORD *your God is with you wherever you go.'*
Joshua 1:9 AMP

'For to everyone who has [and values his blessings and gifts from God, and has used them wisely], more will be given, and [he will be richly supplied so that] he will have an abundance; but from the one who does not have [because he has ignored or disregarded his blessings and gifts from God], even what he does have will be taken away.'
Matthew 25:29 AMP

...As I finished the phone call, all around me was busyness. Stood in the bustling, busy train station, passers-by scuttled from one place to another. Announcements rang, screens flashed and sirens echoed outside. It was noisy! But all I could sense was a stillness, in this 'oh my goodness' moment; a 'what have I got myself into?' kind of moment. We'd been awarded the contract. This was to be the largest, most demanding work I'd ever been involved in. Taking this on meant working in territory never walked before. Something inside kept reminding me; God had. Holy Spirit was reassuring me to forget the doubts and instead, to follow His lead.

Unbeknown to the corporate client, bit by bit, the Holy Spirit set to work within as the plan, the insight and ideas flowed with a level of creativity I'd never previously experienced. It was unpredictable, unforced, exciting and specific. Thoughts materialised into concepts that naturally evolved into design. In super-fast time, an approach was formed that broke ground. This was risky and would challenge the leaders involved to new heights. Behind the scenes, an excited confidence grew. Until, that is, the night before the launch...

As the top fifty leaders arrived at one of the world's most exclusive venues, this critical event had the power to make or break things. The design was edgy, stakes were high, expectations were even higher and tension filled the air. The initial doubts, once supressed in the busy train station re-surfaced. Could we land all this to a bunch of highly intelligent, often-sceptical, ambitious Directors? 'What if they weren't ready for this? What if they didn't engage? What if we'd read the situation incorrectly? What if the whole thing failed? What if I was not good enough?'

Then came the moment of truth. Waiting in the wings whilst the President opened events, the first key note speech was ready. Everything was meticulously planned; all based on the lead I sensed (and now earnestly hoped!) the Holy Spirit had given. Ten minutes to go, but where on earth were my prompt cards? In a paralysed panic, my jumbled mind tried in vain to remember the intended launch messages. As the opening music faded, as if in slow motion, I found my legs were walking to the podium. But what on earth would I say?...

What is heightened ability?

This is about experiencing the natural flow of an ability that is beyond what we independently would ever achieve. It is when our natural gifts seem to flow and converge as God multiplies the impact of what we are capable of. In these moments, we tap into the real potential He places inside us, as God anoints us with empowerment. As He does, our effectiveness and impact are magnified.

The chances are you will have experienced moments like this. Think of the times you have done, said, prayed, imagined, created, written, or made something really good. It may be that you stand back and actually think, 'wow; was that really by me?' The answer is both yes and no! Yes, it was the culmination of all your experiences; the practising, learning and development of your God-given abilities. And no, because operating independently, it would not have been possible. What made it possible was God working through you.

This can happen every day. Things of big or small consequence, the mundane or adrenalin fuelled, things only you will see or things that matter to others. It may be in how naturally a conversation seems to flow, the sudden alertness when you hear an ambulance siren or an inspired approach that seems to calm the atmosphere of a heated family argument. Maybe it's how you could fix the roof that repeatedly leaks, an amazing photograph you somehow capture or the exquisite taste of ingredients thrown into a pot on the stove.

This ability overtakes all known boundaries of what you are independently capable of. It's when the Holy Spirit guides your ability. Whether in a small or a large way, God is anointing what you do.

Matt Redman captures this beautifully when he describes the experience of writing the amazing worship song '10,000 reasons': 'The song '10,000 reasons' came along late one night. It was at the end of a long day of song writing with my friend Jonas in the South of England. The song came without any hint of a struggle at all. There was something beautiful about the simplicity of its birth – an uncomplicated case of 'four chords and the truth'. As moments go, it was a pretty good one'. ^{10,000 reasons by Matt Redman. Published by David C.Cook 2016}

Contrast this with times you have felt like something is just not working. Times when everything feels like hard work; when things just don't click. In these moments, we become locked into the limitations of our own self. With it comes frustration, stress, wasted effort and heaviness. The times when no-one will listen, the times when the curtain pole won't stay up, the times when you can not find those keys. Or the times when the client keeps saying no, the times when you repeatedly lose to the lower-league team or the community event poster that fails to draw in the crowds.

The supercharged ability available to all of us requires no effort or straining. We just need to be open to receiving it. However, it's not to be confused with lack of preparation. It doesn't mean we have a license for laziness and doesn't work on the assumption that 'God will just show up.' If anything, this might prevent us receiving, due to the interference of nerves or lack of confidence if unprepared. That tends to make us even more conscious of what's going on in our head, not what's being released through our spirit. God's empowerment doesn't work alongside our ego. It has to replace it.

God is our omnipotent all-powerful God. In Him is all the ability we ever need. Yes, we need to take the responsibility for developing and stepping out, but the truth is, it's His power in us that makes the biggest impact. All we need to do is trust He wants to release it.

When you learn how to live the Zoe kind of life, you will experience this heightened ability ever frequently. Not just when you need a breakthrough or super-human impact. Through every situation in your day, His anointing can be released on all you think, speak, touch and do.

What His empowerment can bring

'So it was, when the Philistine arose and came and drew near to meet David, that David hurried and ran toward the army to meet the Philistine. Then David put his hand in his bag and took out a stone; and he slung it and struck the Philistine in his forehead, so that the stone sank into his forehead, and he fell on his face to the earth. So David prevailed over the Philistine with a sling and a stone, and struck the Philistine and killed him. But there was no sword in the hand of David.'

1 Samuel 17:48-50 NKJV

Living the Zoe kind of life, there is a way for God to multiply your effectiveness, replacing grinding effort with natural flow. When you access His empowerment, you activate your heightened ability. This becomes your confidence.

Imagine your own life for a moment and consider what the impact of this could practically mean to you. The more you develop this, the more you will:

- Find you achieve things faster and avoid mistakes.

- Deliver natural and supernatural gifts in an authentic, intuitive and innate way.

- Find clarity, ideas, creativity, problem solving or pioneering thoughts come to you.

- Find when this happens, you experience a calmness in the moment. You will feel grounded, which releases an air of authority. This is the presence of God working through you. What you say or do will be magnified as you act with greater boldness.

- Find when this happens, you flow. You will intuitively let go of forced cognitive thought and go with what is given to you. In this moment, you won't have to overly think.

- Find if challenged, your response doesn't come from feeling defensive or vulnerable.

- Notice a multiplication of what you are used to doing. You will see the impact of God strengthening, adding and elevating what you know you have done, said or achieved. His hallmark will show in both the outcome and the manner in which you hold yourself as it happens.

- Find the degree of connection and empathy that flows, creating a heartfelt link with people you are around. As God floods His anointing over you, He simultaneously floods His essence through you. You will be immersed in His presence. It is this that your countenance carries.

- Find the atmosphere carries heaven's culture. This will infect the climate, the energy dynamics and the power of anything spoken (prayers or otherwise).

- Find you feel vibrant. It will be as if you are totally aligned to what you were actually created for. In the moment when this heightened ability flows, it will feel the most natural thing in the world; you will just know you were meant to be doing this.

The power of His empowerment

'For God has not given us a spirit of fear, but of power and of love and of a sound mind'.

2 Timothy 1:7 NKJV

God has planted so much more within us than we will ever know. When we live in Him, His empowerment is what enables us to tap into this potential, so we are equipped to think and do with ease. When this happens, we are left feeling in perfect harmony with what we have been made for. In Him we are never incapable, limited by our past experiences, or 'just' good enough. Instead, we get to experience our real potential. This effectiveness enables us to make a better impact and a greater difference, so we can pro-actively influence and change the world around us.

Are there situations in your life where more of this would help you right now?

In the Zoe life, we are honoured to receive this empowerment. This flow, heightens our capability, which multiplies confidence in our effectiveness. His anointing is the source...

... You could hear a pin drop. As the conference music stopped, with expectant eyes upon me, I took what seemed like the longest pause. 'Trust me', came the gentle whisper of a God hearing my racing heartbeat. His presence had descended like a cloud. So, letting go of what I had only minutes before scrambled to remember, I did. Looking into the alert faces of the audience, I started to hesitantly speak - and knew what to say. As I spoke, His anointing fell. The fluency, the links, the clarity; everything landed with poise. Everything fell with presence. God was in the room. In those first few tentative moments, the atmosphere turned from a large disconnected space, to the smallest most intimate venue - heaven itself had pulled everyone into a bubble of connectedness. What existed was the energy of something that together, we were holding. Unbeknown to the audience, it was the presence of God. People were leaning in; stern faces gave way to warm expression and eyes glistened with connection. As the words arrived, hearts were being stirred. Minds were being captivated. Decisions were being influenced. This, was the power of His ability at work. For all the preparation, prayer and practice, this kind of impact could only come from one thing. It came from who was working through me. All I needed to do was get out of His way!

'My message and my preaching were not with wise and persuasive words, but with a demonstration of the Spirit's power, so that your faith might not rest on men's wisdom, but on God's power.'
1 Corinthians 2:4 NIV

Reflections

'Now the LORD said to Moses, "See, I have called by name Bezalel, son of Uri, the son of Hur, of the tribe of Judah. I have filled him with the Spirit of God in wisdom and skill, in understanding and intelligence, in knowledge, and in all kinds of craftsmanship'.
Exodus 31:1-3 AMP

Whether it is through our words, our actions, our thoughts or our natural gifting, God wants to multiply our ability every day. His anointing can increase the effectiveness of anything we try to do in our own forced might. Thinking of your own life;

- Where do you recognise this type of heightened ability the most?

- Where do you recognise it the least?

- Is there anything you would like to change about this?

- How would it help your life and this world if you did?

In part two we will look at how this can become your reality.

8

His sovereignty – our supernatural might

The combination of our character, spiritual gifts and faithful expectation, releasing God's will into our world.

'It has seemed good to me to declare the signs and wonders which the Most High God has done for me. How great are His signs, And how mighty are His wonders! His kingdom is an everlasting kingdom. And His dominion is from generation to generation.'

Daniel 4:2-3 AMP

'I pray that the eyes of your heart may be enlightened in order that you may know the hope to which He has called you, the riches of his glorious inheritance in His holy people, and His incomparably great power for us who believe. That power is the same as the mighty strength He exerted when He raised Christ from the dead and seated Him at His right hand in the heavenly realm.'

Ephesians 1:18-20 NIV

...Everything seemed to be in slow motion, unable to digest what had just been said. Our baby. Our boy. Our little miracle. At five months old and not yet crawling, here we found ourselves, under the watchful eye of the hospital Doctors. Earlier that afternoon, finding the large, soft, cushiony swelling on Jacob's head was only the start of the nightmare.

The subsequent X ray revealed a six-inch fracture, the entire length of Jacob's skull. As yet, both the cause and the consequence were unknown. With the life-threatening risk of bleeding on the brain, decisions were needed – and so were answers.

'How did it happen? This isn't just a slight knock - something really hard has impacted on his skull. A fracture so large is only possible from a massive trauma to the head. Did you see anything, did you do anything?' Why don't you know how it happened? You must know something? What is it you are not telling us?' The eyes of accusation were upon me, as I stared at the unbelievable picture in front of me. For hours, questions were unrelenting, tumbling one after the other. Jacob had been with me and my Mum, in our constant care whilst away from home. Between us, we were utterly at a loss as to what had happened, or even what to say.

Jacob, too tiny for the usual CT scan, was under close observation. But this was no longer just a medical diagnosis. It was now a social-services led interrogation. The prayers for healing were abruptly interrupted. Until the cause of the injury was known, we were under examination. A stabbing horror arose in my chest – we were under the mercy of people with the power to take our little miracle baby away...

What is supernatural might?

This is when God, in His sovereignty releases supernatural power in, through and around us. These are the times when God's mandate is carried into the world. This is the domain of miracles - when the full force of heaven is released tangibly into the natural realm.

It may result in supernatural interventions such as the softening of hardened hearts, deliverance or healing. Or it may result in a change to circumstances, such as to bring protection, breakthroughs or certain decisions into being. It could be the release of spiritual revelation such as words of knowledge, pictures, prophecy or discernment of spirits. Sometimes it's the transference of a gifting or quality needed, such as supernatural faith or perseverance. Or it could be how He shifts an atmosphere, changes an energy or creates a domino of interconnected happenings. Sometimes it's simply that we experience the weight of His glorious presence within. Unexpected provision, blessings or touches of His grace; all are marks of God's supernatural involvement. It can happen in the daily routine, such as enabling you to bump into just the person you need to speak to. Or it can happen in something more profound like healing a life-long illness.

God sovereignly chooses what favour to release. It can't be forced, it can't be controlled and it can't be manipulated. This is the purest form of God's unlimited power on earth, always sent for the benefit of mankind.

This isn't something that only the well trained or well experienced can encounter. Every time you pray, you're engaging with the supernatural. You're calling heaven's authority to earth. This is something that is available to all of us. When it comes, every element will be perfect for the situation needed – and that includes when it happens.

Joyce Meyer often says 'God is rarely early, but never late.' Ten years into a dream to have our own family, I can testify personally to how well that lesson was drilled into me! So, part of trusting His supernatural power exists, includes trusting His timing.

I will often pray for protection and remember one particular occasion where those daily prayers were answered. At around 3am. I was awoken in the night, with an urgent prompting. Holy Spirit's unusually directive, but unmistakable guidance was instructing me to pray immediately for the security of our home. In that moment I had the strongest sense that people were outside planning to break in. Tucked up in bed, following the orders, the presence of God was thick. After what was probably ten minutes, a peace fell, the intensity of the moment passed and I knew the prayers had been answered. There was no need to get up, wake my husband or check the doors. I knew God had intervened, protection had been placed and the risk had disappeared, such was the strength of the shift in the atmosphere. Sure enough, the next morning we found that one of the garden sheds was wide open. Nothing had been taken. Whoever it was, something had led them to abandon any plans. I know what that something was: it was God's sovereign power.

However, talk of the supernatural can sometimes come across as sensationalised hype or an elusive rarity. Whether wholly accurate, embellished or otherwise, stories circulate about extraordinary events that can seem out of reach for most of our day-to-day normal lives.

The leg that grows centimetres in minutes. The addict that quits heroin overnight, without cold turkey or medical help. The fiercest atheist gang lord who becomes a champion for the gospel. Even the closer to home needs can sometimes seems so scarce. The finances to pay the monthly bills. The new job. The sick neighbour. The wayward child. Yet there are often so many hallmarks of God's divine power at work in the day-to-day rhythms of life - if only we would stop to notice. How many times have you recognised in hindsight, 'so that's why that happened'? Or stumbled across a seeming co-incidence and started a conversation with the words, 'you'll never guess what just happened!?' Friends, God is at work all the time, in the front-of-mind ways we can see - and in the behind-the-scenes ones we can't.

When it comes, this is not some flaky, manufactured, weird manifestation. From personal experience, I have found God's supernatural power falls in a very, very natural way. In his brilliant book, Spirit Contemporary[2], Leon Fontaine writes: 'Some have confused the work of Holy Spirit with the outward reaction to that work. One is a gift from God; the other is a personal response to that gift. People may have all kinds of emotional and physical reactions to Holy Spirit's power. That does not mean that the way one person reacts is a pattern for all others. In fact, there are too many cases where people who make dramatic or showy responses to Holy Spirit do so because they are looking for attention. That's tragic because God is magnificent enough on His own; we don't need to dress up our interactions with Him'. [2. The Spirit contemporary life. Leone Fontaine. Published by Waterbrook 2016]

My own experience is that God's grace provides whatever we need in those moments, to enable a response that's appropriate to the situation.

When once working with a secular Board, the power of God fell in the most tangible way. For a time, no one said anything, but everyone knew the environment felt very different. Yet it also felt very natural. People started speaking with honesty and the once guarded veneer of superficiality was broken. In a culture where self-protection was critical, open transparency flowed. The real conversations long-needed bore fruitful long-term changes. It was the doorway for many lives to be altered. Not only with the people in the room, but also for the countless thousands of people they led. From this supernatural invasion of Glory, the culture of an entire organisation started to shift.

This is something that can't be bottled. God's power can fall when we least expect it. Or it can fall when we are intentionally calling down fire from heaven. It can be something you tangibly touch, see, smell, feel or taste. Or it can be something only evident in the spiritual realm. It can happen when we are alone, or when in the company of others. It can happen immediately. Or it can happen gradually. There simply is no A to Z guide that pinpoints how this all works. This is God acting in His sovereignty. Only He understands and knows the perfect way His power will be released.

However, there are two patterns that often emerge. The first is He will rarely (if ever?) release more than the circumstance can handle. The second is that the degree of experiences we witness tend to have one common denominator: It's our proximity to Him. The more we live in His presence and radiate His love, the more supernatural power we seem to experience. In some respects, this is the culmination of all the previous five promises we've explored in motion. The more we develop the Zoe life, the more aligned we become for the Holy Spirit to create a channel for God's power to be released on earth.

When that happens, it rocks the natural out of all balance and meaning. This is when only the power of God makes sense. God sovereignly intervenes. He directly impacts what is happening and changes the outcome. That's when we see Him shifting the world around us as we know it. The end of The Book tells us that one day, every knee will bow to Him. But in the meantime, let's not forget He still has all authority, over every situation in the here and now. (Col 2:10)

When you learn how to live the Zoe kind of life, as your spiritual maturity develops, the degree of the supernatural you are equipped to experience is released. This will become your expectation, not your desperate hope. As supernatural manifestations of God's power increase, so does your faith. The more you see, the more you believe for.

What supernatural might can bring

'The mountains melt like wax before the LORD, before the Lord of all the earth'.

Living the Zoe kind of life, there is a way to experience the supreme power of God and take dominion.

When you access His sovereign power, you activate your supernatural might. This deepens your faith.

Imagine your own life for a moment and consider what the impact of this would be like for you. The more you develop this the more you will:

- Feel anchored and certain of everything God is. You will just know He is at work. And you will be surrendered to His higher power. You will instinctively know you just have to get out of the way for Him to move. It will be as if you just don't matter. You will find your heart utterly prostrate before him.

- Find that often when this power falls, you will sense something in the atmosphere. This shows up in different ways. Sometimes it may change from heavy to light, sometimes from frenzied and frenetic to still and weighty. Sometimes you may instinctively move from passive to alert.

- Find you may feel vulnerable, small and mighty in equal measure. Vulnerable because you will surrender everything to Him, small, because you will literally bow to how huge He seems, and mighty because of the supernatural power you know He is releasing upon, through and around you.

- Find your natural reactions and behaviour will change. Where you may naturally experience stress, you will experience peace. Where you may naturally experience insecurity, you will experience certainty and courage. Where you may naturally experience fear, you will experience love. Where you may naturally feel procrastination, you will experience a conviction to act. Whatever the shift, in those moments, you will be able to maintain the consistency of this state with no effort.

- Find that people, circumstances and outcomes change. You will witness miracles, with no other plausible explanation. As this happens, your level of expectancy will grow. These outcomes will have no geographical limitations. You may be praying in Dundee about something that is changing in Delhi.

- Find that doubts will become redundant. And even if you slip back into human fear, it will be as if invisible arms immediately restore you to the certainty of God's faithfulness.

- Sometimes find the outcome quietly changes without any spiritual fanfare at all. Whilst at others, in unique moments, the full weight of heaven will seem real and as close as a breath. It will be as though all the spiritual heaviness of all God's power is being brought to bear down and wage warfare on anything that gets in its path.

- Find that in the epi-centre of those unique moments, there will literally be nothing that would surprise you. You will utterly believe there is nothing God cannot do. These are the times when tumours disappear, bad backs are healed, when justice is served and when 'only God' could have done it; you will know His kingdom has come.

- Find in the unique moments, many people who are unaware of the spiritual manifestation taking place, may feel or sense something they cannot put into words. Even non-believers may be left visibly impacted.

- Find after these unique moments, you may well find yourself on your knees in worship, reverence and awe. No words will be adequate to describe the potency or the power of God's presence experienced.

The power of God's sovereignty

'For the kingdom of God is not based on talk but on power.'
1 Corinthians 4:20 NIV

God's supernatural power can release Kingdom sovereignty into our everyday lives. When we live in Him, there is never hopelessness, limitation, the mundane or defeat. Instead, we are His warriors as we get to experience the fullness of His impact. This is when we see divine miracles showing God's favour and Glory to all around. This supremacy enables us to take ground and establish God's dominion over the issues in our lives and in the matters of this world.

Are there situations in your life where more of this would help you right now?

In the Zoe life, with reverence and awe, we experience His supernatural impact ever more. As this is released in, through and around us, His power replaces all earthly limitation with the impossible...

... Hours of exhausting cross-examination passed. Set against the backdrop of worry about Jacob, something was shifting. A lucid calmness had fallen. The fervent prayers in my mind were being answered. Fear and intimidation were being replaced with certainty and composure. The dark blackness in my mind was becoming lighter, the heavy oppression exchanged for quiet inner authority. Different people came in using different approaches. The inner steadiness held its course. Some were kind, some were harsh, some were clinical, some explained things well. 'Stay centred in me', came the clear voice of Holy spirit within. A knowing started to flood my being - it was all going to be fine. Whilst at total odds with everything happening around me, I could sense God's power at work.

Then, eventually, came the breakthrough as a flashback of how I'd found Jacob that morning appeared in my mind. Curled up like a little cat in the corner of his travel cot, it later transpired the base had come loose, to reveal spiky metal grips. What was intended to hold the base in place had instead knocked Jacob unconscious in his sleep. When finally re-united with my baby boy, the same divine whisper came again; 'he's going to be fine'. After test upon test, when we finally drove him home, I knew Jacob had been delivered. Incredibly, despite the extent of the injury, there were no lasting impacts of the trauma to his tiny brain. Without any home visits or further investigations, the social-services case was permanently closed. A spiritual battle had been fought and won by a sovereign God. A God who is greater than anything in this world. A God who can literally move mountains.

'For You, O Lord, will bless the righteous; with favour. You will surround him as with a shield.'
Psalm 5:12 NIV

Reflections

'As a result of the apostles' work, sick people were brought out into the streets on beds and mats so that Peter's shadow might fall across some of them as he went by.'
Acts 5:15 NLT

The courage and faith from the release of God's sovereign power is available to all of us. This is the ultimate display of His glory.

Thinking of your own life;

- Where have you experienced the supernatural might of God before? Think about the big and the small.

- Are there ways you would want to experience this more?

- How would it help your life and this world if you did?

In part two we will look at how this can become your reality.

9

Promise 7
His strength - our victory

The conquering spirit that enables us to deal with
anything - and win!

---

*'For who is God, except the LORD? And who is a rock, except
our God? It is God who arms me with strength, And makes my
way perfect. He makes my feet like the feet of deer, And sets
me on my high places. He teaches my hands to make war, So
that my arms can bend a bow of bronze.'*
Psalm 18:31-34 NKJV

*'But he said to me, "My grace is sufficient for you, for my
power is made perfect in weakness." Therefore I will boast all
the more gladly about my weaknesses, so that Christ's power
may rest on me. That is why, for Christ's sake, I delight in
weaknesses, in insults, in hardships, in persecutions, in
difficulties. For when I am weak, then I am strong.'*
2 Corinthians 12:9-10 NIV

... I paused momentarily to allow the impact of the words I'd just spoken to sink in. Here we were, after six months of chemotherapy, in an emergency meeting with the oncologist, surgeon and breast care nurse. I'm not sure they could quite believe their ears, as I first explained my beliefs, then the decision that I didn't want to proceed with either the mastectomy or the radiotherapy. I was so sure, so calm and the grace of God was flowing, giving me the strength to speak out the unwavering conviction my faith had given me. Getting to this point had pressed me into the deepest point of surrender yet and held my feet to the fire of contemplation. Did I *really* believe every word in that book? Did I *really* believe Jesus never half way healed? Did I *really* believe He's the name above all names; even the name of cancer re-occurrence? For this is what the dilemma demanded.

In the medical world, all treatment so far was inferior to the most important element of the whole programme - removing the tissue from where this cancer had once started. With hugely compassionate hearts, the medical team explained their experience of such scenarios and described in detail how the cancer cells may lay dormant, only to re explode, spreading the disease rapidly through all parts of the body. It was sobering to hear and starkly brought home the aggressive and unforgiving nature of the beast we all call cancer. However, simultaneously, something wonderful was also being spoken inside me. Every scripture, every promise, every revelation God had given me was as vibrant and compelling as the times I'd poured over them in the many hours of the day and night. The certainty that had held me for months was unmoved. Not through my own will or a weird wonder woman type of strength - from the spirit of Jesus in me, giving me all the courage of The Man himself.

What is victory?

This is when regardless of the circumstances, we are able to conquer. These are the times when no matter what hold the situation seems to have, from an ascended perspective, we are left untarnished and unharmed from its impact. These are the times, like Jesus before us, where we can sleep in the boat - despite the raging storm, and still know we will conquer its icy blasts.

Spiritual victory does not relate to what is happening externally – it relates to what is happening internally. **When life is rocking the boat in which we live, it is our response to it that determines our victory – not the outcome of the storm itself.** These are the times when the full strength of Jesus within us provides the fortitude we need to be still and know He is God. (Psalm 46:10) To trust His lead – without any fear, then to follow. This is when we become untouchable, with a triumph that is supreme to anything the fragile circumstances of life could ever provide assurance of. With the supreme strength of Jesus within, we have the ability to conquer anything that tries to ensnare us. We win.

However, victory in line with God's will may look very different to victory in line with our own. Being surrendered to this, is part of our victory. For in submission to the belief God's sovereign will is perfect, we enable The Victor to lead the way. There is no greater assurance of the right outcome than to trust the one who has already walked the path before. So, victory does not come from our limited understanding of what the outcome needs to be. Nor does it come from the end result itself. It comes from trusting the one who knows what the right outcome is. Victory is possible through-out the journey to get there – not just at the end of it.

Our victory comes from our freedom. The freedom from any weight that ties us to the ocean bottom. Fear, anxiety, stress, busy entangled minds, toxic emotions – all are signals that we holding onto what keeps us under the waves, rather than holding onto The

Anchor that keeps us afloat. Our victory is the contented wholeness that comes from this trust – not our trust in the end result itself.

When we are unmoved by the situations in life, whether a storm or a gentle breeze, we will vanquish anything before us. Not through any inner determination we can conjure up. It's through the strength of Jesus within us. He is our victory. We move from it, not towards it. He gives us the strength we need to withstand any trial, pain, inconvenience, discomfort or suffering the situation may present. In His strength, we can ride it with a dignified countenance. This means that all the aspects of His being are free to flow through us.

His peace, His significance, His perspective, His nature, His empowerment, and His sovereignty can all operate under the governance of His strength. This frees us to access every aspect of His character, which liberates us to walk it out the way Jesus would. There is no greater victory in life than that. And as we do, we become a magnet for God's favour. Our assurance in His assurance creates our victory. And when yielded to His will, the most incredible things can happen. The most incredible things do happen.

However, what happens will always be inferior in contrast to the beauty of walking through it this way. What we receive of God through the process is priceless and will always eclipse the outcome at the end – regardless of how wonderful that may be. The healing may come, the finances may return, the wayward child may come back to the Lord. All brilliant outcomes. But they are not the victory. **The victory is who God becomes to us through the process.** More of Him is our prize. As we seek Him first above everything, God releases even more favour. (Matt 6:33)

What victory can bring

'Then David said to the Philistine, "You come to me with a sword, a spear, and a javelin, but I come to you in the name of the LORD of hosts, the God of the armies of Israel, whom you have taunted.'
1 Samuel I 17:45-47 NIV

Living the Zoe kind of life, there is a way to experience ultimate fulfilment in Him, whatever the circumstances of your life look like. This will attract God's favour. When you access His strength, you activate your victory. This becomes your wholeness.

Imagine your own life for a moment and consider what the impact of this would be like for you. The more you develop this, the more you will:

- Filter every situation through the lens of assured certainty. Nothing will catch you out or rock your boat. The rock you stand on, will weather any storm. Despite the situation, you will feel light, vibrant and alive.

- Find that whatever happens, the sense of jubilation is constant. When pain, trial, inconvenience or discomfort come your way, you ride them with the same consistent strength. When the enemy tries to grasp you, it will be as if trying to wrap his arms around a ghost. Nothing he can do will pin you down.

- Find you don't need to know the next step, where you are going or what the outcome will be. Instead, you are content in knowing you are where you are meant to be on that day; content and secure in the process of where God is taking things.

- Find your prayers are not focussed on rescue or on finding answers to the problem. They are focussed on God and finding more of Him.

- Find at times, that regardless of the onslaught, you will actually laugh out loud, the attacks will seem so useless. You will actually revel in the apparent hopelessness, as you know it means God has to step in. The anticipation of what He will do will actually excite you and supersede any negative human reaction.

- Experience such a weight of God's love for you that at times, you won't be able to speak. This will make you feel so protected, you will feel invincible. From this assured safety, a courageous valour you never knew existed will naturally rise.

- Know God is using the situation to show His power. You will feel so privileged at being used for His Kingdom, you will gladly make any sacrifice.

- Find people will not be able to understand your composure. They may even be antagonised by it. This may result in people bombarding you with alternative views. This could include miss-placed, albeit well intentioned sympathy or advice.

- Not be impatiently waiting for God to act or bring the end victory. Both are present every day. You live with a consciousness of God's daily grace. You live with a step in your stride. His grace is your daily victory. You will feel victorious, regardless of what you are experiencing.

- Expect God's favour and you will see it.

The power of God's strength

'The king rejoices in your strength, LORD. How great is his joy in the victories you give!
Psalm 21:1 NIV

God's strength within us provides the courage we need to face any situation before us. Our commitment to His will provides the valour we need to live each day knowing victory. When we live in Him we are never too weak, too small, too fearful or too vulnerable. Instead, we are armoured with weapons not of this world. Our victory comes from winning the inner battles, so we are victorious whatever the external circumstances may be. This brings harmony to our soul. Through this unity, we are able to master anything that tries to master us, creating a rest which means we are not at the mercy of our circumstances or our reaction to them. Our circumstances no longer control us and we are freed to enjoy every day – whatever.

Are there situations in your life where more of this would help you right now?

In the Zoe life, with contented wholeness, we experience victory ever more. ...

... The medical team - from a place of the purest intent, were willing me to re consider. Along with many members of my family and friends, in their eyes the mastectomy and radiotherapy were life-sparingly critical. In their eyes I would die without it.

Burdened with the immense external pressure, how could I look my mum in the eye, knowing the fear of 'what if', would most likely plague her forever? How could I reassure Jacob in years to come, that his mummy won't die before her time? The enemy will ride fear like a champion jockey, tormenting a soul until he wins the race in someone's mind. Yet how could I live with myself if I wasn't true to my beliefs? How could I deny my King and the sovereignty He possessed?

The internal conflict of faith joined the wrestling match in my mind. It came back to those questions again. Did I *really* believe what I've based the last 18 years of my adult life on? Did I *really* believe that

God is above all, even the deadly disease that is cancer? Could I *really* look my husband in the eye without worrying he'd be raising Jacob on his own in a few years-time? Could I *really* look at the sleeping frame of our little miracle each night without wondering if I'd see him graduate from school? In that moment everything seemed so black and white. I needed to be sure I was sure. And even in the face of all those questions and terrifying possibilities, I knew that I was. *This* is the gospel. Every word is true. On that I stake my life.

'I'll support you 100% whatever you decide to do', came the incredible words of my husband. Whilst I knew he desperately supported conventional treatment, I also knew he was genuine in that commitment. 'Go and chat with the big fella', he wisely said - the best steer he could have given.

Hopeless at maths, at school I quickly learned to sit next to the brightest kids who weren't. When the answer seems impossible, I learned a long time ago, stay close to those in the know. Running through question after question in my own mind would get me no-where. I needed a breath from heaven.

Laying it all at His feet, a glow of realisation slowly built inside me. Like the dawning of the sun over a beautiful summer meadow, a gentle warmth, colour and energy grew into my consciousness. This glow brought with it the message I so greatly needed to hear… I knew God knew my heart. And that was actually what mattered. God knew my faith and that I would stake my life upon it. Whether to follow conventional treatment or not wasn't the real issue. Ironically cancer wasn't even the issue. It was the purity of where my decisions were coming from that was. As this truth was whispered into my troubled soul, a peace and a stillness returned.

This was not just about me, it was about so many others. As the faces of precious family and friends floated across the tunnel of my mind, the answer God breathed was love. In that moment I had my decision – conventional treatment was my act of love – a pathway followed, for the relief of those I treasured.

On a day that climaxed into tormented uncertainty, turmoil was replaced with victorious certainty. Anguish was replaced by victorious inner peace. The decision was not the victory. My victory was rest - in spite of the decision.

'But the wisdom from above is first of all pure. It is also peace loving, gentle at all times, and willing to yield to others. It is full of mercy and good deeds. It shows no favouritism and is always sincere.'
James 3:17 NLT

Reflections

'Oh death where is your victory? Oh death where is your sting? The sting of death is sin, and the power of sin [by which it brings death] is the law; but thanks be to God, who gives us the victory [as conquerors] through our Lord Jesus Christ.'
1 Corinthians 15:55-57 AMP

The courage and strength to retain our victory is available to all of us. This is the ultimate display of God's glory.

Thinking of your own life;

- Where have you experienced victory like this before? Think about the big and the small.

- Are there ways you would want to experience this more?

- How would it help your life and the world if you did?

In part two we will look at how this can become your reality.

10

To be or not to be?

'His divine power has given us everything we need for a godly life through our knowledge of him who called us by his own glory and goodness. Through these He has given us his very great and precious promises, so that through them you may participate in the divine nature, having escaped the corruption in the world caused by evil desire.'

2 Peter 1:2-4 NIV

It is God's word that promises the Zoe kind of life. He does not offer what He cannot give. What enables the Zoe life is God. This is grace. The grace that provides everything we need.

As we spiritually develop, we become ever closer to the fullness of life Jesus declared He came to give us. Living in Him, God promises us:

1. His presence – our spiritual intimacy.
   This personal love replaces our empty independence with the blissful stillness of inner communion with God. This is a spiritual intimacy that leaves us feeling secure, supported, and captivated. In Him we are never rejected, alone, unheard or uncared for. Instead, we are adored as we get to experience the deepest constant, faithful love. From it we know we are protected. This brings an anchor that can withstand any storm. Our provision is inner peace.

2. His significance – our renewed identity.
   This divine ranking replaces our uncertainty with the confidence of knowing we are a child of The King. This reveals our full

inheritance, so we are confident in who we are, courageous, humbled, yet assured. In Him we are never low in self-worth, useless, inadequate or belittled. Instead, our promotion brings a stride to our step and a conviction to be bold. This brings an authentic gravitas that carries God's presence. Our provision is authority.

3. His perspective – our ability to hear God.
   This clearance enables our limited thoughts to be replaced with accurate, precise messages from God. In Him we are never lost, trapped or going around in circles. Instead, we experience Kingdom inspired revelation, which enables us to make wise choices. This brings a clarity that enables us to see things through heaven's perspective. Our provision is joy.

4. His nature – our accelerated change.
   This servant-heart fuels our desire to replace our old default ways, with the heart, mindset and behaviour of Jesus. In Him we are never a lost cause, incapable of change or mediocre. Instead we are freed as we conquer our old ways and replace them with fruits of the spirit. This maturity positively changes outcomes. These virtues accelerate our change and give us the hunger to pursue our ongoing transformation. Our provision is motivation.

5. His empowerment – our heightened ability.
   This anointing replaces grinding effort with natural flow, by the convergence of God's multiplying power with our natural abilities. In Him we are never limited by our past experiences, 'just' good enough or incapable. Instead, we experience ever more of our potential, as he heightens what we would ever be capable of without Him. This enables us to do things that surpass any expectations, so our effectiveness enhances our credibility. This inner assurance outstrips any pressure. Our provision is confidence.

6. His sovereignty – our supernatural power.

This supreme power releases God's will, as the rules of His Kingdom are released and replace all earthly boundaries. In Him there is never lost hope, limitation, the mundane, or the impossible. Instead, we are privileged to experience the divine sovereign hand of God, changing our lives and our world. Through it we take dominion. This increases our trust that He is who He is. Our provision is deeper faith.

7. His strength – our victory.
   This fortitude fuels the courage and perseverance to stand up to any situation. In Him we are never too weak, too small, too fearful or too vulnerable. Instead, we are armoured with weapons not of this world, so we win the inner battles that bring victory whatever the external circumstances may be. This victory comes from our proximity to Him. God is the strength we need. More of Him becomes less of us, bringing fulfilment, contentment and harmony to our soul. Wholeness is our provision.

All this is grace from the giver. He is our provision to access everything He ever promised.

The sacrifice of Jesus was never to just get us into heaven. It was also to set us free from the constraints of this world, so we could live life to the full until we get there.

'Our old sin-loving nature was buried with him by baptism when he died; and when God the Father, with glorious power, brought him back to life again, you were given his wonderful new life to enjoy'.
Romans 6:4 TLB

Let's get real

The Word is The Word. We are promised it does not return void. (Isaiah 55:11) The Word does what it says. But in this demanding fallen world, can this Zoe kind of life become a reality? You may believe the promises are true, but could the reality of being able to live them – consistently, just be the wishful, deluded, naïve view of a positive minded, half-glass-full type of thinker?

Twenty years ago, I would probably have thought so. I don't say that through the patronising belief that I've personally cracked this in every situation, every day. I'm a walking work in progress – the Zoe kind of life is unmistakably a life-long journey.

But would a loving father really re-enforce such possibilities so many times, only for them to be so elusively out of reach, they become nothing more than an aspiration? Think about it. Would you tease your own children with a gift you knew you would never be able to provide? A gift they would never actually be able to receive?
So, to answer the question of whether it's really possible, we have to remind ourselves of who this God of ours is. What do you know of His character, His goodness and His faithfulness?

Well, is it only possible for the spiritually elite then, you may ask? God may be able, but am I? Is there something particularly unusual about those who get closer to the Zoe kind of life we are promised?

In times gone by, I would have compared myself to others, automatically concluding I am 'less than'. At that point, all this may have seemed out of reach.

Born into a normal working-class family, whilst my biological father left when I was small, the love from my Mum more than compensated. Raised as a Christian, good seeds were sown from an early age. But through tricky circumstances and bad choices in my teenage years, I was soon to fall away from that grounding. Middle-of-the road academically, the world of work became my focus from a young age. Married at eighteen, divorced at twenty one, heartache was something I knew. Success did not come without many punishing hours, extra curricula study and a lot of determination. So you see, there really is nothing unusual about me. I dare say that if we were able to chat over coffee, we would find so many parallels in the reality of our lives.

But – and this is the key - there is someone exceptional who lives in me. If you are reading this book, the chances are, He lives inside you too. **This is the key to accessing the fullness of the Zoe life we're promised - living in Him, instead of in ourselves.** One day at a time, one step at a time, (if you're anything like me) - with a few backward steps in-between. If we apply ourselves to it, change really is possible. If it can be for me, it can be for you too. All it takes is a decision.

Even a cursory glance back to the challenges of life remind us how we are often so limited. In contrast, the promises of the Zoe life show us the brilliance of what is available. So, what is it that gets in the way? In short – we do!

We set the limit

'And I will ask the Father, and He will give you another Helper (Comforter, Advocate, Intercessor—Counsellor, Strengthener, Standby), to be with you forever'.
                    John 14:16 AMP

We know we are made in the likeness of God (Gen 1:26-27). God is Spirit. And so are we. But here on earth, we also have a soul and the body in which we live (1 Thess 5:23). When we die, our body and soul fall away, but our spirit lives on eternally.

'Therefore we do not lose heart. Even though our outward man is perishing, yet the inward man is being renewed day by day.'
                    2 Corinthians 4:16 NKJV.

In the New Living Translation, the term 'inner man' is referred to as spirit. At any time, we have three distinct sources of consciousness available to us:

- What our spirit says – our inner man.
- What our soul says - our mind (how we think), our will (what we want) and our emotions. (how we feel)
- What our body says - what we physically experience.

The trouble is that in the noise of this complex, fallen, demanding world, our level of spirit consciousness is often drowned out. It's our soul and as a consequence, our body who often run the show.

The degree to which we live the Zoe kind of life does not depend on our circumstances, our upbringing, our status in life or what the enemy tries to throw our way. It's about how we respond to the reality of that world. This is why God sent us a helper.

How we respond is changed when we live in Him. We live in Him by the power of His Spirit within us – The Holy Spirit. If we allow Him to, God is the one who can influence our own spirit and this is what releases the Zoe life within. **The Zoe kind of life is possible when we think, feel and do what the Holy Spirit guides us into.**

God's abundant favour

'You are their strength. What glory! Our power is based on your favour! '.

Psalm 89:17 TLB

Incredibly, the amazing promises we've explored only reflect a fraction of what God can do in and through our lives. Whether we proactively partner in this or not, in His grace, He never stops working, wooing and willing us to more. None of it comes through what we deserve, desire or earn our way to.

Maybe you have experienced glimpses, seasons or times when many of the promises He offers are a reality for you? Or, maybe those experiences seem to come and go? When we see them, God is leading us into the truth of what He can do for us. Through each experience, He shows us the possibility of what our life can be like when we follow His blueprint. The blueprint of how He's purposefully designed our lives to work effectively here on earth.

In John 14:12 Jesus himself said: *'Truly, truly, I say to you, he who believes in Me, the works that I do, he will do also; and greater works than these he will do; because I go to the Father'*. This always blows my mind. However, if He said it, it's available - the unlimited abundance of all this favour. If we choose to walk this way - if we chose to press in and develop the Zoe kind of life.

What do you choose?

'Your Kingdom come, your will be done, on earth as it is in heaven.'
Matthew 6:10 NIV

All around me, on a daily basis, I hear of people who have the most awful struggles in life. Some of it is not of their making. Some of it is. There is no judgement here. I could be talking to myself as I write this.

For so many years, I would regularly experience stress, restlessness, pain, compromise, fear and burden. I found it very difficult to experience peace and rest. Even now, there are times when I can find myself going around the same issue, having doubts and feeling the pressure. In a split second, there are occasions when my soul overtakes my spirit. Left unchecked, my thoughts, feelings and behaviour would spiral downhill from there.

Internally I have experienced more worry and exhaustion than I can now bear to imagine. I have wasted so much time trapped inside the prison of my own mind, caught up in tensions of my own making. I have repeatedly felt lacking and have not addressed things I need to, making more bad decisions than I can care to remember. Being salt and light has felt like hard work! Being 'nice' has taken my best fake Sunday face and I have struggled not to just react to situations. In these times, I am ashamed to say I have been a very poor walking advertisement of the Jesus who is in me. Even in the good days, I have still, eventually got to a point of feeling that gnaw of discontent, despondency and loneliness. Because nothing compares to doing life with Him.

Through all this, I have experienced more turmoil, pressure and rollercoaster rides than Disney could create. Some of it has been my making. Some of it has not. But my life, lived independently of the Holy Spirit's lead has always been just too hard, too inconsistent and too empty.

Think about your own life for a second. What kinds of problems, situations, challenges and resulting consequences might you have avoided in your life, if you had instead developed the Zoe kind of life?

It doesn't need to be this way. Just for a second, imagine you are God. You know the world is fallen, you knew all along Jesus would be the only solution to redemption. So, despite the cost, you sacrificed Him for this. In perfect precision, Jesus showed us the way and when He returned to heaven, the Holy Spirit was sent to be our guide. You specifically chose your people and made your commission clear. You gave the help needed and access to the power of heaven itself. But your people don't use it. Instead, you see brokenness, turmoil and hardship. Your people may love you, may pray, may do lots of good things. They may even seem fine, but they do not access the help you have sent. Instead you see your people struggling, yo-yoing, resisting, getting weighed down, making mistakes you know that will hurt. Even with sincere hearts, you see the daily battles people wrestle with. You have made it as accessible and clear as you can; 'The Holy Spirit is right there within you' you impress again and again. Somehow lives just don't embrace or embed this provision. And there's a cost. Because without living in Jesus, you know your people will always fall.

How do you think God feels? I reckon it breaks His heart to see His people limited, marginalised or suffering as we can do, when the answer has been placed within us. Not to mention, that this is *the* enabler for us being able to truly reach others and make real disciples. If we aren't sorted, how do we ever attract the world? Jesus was the most perfect, powerful person that ever walked the earth. To infect this world, as His followers, we need to radiate who He was. To do this, we need to develop the Zoe kind of life. The choice for you right now is, do you want to?

Reflections

At the end of each chapter in part one, we stopped to reflect. Whilst you may have experienced some of what we explored, there is always more. God doesn't want us to miss out on a thing, which is why The Word says:

'Test yourselves to make sure you are solid in the faith. Don't drift along taking everything for granted. Give yourselves regular check-ups. You need first-hand evidence, not mere hearsay, that Jesus Christ is in you. Test it out. If you fail the test, do something about it.'
2 Corinthians 13: 5-7 MSG

In the Living bible, this same passage challenges: 'Do you feel Christ's presence and power more and more within you?'

Do you?

The exciting thing is that the depths of this are limitless. When we live the Zoe kind of life ever more consistently, there is the opportunity to turn these moments into hours, the hours into days and the days into a way of being.

Psalm 42:2 NKJV says *'My soul thirsts for God. For the living God'*. This is because our soul (our mind, will and emotions) will never be fully satiated by anything else.

In part two, we will explore how to develop the Zoe kind of life. The life that will bring an abundance of God's favour through the manifestation of all the promises we have explored. Before we do, look back at your own reflections from the seven promises we have covered so far. Pray and invite the Holy Spirit to help you think about the areas of spiritual growth you would like to develop.

When you're ready, let's go and let's get started.

Part two will show you how.

Part two

How to live the Zoe life

'I am the way, the truth and the life'
John 14:6 NIV

11

The tapestry

'I want you woven into a tapestry of love, in touch with everything there is to know of God. Then you will have minds confident and at rest, focused on Christ, God's great mystery. All the richest treasures of wisdom and knowledge are embedded in that mystery and nowhere else. And we've been shown the mystery!'
Colossians 2:2-3 MSG

My Aunt is a great seamstress. Over the years, she has been gifted to pick up a piece of fabric and turn it into something beautiful. One of her hobbies is weaving intricate tapestries. There is one particular rug which has become a lifetime's work for her. At around 20 feet squared, it is something she needs to lovingly return to over and over again. At the beginning, this piece of fabric was nothing more than a dull cloth, with an image of the design branded onto the fabric. It was just a lifeless, empty, heavy piece of hessian. But it was full of possibility. With precision, patience and perseverance, over the years she has tenderly stranded beautiful coloured yarns through the material. Day after day, she has hovered over small patches at a time, to gingerly create an amazing picture that is now starting to represent the image it was always intended to be.

In the same way, Jesus is the perfect picture we are all branded to look like. If the Zoe kind of life is thinking, feeling and doing what the Holy Spirit guides us into, it is this pattern He is following. What Jesus shows, guides and makes the way for enables this transformation His example, instruction and sacrifice create the perfect picture.

'There is only one Life-Leader for you - Christ'.
Matthew 23:10b MSG

If our life is a tapestry, we need certain strands woven into the fabric of our lives to enable this. The Holy Spirit is the master craftsman. Our engagement with Him provides the strands He needs to turn our stark, dull, messy lives into a co-ordinated vision of beauty. This is how we become everything The Father always intended. It's the perfect harmony of the trinitarian Godhead, three-in-one at work.

There are 7 distinct strands that develop this intended Zoe kind of life. Each of these strands are what enable the seven promises we explored in part one. All are based upon who Jesus is, how He lived and what He said. This is our 'how'.

- Releasing His presence and activating our spiritual intimacy, is developed through strand 1: *Connection.*

- Releasing His significance and activating our renewed identity, is developed through strand 2: *Building relationship.*

- Releasing His perspective and activating our ability to hear God, is developed through strand 3: *Worship.*

- Releasing His nature and activating our accelerated change, is developed through strand 4: *Purposeful service.*
- Releasing His empowerment and activating our heightened ability, is developed through strand 5: *Partnership.*

- Releasing His sovereignty and activating our supernatural might, is developed through strand 6: *Spiritual growth.*

- Releasing His strength and activating our victory, is developed through strand 7: *Surrender.*

For living in Jesus to be possible, we have to stop living in ourselves. These 7 strands of activity are how we learn to do this.

The 7 strands of activity

Strand 1:
Connecting – constantly inviting the Godhead in.

> Increased connection is how God's presence is released within us. The peace this creates enables us to live in the promise of spiritual intimacy. As we experience this, we are stilled and increasingly drawn to:

Strand 2:
Building our relationship – developing deep, constant fellowship and understanding.

> Deepening our relationship is how we come to know who God really is – and the significance of who we are in Him. The authority this develops, enables us to recognise our full inheritance. When we embed this renewed identity, we develop the royal countenance of a child of the King. The depths of what this means captivates our hearts, so we can't help but develop:

Strand 3:
A heart of worship – constant adoration and gratitude.

> Developing a heart of worship is what elevates us to the spiritual realm that changes all perspective. As we increasingly take our eyes away from ourselves and up to God, we enter the throne room of heaven. This always brings joy, which elevates us to see things through heaven's filter. This ascended perspective clears a channel so we are able to hear God's word, will and wisdom. These Kingdom revelations inspire our minds and remould our hearts, ultimately leading us to:

Strand 4:
Purposeful service – wholeheartedly applying ourselves.

Purposeful service is a wholehearted commitment that comes when we want to give ourselves in return for His love. Blossoming from the humility and servant heart of Jesus' nature within us, it stirs an uncompromising motivation. Pursuit of both our purpose and the way we need to change to fulfil it, is what accelerates our transformation into the image of Jesus. This increasingly releases the fruits of the spirit, whilst simultaneously highlighting our ever-more dependent need for God. Our purpose can only ever be achieved through Him, which propels us into:

Strand 5:
Partnership – constantly accessing the Holy Spirit's leading.

Working in partnership with the Holy Spirit is how the promise of God's empowerment multiplies what we could ever achieve independently. As we increasingly turn to this, a restful confidence overtakes our self-imposed limitations, through the heightened ability God enables. This increases our impact and further inspires us to pursue:

Strand 6:
Spiritual growth – maturing into our inherited spiritual stature.

Spiritual growth is how the promise of God's sovereign will is increasingly released into our world. As we experience this, unrelenting faith is developed in tandem with the character, spiritual gifts and wisdom needed for us to be trusted with His supernatural might. When we develop our spiritual stature, we increasingly receive more supernatural power. As heaven invades earth through us, we can't help but be compelled to:

Strand 7:
Surrender – yielding our whole life.

> When we surrender our thoughts, feelings and actions to God's will, He replaces what we let go of with more of Himself. This is what brings us His strength to obey and as we do, we remove all barriers that we separate ourselves from God with. This bonding brings a contented wholeness nothing else can create. With it comes such completeness, that all we can do is fully yield our lives. It is this submission that frees God to lead us into His intended will. Our obedience is a magnet to His favour. His will is our victory. This is what enables us to take dominion over every circumstance in life.

These 7 strands bring the freedom God requires to fulfil every one of His promises. As we increasingly step out of ourselves and into Him, we are lead us into the heart of the Zoe life.

'And [I pray] that the eyes of your heart [the very centre and core of your being] may be enlightened [flooded with light by the Holy Spirit], so that you will know and cherish the hope [the divine guarantee, the confident expectation] to which He has called you, the riches of His glorious inheritance in the saints (God's people), and [so that you will begin to know] the immeasurable and unlimited and surpassing greatness of His [active, spiritual] power is in us who believe.'
Ephesians 1:18-19 AMP

By weaving all 7 strands into the fabric of our lives, the Holy Spirit enables us to live in Jesus. Living in Him gives us the inner provision we need to release the promises of His word.

This is grace – grace is the Zoe life.

The master craftsman

These simple, yet challenging strands are how we develop the wondrous life God wants for every one of us. With a cursory glance, we may intellectually place a tick in many of the boxes. In theory, we get it. In a way it's similar to the executives I often work with. Operating at senior organisational levels, they have been through the leadership development programmes and hold the MBA's. However, there is a huge difference between knowing the leadership text and being an effective leader. In the same way, there is often the same disparity between knowing what our bible says and being it. We may even personally know Jesus, but that doesn't mean we know how to live like Him. Despite our most sincere desire and intentions, it's the inconsistencies that provide the breeding ground for our own struggles. Romans 7:15-20 helps to highlight the challenge, when Paul wrote about his own wrestle between knowing what to do and his inability to do what is right.

The Holy Spirit lives in us to repeatedly weave the full spectrum of all these strands into the fabric of our lives. If some strands are missing, the end picture will not look like it could do. The vibrancy of the colour and the density of the strand impacts on the precision, clarity, accuracy and detail of the tapestry being woven. So, as such, what the final image looks like depends on how well we have engaged with all the strands the Holy Spirit seeks to perfect.

As I reflect back on my own journey, there have been times when all 7 strands have been in Holy Spirit's fingers. Other times I have found that, in different seasons, God seems to have been focussing on strengthening one particular strand at a time. The Holy Spirit knows exactly what elements we need to develop when. In different sequences, for different reasons, if we engage with Him, He will navigate us through deepening the texture of each and every one.

We will never understand all the mysteries of heaven this side of eternity. Nor can we contain or in any way control the workings of the Holy Spirit through what we do. However, we can learn how to open ourselves to His influence. Working hand-in-hand with The Master Craftsman, part two will show you how.

What comes next?

Part two is about how to live the Zoe life. It aims to provide useful guidance, along with very practical ways you can implement these seven strands into your life. This can help:

- Challenge the depth of the Zoe life you currently experience
- Enhance the consistency of how you already live parts of the Zoe life
- Help you activate and grow into a new depth of spiritual maturity
- Provide encouragement and reminders of how to maintain the Zoe life.

All of this is dependent on four key things:

1. Prayer is intrinsic to every element.
2. The activities don't replace your ongoing study of the word. They supplement it.
3. The Holy Spirit is the source for all progress.
4. It requires your ongoing engagement.

Whilst this book is intended to repeatedly be picked up and put down, ongoing momentum will bring the best results. Without these four things, the strand will be weakened. Left untied, the cotton will gradually unravel from the fabric of your life. As this slowly unravels, the tapestry does not remain the same. The good progress you start with can gradually look less like the image of Jesus it once began to portray. Perseverance is the key.

To help, together we will explore what each of the seven strands involve, the inner provision they bring, why each one is so critical and how to strengthen them in our lives. However, this does not come in an A-Z, 'step-by-step' guide. The Holy Spirit can't be tamed and we should never assume what is needed. He knows what is right for each one of us. We are all at different points, so He meets us where we are. This may also mean that He deals with different strands in different sequences. In partnership with the Holy Spirit, He guides us through this.

However, we know that for us to get close to the perfect mind of God, He often gives a pattern to follow. Think about the instructions for the building of the tabernacle, as just one example. That pattern related to building the vessel that would carry the very presence of God. In the same way, the pattern we will consider helps build the vessel that holds God's presence now. It builds us.

Eighteen years of personal experience have been validated by an ongoing discovery of Biblical truths. In its pages, every direction we ever need is provided. How many times do we read a psalm, to find the writer's initial turmoil is replaced with peace and security in a matter of a few sentences? Or when mining the depths of a parable do we see a buried clue? What about the stories of old that provide both metaphorical and literal application to how we respond to so many of life's conundrums? Embedded in the text is all the guidance we need. Biblical treasure hunting has pieced the pattern we will follow together. (Prov 2:4-5)

Lifted straight from The Word, this pattern includes suggested loops of activity we can give the Holy Spirit to work with. Their application will be different for everyone, but personal examples have been given to help get you started. These are simple, easy to use activities, many of which you may already naturally do. Whether sporadically or consistently applying the pattern in each strand, the full power is in the cumulative effect of a life that is lived this way – always. This is our challenge – to embed these patterns into a natural way of being. An increasing Zoe life is our promise if we increasingly do.

Pursuing the Zoe life requires our intentional engagement. No amount of reading or knowledge gained will in isolation, enable its reality. Preaching, teaching, conferences and bible study will only do so much. At some point, application is required. You are the only person who can do this.

To help you, with the Holy Spirit's lead, we will regularly pause to process, contemplate and practice. This is as important as the understanding that sits alongside it. Each chapter has been designed to first elicit reflection, then to be as practical as possible, with biblical references, stories and ideas to help you turn good intentions into simple actions. These can become key tools for you to come back to again and again. With regular application, what starts as conscious practice can turn into healthy habits, which when embraced, become the most natural unforced way of being. This is our journey into the fullness of the Zoe kind of life.

This isn't something to scramble towards. God is a good God, who is willing you to the more He always intended. However, there's no need to rush, force, or pressure yourself in any way. Right now, some of you may want to push straight into the content. Just in this moment, my encouragement is not to. Instead, take a moment to pause. Allow yourself to be stilled and consider the following three questions:

- What do you most want to get out of this?
- How might your life be changed?
- How might it impact others and the world around you?
- What, if anything, concerns you?

As you ponder these questions, spend some time praying about what you discover. Allow this to organically merge into a conversation with your Father. Allow time for silence and consciously allow the Holy Spirit to flow. Breathe Him in and just see where His nurturing arms take you. What else does He have to say?

When you're ready, we can now begin.

12

The 1ˢᵗ strand

Increasing connection
Inviting the Godhead in.

How to release His presence and activate our spiritual intimacy.

'So I say to you, ask and keep on asking, and it will be given to you; seek and keep on seeking, and you will find; knock and keep on knocking, and the door will be opened to you. For everyone who keeps on asking [persistently], receives; and he who keeps on seeking [persistently], finds;   and   to   him   who   keeps   on knocking [persistently], the door will be opened.'
Luke 11:9-10 AMP

Connection is the key that unlocks the Zoe life. It opens the door of our heart, something that is only possible through invitation. Whether stuck in the autopilot of life, or whether wilfully operating in our own strength, it's this invitation that lets God in.

Whilst the Holy Spirit comes to live inside us, the reality is, we are as close to Him as we choose to be. Connection is about consciously making a decision to open ourselves up to God's support. When we invite the Holy Spirit in and connect our spirit to Him, this enables us to be constantly refilled with all He is here to bring us. It was Jesus himself who assured us that if we ask, we will receive. In exchange for our invitation, we open up the channel to receive all of Jesus today.

We may connect in this way when we are in the mood, not shaken by conflict, or overcome by the busyness of the world. But how often do we live there? This is about a consistent connection with the Holy Spirit, regardless of our external situation.

The truth is that all too often, we effectively put up invisible barriers that block this support. We can become so consumed by the world around us that our soul takes all our attention, not our spirit within. Often, to invite anyone in can feel risky. It means opening ourselves up, which can often make us feel vulnerable. But in a Spirit-fuelled life it is critical.

In some respects, this is the antithesis of common culture. Much of social conversation these days seems to be at such a superficial level. Just think about the typical pleasantries you exchange with your neighbours, friends, work colleagues and even family members. Often behind the screen of technology, meaningful engagement can be scarce. In contrast, think about the times you have been in conversation with someone, when you have slipped easily into a deep exchange. As you have both spoken freely, you have been fully present with each other and you often don't know where the time has gone. These are the times when you've let your guard down, you've stopped to really listen and you've invested in what the other person is sharing. Often, they can be moments of intimacy. For many, these moments are rare.

In today's world we over rely on either self-sufficiency (I will sort it), self-protection (I don't want to get hurt) or self-preservation (I don't want to get that involved).

The Holy Spirit is always willing us to get beyond these self-imposed restrictions. Without constant connection with Him, we are throwing ourselves at the mercy of life.

In the amplified Bible, John 14:16 says the Holy Spirit is our standby. In the Oxford Dictionary, this word means 'ready for duty'. The Holy Spirit will not force himself upon us, but waits patiently to be called upon. This is about being prepared to open ourselves up to his leading, investing our faith in this and talking honestly about the support we need. Connection is not a one-off decision. It is a minute-by minute daily one.

When we do this, we encounter love. Pure, holy love.

God's love is perfect and constant. He loves because that is who He is. It's the very expression of His being. In Greek, this type of love is described as 'Agape', but we have no English equivalent word for it. In our humanity we can never fully understand the incredible depth, purity and unconditional nature of it. We are wiped off our feet with the potency of it. The more time we spend with God, the more we will start to know, believe and become this love.

These are the moments when we get to experience the very heartbeat of God. As this happens, we step into more and more of His presence. I often feel like just one touch from God is enough to keep me going for weeks. But the good news is that He wants to renew this every minute of every day.

Time and again Jesus was able to love, in the most incredible circumstances. In Gethsemane He healed the ear of the centurion arresting him (Luke 22:51). On the cross he forgave the people who eventually murdered Him. (Luke 23:34) Such love could only come from the pure love of God. We know from His life how Jesus constantly served then retreated to be re-filled by His father. Our connection with God is the source behind our provision. **His presence is our power.**

The provision is peace

1 John 4:18 tells us that perfect love casts out all fear. It's true. When we are immersed in the presence of God, this connection leaves us in total peace. This, is the outcome that takes us further into the Zoe life. The greater and more consistent our connection, the greater and more consistent our peace. This is our provision. **Connection brings peace.**

The oxford dictionary says the definition of peace is the freedom from disturbance. Tranquillity. Mental or emotional calm. A state where there is no war.

'Trust in, lean on, rely on, and have confidence in Him at all times, you people; Pour out your hearts before Him. God is a refuge for us (a fortress and a high tower). Selah (pause, and calmly think of that).'
Psalm 62:8 AMP

The peace God brings has the power to supersede all anxiety and distress. **Whatever our situation on the outside, in His presence, this is peace that abides.** It never leaves. This is a state of mind that allows no disturbance to penetrate the protection this covering brings.

God really is our mighty high tower of refuge from the bombshells of life. Whether we are at war in our heads or in our circumstances, under His wings, peace can be a place in which we live. **This is abiding peace;** a peace that is different from the tranquillity of mind we can ever find through our own meditation or introspection - no matter how serene the environment. Abiding peace stays – no matter what is going on around us. It does not depend on a self-calming centred state of mind or beautiful surroundings. **It depends on being in the presence of Jesus.**

Stop to reflect on your own life for a moment.

- How often do you consciously live in the peaceful presence of Jesus?
- Conversely how much time do you spend living in worry, isolation, or in negative emotions such as impatience or fear?
- What would your life look like if you could replace all those times of uncertainty with a permanent state of abiding peace?

Connection is the strand we must increase to release this provision.

The missing strands

If we don't consciously let God in, we won't let what binds us out.

The Zoe life is impossible without this strand, as the demands of this world will constantly try to rock our Kingdom composure. Without constant connection to the presence of God, we limit our ability to live in peace, or ride the rough with the smooth. However, it is often either missing or not consistently prominent enough in the tapestry of our lives. Let us start by looking at three key reasons why:

1. Because our busyness crowds out God's presence.

'Let me put this question to you: How did your new life begin? Was it by working your heads off to please God? Or was it by responding to God's Message to you? Are you going to continue this craziness? For only crazy people would think they could complete by their own efforts what was begun by God. If you weren't smart enough or strong enough to begin it, how do you suppose you could perfect it? Did you go through this whole painful learning process for nothing? It is not yet a total loss, but it certainly will be if you keep this up!
Galatians 3:3-4 MSG

This paragraph in the Message Bible actually makes me laugh out loud at myself, such is the punch of its truth. If we don't consciously invite God in and connect with Him, eventually we will fail and fall. For many, our days turn into weeks, which then turn into months and years of a constantly turning hamster wheel. As we juggle with the priorities and complexities, we can get accustomed to just getting on with things. When we do, we often forget to consciously include God in the process. Or we make a decision, act and then pray God's covering over it. We can become so preoccupied by life, that we forget we are spiritual beings at all. Instead, we focus on the immediacy of the world we see around us. Our soul (mind, will and emotions) takes our focus. When this happens, we tune out from our spirit.

'As soon as Jesus was baptised, he went up out of the water. At that moment heaven was opened, and he saw the Spirit of God descending like a dove and lighting on him. And a voice from heaven said, 'this is my son, whom I love; with him I am well pleased'.
Matthew 3:16-17 NIV

Despite being the son of God, Jesus insisted he was baptised by John the Baptist. As this happened, we learned how the Spirit of God descended and rested on him. In this symbolic act, Jesus showed us that we all need to invite Holy Spirit's presence into our lives.

In the Old Testament, we read over and over how King David constantly asked for God's advice, intervention and help. We also know how it cost him when he didn't. Sometimes we may consciously avoid giving God this permission, for fear of what His involvement means. Had David connected and invited God in when he was experiencing the lust for Bathsheba, the story would have turned out very differently.

There have been days where I have felt that my shoulders have metaphorically been up by my ears. The days when I have been so busy that tension is a constant. But as soon as I realise and ask for Holy Spirit's support, the burden flees and my awareness of Him in me returns.

In the mix of busy lives in a busy world, if we don't stop to invite this connection, we will make so many mistakes without it. Think about a typical working week and the juggling of family, work, social, sporting, leisure and church commitments. That's on a normal week, before you add in emergencies such as a sick child, an elderly neighbour who takes a fall, a disaster at work or a leaky roof on the house. Often the enemy's most successful tactic is to distract us.

When we find ourselves filling every day to the brim, with no time even to breathe in between, we lose connection - connection with our spirit (we get absorbed by earthly stuff); connection with ourselves (we ignore the symptoms that say we need a good night's sleep); connection with others (we engage in small talk but at the same time we are thinking of other things in our busy minds) and connection with God (we may 'do church', but the daily, ongoing communion we need just never gets to the top of the pile).

This was the connection Elijah so greatly needed after his great show down on Mount Carmel. (1 Kings 19) The all-encompassing nature of his quest left him exhausted and vulnerable, as he flee from Jezebel in fear of his life. His natural reaction was to run away and hide. What he really needed was an infilling of God

2. Because we leak.

'We must pay the most careful attention, therefore, to what we have heard, so that we do not drift away.'
Hebrews 2:1 NIV

I love cycling. At the top of a hill, I can take my feet off the pedals and allow the momentum to propel me forward. But at some point, I need to start peddling again, or I will eventually come to a stop. Being refilled is a constant process. Because in a fallen world, life can be tough. Without this connection, we quickly lose our power.

The reaction of our soul can be so strong, deep and fast. Within an instant, circumstances can pull us down into the turmoil of our mind, will and emotions. In every minute of every day, we need to determine to stay connected. We can't afford to unplug from our power source for even a day. With a young boy who (still!) often wakes in the night, there are mornings when I humanly feel exhausted. Left unchecked, it can affect my mood, my perspective and my resilience. But the minute I invite Holy Spirit in to refill me with strength for the day, the minute my tiredness starts to change into energy. The Holy Spirit wants to refill us deeper in every situation, every day. All He needs is an invitation.

I remember once handling a tricky issue with the tax office. My accountant had sent a duplicate form in to their offices and as a result, I was incorrectly being asked to pay double the amount due. Speaking to the relevant tax officer didn't seem to help. Without praying beforehand, instead, receiving the demand letter, I rushed straight to the phone and the unhelpful conversation that unfolded. Filled with frustration, anxiety and impatience before the call even got going, midway through, (when getting nowhere), in the quiet of my heart I asked the Holy Spirit to help. That's all I said: 'Help'. Explaining the predicament once more, in the very next sentence, the officer decided to transfer me to another department. After further explanation, the matter was promptly resolved.

That was a practical issue. But the Holy Spirit is also on standby to help us with the deepest, most long-standing issues of our lives too.

I have a very dear friend who has suffered a lot of pain in her life. Rejection, betrayal and loneliness have been the hallmarks of her life for over fifty years. So, despite being a believer, God was kept at an arm's length. In her own words, she once said 'I encased myself in steel so much; no one was getting in'. Circumstances caused her to build a wall around her heart, so whilst on the surface she could portray forgiveness, deep down the hurt still gnawed away. She was fiercely independent, doggedly determined and never asked anyone for help. One day (through the incredible working of the Holy Spirit), she took the step to reconnect and invite God in. In a very simple prayer, the Holy Spirit immediately made Himself known. She describes how in that instant, it was as if a cork had been popped open. All the pain she had ever held onto was literally sucked out from inside her. As this happened she said she felt the sparks and embrace of a love beyond words. Those few moments literally changed her life forever.

3. Because we need to get over 'self'.

'He must become greater and greater, and I must become less and less.'

John 3:30 NLT

In this statement, John the Baptist laid out a central principle to the Spirit-led life. Some bible translations use the words 'increase' and 'decrease'. In essence, it's saying that our focus needs to shift from ourselves to the work of Jesus. The Holy Spirit enables the work of Jesus in us. But it's incredible how strong our sense of 'self' can be. Over the years, we learn to operate in this 'self'. This covers all manner of purposes, but here are just a few:

- Self-protection (e.g. 'I won't let anyone hurt me')
- Self-interest (e.g. 'What's in it for me?)
- Self-righteousness (e.g. 'My view is right')
- Self-sufficiency (e.g. 'No one else will do it for me')
- Self-centred (e.g. 'What I want is')
- Self-hatred (e.g. 'Why would anyone help me?')
- Self-esteem (e.g. 'I have to prove myself')
- Self-help (e.g. 'I can make it happen')
- Self-effacing (e.g. 'I'm not good enough')
- Self-confidence (e.g. 'I believe in me')
- Self-preservation (e.g. 'I need to look after myself here')

Andrew Owen once referred to this as the 'sovereign-self' – when we effectively become our own messiah.

In her book 'Limitless', Charity Bowman-Webb speaks much about the creativity God has placed in us. In it she says; *'the more freedom we allow the Spirit, the more freedom we will find for ourselves. We are supposed to be the temple for the Holy Spirit living in us (1 Corinthians 3:16), not the walls; but we can become the walls, the parameters, as we set boundaries and limitations for God. We need to allow the Spirit new levels of liberation.'* [3. Published by Blue Flame 2016]

It is our sense of 'self' that can be the walls that block the Holy Spirit from leading us. When we are holding onto 'self', whether intentional or not, we have taken over. When our 'self' is in control, the Holy Spirit is not. It's only when we let these barriers down that we allow the space for Him to be our 'more'. When we connect, it helps us to be focussed on our 'self' less.

Just pause for a moment.

- When does your busyness crowd out God's presence?
- When do you leak and revert back to unhelpful ways as a result?
- What sovereign-self behaviours block the Holy Spirit?

As you reflect, spend some time praying about what you discover. Allow this to organically merge into a conversation with your Father. Allow time for silence and consciously allow the Holy Spirit to flow. Is there anything else He says?

The pattern to living it

In each chapter, we will explore the pattern that helps develop, strengthen and embed each strand. **The purpose of the pattern in the strand of connection is to increase our inner sense of abiding**

peace. It is how promise 1: His presence – our spiritual intimacy is released and activated.

This pattern has been broken down into the three key loops of activity that each strand can make. These loops will need to be woven over and over again by the expert hands of the Holy Spirit within us. With each and every loop, the definition, depth and profile of each strand in the fabric of our lives will become more and more striking. This is the arresting impact of the Holy Spirit causing the tapestry of our lives to stand out and reflect the beauty of Jesus.

How to develop the 1st strand of increased connection.

'When Jesus saw him lying there, and knew that he already had been in that condition a long time, He said to him, "Do you want to be made well?"'.

John 5:6 NIV

1st loop: Decide

This begins with a conscious decision. Set your mind every day to invite and include the Holy Spirit in everything. This is about intentionally determining to engage with God in all issues, not just the critical ones and not just when you remember.

'Do not cast me away from Your presence, And do not take Your Holy Spirit from me.'

Psalm 51:11 NKJV

2nd loop: Invite

Ask God in. It may be in relation to something specific, or in relation to the day at large. Something happens in your soul when you externalise the request. You become ever more conscious of the

Holy Spirit's presence. Allow yourself to be refilled. When you do this, in an instant you can bypass the noisiness of your own thoughts, to be God-focussed instead of situation-focussed.

'The [Holy] Spirit and the bride (the church, believers) say, "Come." And let the one who hears say, "Come." And let the one who is thirsty come; let the one who wishes take and drink the water of life without cost.'
Revelation 22:17 AMP

3rd loop: Dwell and soak

Hover in His presence. Visualise Jesus as you do. Determine to remain present yourself, as the power of the connection saturates you within. Speak intimately, from the deepest part of you and allow His responses to fall. Jesus frequently asked people what it was they wanted, so be specific and linger upon His response.

'How lovely is your tabernacle O Lord of hosts! My soul longs, yes, even faints for the courts of the Lord; My heart and flesh cry out for the living God.
Psalm 84:1-2 NKJV

Practical suggestions

As you engage with the Holy Spirit to weave these three loops more consistently into your life, constant connection will start to become the most natural thing in the world. After all, we were created to live in His presence. You'll start to feel odd doing anything without it. Of course, there will be days when you may feel less 'umbilically' connected than others. Over time, even that sense will start to become so acute that you quickly press back in for more. This connection brings a feeling of 'oneness'. The more you experience it, the more you start to feel lonely without it!

There is no set 'formula' for accessing the Holy Spirit's connection. We can't reduce our actions to following a set of religious steps. However, people often ask how they can get better at this. What works for me may not work for you, but what comes next are practical suggestions to help your momentum. This is what can help you to receive the love and protection from God's ongoing touch. These may become useful tools. No doubt you will have other ideas of your own you can add over time.

Loops	Practical suggestions
1. Decide	• Set your intention for connection beforehand, in both the good and the bad circumstances of life. This can be in general at the start of every day, or before a specific situation. Ask the Holy Spirit to help you remember and tune into this connection as your day unfolds. • At the end of each day, review how many times you have connected and invited God in. Stay conscious of this tomorrow. Stick with it. Even when you go through spells where you don't sense an immediate response, keep inviting. When you review, consider the triggers that seem to break the connection, then pro-actively consider what you can do to prevent this tomorrow. • Press reset. If you realise you haven't included God, it's never too late. Consciously decide to press reset. Ask the Holy Spirit in at any point. He will always respond positively to your decision and desire. One word is often enough; 'Help, Speak, Show, Hello'.
2. Invite	• Still your soul to calm your mind, will and emotions

	- If certain things help relax you into this, use them (music, exercise, looking at nature, etc.) - Eliminate any other distractions that could get in the way of opening this channel. • Speak your invitation, either in your mind or out loud. - Tell Him you need Him, tell Him you want to connect, tell Him you are opening yourself up for Him, tell Him you want to just be with Him. - Invite Him to reveal what may be on His mind. Real connection is a two-way dynamic. Open yourself up to what He may want to impart to you through this unity.
3. Dwell and soak	• Visualise His presence and company. - Imagine Jesus is right next to you. It can be difficult to get your mind off yourself, so creating this mental picture will help you bypass your own thinking. - Tell Him the stuff you are carrying, but don't dwell on it yet. This is your way of creating a momentary pause from its interference. - Visualise placing it all at the feet of Jesus. This is so you can take your gaze away from your 'stuff' and onto Him. • Remain present yourself. - Breathe in His presence. Slow your body and take a few deep breaths. Remain still. - Even if for a few seconds, allow the embrace to fall upon you. - In silence, hold the stillness of His presence. - Consciously hold your awareness of this presence. Even if you move away from this, in an instant,

intentional conscious thought of it will return you to its hold.

- Speak with Him intimately and allow His response to fall.
    - Thank Him for being with you and thank Him for staying.
    - Be honest about anything on your heart, on your mind or in your life. These are likely to be things you may never share with anyone else. Share your feelings, your thoughts and your circumstances in the most unfiltered, raw way you can. This is not about polished prayers. It's about letting out the gut wrenched transparency of your deepest inner self.
    - Ask Him to reveal more of Himself.
    - Soak up whatever you receive. Linger in this moment. As you do you are elevating yourself from being stuck in your stuff, to being stuck to Him.
    - Even if for a few seconds, as you connect in this way, hover to see if there is anything you sense He is revealing, showing or saying to you. Allow the space to let His love flow.

The mirror

'Peace I leave with you; my peace I give you. I do not give to you as the world gives. Do not let your hearts be troubled and do not be afraid.'

John 14:27 NIV

The vulnerability that comes from sincerely connecting and letting God in changes our heart. It is this that opens the door to experiencing His presence. This brings an abiding peace that surpasses all understanding and brings an ever-increasing intimacy with God. An intimacy that goes beyond knowing about Him, believing in Him or even praying to Him. It's an intimacy that comes from the closest of encounters. Through it we are stilled by its purity.

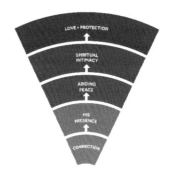

This is the Zoe wheel of life. The power of Christ in us. As we develop the strand of connection, it enables us to live in His presence, releasing an inner provision of abiding peace, so we activate the promise of spiritual intimacy. This makes a difference to our lives through the love and protection it brings us.

Reflections

Before we move on, my encouragement is to take some time to review the tapestry of your life. Rather than rushing through these prompts, allow some space to mull these over. Pray with and consciously invite the Holy Spirit to bring His insight into your awareness.

Consider the current pattern

- How frequently and consciously do you invite God into this type of connection?
- How frequently and consciously do you experience the presence of Jesus within you?
- What is the level of abiding peace you mostly live with through your day? Consider different situations.
- What degree of loving spiritual intimacy do you regularly experience?
- How stilled and safe do you feel by God's love and protection in your soul (your mind, will and emotions) on a day-to day basis?
- What triggers it's passing?
- What enables it's return?
- What are the largest canyons where these things are missing?
- Do you ever feel any of the following: isolated, stressed, fearful, frustrated, anxious, disconnected, emotionally closed down or guarded?
- Conversely how often do you feel steady, tranquil, serene, stable, restful, stilled, loved?

Consider what you need to grow

- Reflect on promise 1 from part one. Of the examples of what His presence brings, what do you need to develop?
- How would this help your life, others or the world?

Consider how to develop further

- How much of your day is spent on automatic independent pilot, verses intentionally engaging with the Holy Spirit?
- How frequently do you stay to dwell and call upon His presence?
- How consciously do you tune into what God wants to release?

As you reflect, spend some time praying about what you discover. Allow this to organically merge into a conversation with your Father. Allow time for silence and consciously allow the Holy Spirit to flow. Is there anything else He says?

Stay connected, then review the suggested loops of activity you can take to help you grow in this area. Add any other activities that would work for you. Prayerfully consider these and then create a plan.

- What will you do, when and how?

- Visualise the impact

- Now get practising!

This increased connection is how the promise of God's presence is released within us. Once we experience this, nothing else compares to this intimacy and the abiding peace it provides. This seduces us into the desire for an ever-deeper relationship with Him.

When you are ready, the pattern in the second strand shows you how.

13

The 2nd strand

Deepening your relationship
Developing constant fellowship with God.

How to release His significance and activate our renewed identity.

'Jesus answered and said to him, "If anyone loves Me, he will keep My word; and My Father will love him, and We will come to him and make Our home with him'.
John 14:23 NKJV

If connection is the key that unlocks the peace of Zoe life, relationship is the door we must walk through to apply it. As we increasingly experience spiritual intimacy, this doorway takes us from religion to a deep, vibrant, personal interaction with a living God. As far back as the Garden of Eden, when God walked with Adam and Eve through the cool of the day, He made it clear: He wanted a relationship with us. He is not some distant, far removed God. But He wants this through an open heart, not through His command. This is why from the tree in the middle of that Garden, up to the present day walk of life, He makes it a choice. We are given free will.

If you asked me the top three ingredients for a thriving long-term relationship, I would probably say deep understanding, honest communication and trust. When we have total faith in these ingredients, we will never worry about anything we need; for we know and believe in the character of who is involved. So, strengthening the strand of relationship is about investing the time to develop deep understanding, honest communication and trust with the Godhead. Nothing will build our faith in the character of God more.

We may be inclined to build our relationship with God when we have time or when it caters to our requirements. But what if God is seemingly quiet, has an alternative view, works to a different timescale or agenda to our own? What if life is going well and feel we know His character already? Even when we are aligned, how diligently do we mine the depths of our faith?
This is about deepening our relationship as an ongoing life-long vibrant affair.

Wherever He went, Jesus loved the unlovely. His entire life was a walking demonstration of the nature of God's love. When we are loved, we feel accepted. When we feel accepted, we start to feel worthy. When we feel worthy, we feel like we belong: we belong to something bigger than ourselves. As we understand more and more of God's character, the draw of His love gives us the confidence to put our trust in this. It's the seal that tells us 'you are mine'. We start to see ourselves in a totally new way - as someone who is cherished. Someone who has position. Someone who is seen as priceless, just the way we are. We have to be, for Jesus to have died on our behalf. There is no greater demonstration of the father's love for his children.

'For God so loved the world that he gave his one and only Son, that whoever believes in him shall not perish but have eternal life.'
John 3:16 NIV

As this love organically grows within us, we start to see others as God does. We love them in a whole different way. And that includes ourselves!

Cultivating this relationship takes focus. It takes allowing ourselves to be seen by God, in all our mixed-up vulnerability. As we develop our understanding of who God is – and who we are in Him, a confidence grows - the confidence that comes from knowing we are a child of the King.

'You, dear children, are from God and have overcome them, because the one who is in you is greater than the one who is in the world.'
1 John 4:4 NIV

The deeper we embed this truth, the more we realise the significance we have been graced with. With it comes authority.

The provision is authority

Matthew 28:18 tells us all authority was given to Jesus. Ephesians 1, Romans 8, Colossians 2, to name but a few, all confirm that we are children of God and joint heirs with Christ. The very moment we receive Jesus as our saviour, we are spiritually raised up and seated with Him at the right hand of the Father. The authority of God that's in Jesus is shared with us. When we fully internalise the truth of this - our real identity, we no longer desperately cling to the hopeful notion of this authority. We know to who we bow. We know to who we belong. We know to who we are yoked. We know we *are* authority. The deeper our relationship, the more embedded this authority becomes in the countenance of how we walk through every day. This, is the outcome that takes us further into the Zoe life.

At the start of His earthly ministry, when tempted by Satan, Jesus knew who He was and knew all He commanded. (Luke 4:1, Matt 4:1, Mark 1:12) This gave Him the authority on which to make His stand. How many times was Jesus questioned about on whose authority He acted? Authority is critical for us to know what is truly at our disposal. To know our level of authority, just as Jesus did, we need to know who our Daddy really is! (John 14:10) Authority is our provision. **Deep relationship brings this authority.**

The Oxford dictionary says the definition of authority is the power or right to give orders, make decisions and enforce obedience. When we are authorised, we are able to control, influence and change things.

The authority God gives us has the power to supersede all worldly protocol. With it comes the permission that can be asserted over every situation in life. God really is the name above all names) and we really do have the license to command every knee to bow to this. (Phil 2:9-10) Whether we need to stand up to illness, organisations, people, systems, or the doubts in our own minds, under His identity, such authority can be a place in which we live.

This is unshakeable authority; an authority that is different from the re-assurance we gain through position, status or inner belief in our rightful place – no matter how conventional culture would regard things. Unshakeable authority outranks any earthly entitlement or domain. It does not depend on our training, our title or our ability. **It depends on our significance through who Jesus is.**

Stop to reflect on your own life for a moment.

- How often do you live in the unshakeable resolve of your rightful authority?
- Conversely how much time do you spend living in vulnerability, doubt or insecurity, feeling at the mercy of situations? Do you overly-require encouragement from people, or experience negative emotions such as feeling offended, hurt or the weight of burden?
- What would your life look like if you could replace all those times of uncertainty with a permanent state of unshakeable authority?

Relationship is the strand we must deepen to release this provision.

The missing strands

If we don't get to know who God is, we will never know who we really are.

This strand is critical, as without it, our faith can be rocked. When we know that we know who He is – and who we are in Him, nothing can shake that foundation. The reality is, that when life collides, this confidence can seem like an abstract theory rather than a living reality. It is often either missing or not prominent enough in the tapestry of our lives. Let's start by looking at three key reasons for this:

1. Because we need an understanding of who God really is.

'Don't let anyone capture you with empty philosophies and high-sounding nonsense that come from human thinking and from the spiritual powers of this world, rather than from Christ.'
Colossians 2:8 NLT

The world is loud. All the time it shouts its message. Through media, through social values, through how we are raised. It bombards us. But often these messages are not in line with God's Kingdom. The more we are immersed in a culture, the more desensitised we can become to the differences between what seems to be the norm and God's way of looking at things. We are inundated with principles that are counter to who He is. You only have to follow the story line of any soap opera to get a sense of this. As time passes by and as our exposure to more and more of what is counter to God's word increases, there is a danger that we can start to dilute truth.

We are told we are made in God's image, so we need to know what that image is. (Gen 1:26) Our view of who we are is massively influenced by our view of who God is. So, our perspective needs to be accurate. We need to know God's truth, His character, His word. Tozer once famously said, *'I don't want the world to define God for me. I want Holy Spirit to reveal God to me'*.

I recently found out I needed to change the prescription of my reading glasses. For a while, I noticed I had been struggling and started to experience powerful headaches as a result of the burden being placed on my eyes. If we don't use the right lenses, we can spend a lifetime seeing things in a blurred way. This actually hinders us and causes long-term damage to what we see.

My own relationship with my natural father was once the lens through which I saw my heavenly Father. Now, instead of being distant, uninterested and uncaring, I know He is so close, so concerned and so loving of me. I needed to unlearn what the world taught me, to relearn what is really true.

This is key, because if we don't know who God really is, how do we know what to place our trust in? Are there ever times you wonder if what you're hearing is from God at all? There is one sure-fire way to distinguish truth from a deceptive lie: is it in line with the character of God we find in the scriptures? The world bombards us with its perspective and religion does the same. We have to move from head knowledge to a heart experience. The only way to truly know God's character is when we invest time in getting to know Him - *really* know Him. When this happens, we never live in fear again - of anything.

2. Because we need ongoing communion.

'But Martha was distracted by all the preparations that had to be made. She came to him and asked, "Lord, don't you care that my sister has left me to do the work by myself? Tell her to help me!" "Martha, Martha," the Lord answered, "you are worried and upset about many things, but few things are needed—or indeed only one.

Mary has chosen what is better, and it will not be taken away from her."

Luke 10:40-42 NIV

Jesus showed us the value of hanging out together and 'being', rather than always 'doing'. God desires it and we need it! It's in the place we deepen our affection, broaden our understanding and build up precious memories. Memories of times with God.

The Lord's prayer includes the request 'give us this day our daily bread'. In this, it is made clear. We need a daily infilling to thrive in this world.

Think of it like other relationships. My husband and I have been married now for twenty years. It has taken dedication to put time into our relationship. It has taken time to understand how we tick and what we are about. It has taken conversation and effort to create shared experiences, for us to access the depths of what we now share. It is this focus that builds up a precious shared history.

God wants this deep communion with us because He loves us without measure and because He knows we are safest when we are with Him. If we don't go to God with our life, we will invariably go somewhere else. This is when our grasp of who we are and the authority we carry can seem to ebb away.

'Keep and guard your heart with all vigilance above all that you guard, for out of it flows the springs of life.'

Proverbs 4:23 NIV

Throughout His life, we learn how Jesus regularly spent time alone with God. On one such occasion, Jesus had miraculously fed the five thousand-plus people with five loaves and two fish. In Matthew 14:23 we learn that 'after he had dismissed the crowd, he went up on a mountainside by himself to pray'. No doubt Jesus was already exhausted and this would have taken a lot of energy, but he was purposeful about spending time alone with His Father. This was His re-fuelling. **Authority can only stand as long as we stand in its strength.** As we do, the fullness of His incredible authority becomes so real, we will stake our lives upon it.

3. Because we won't experience pure love without it.

'There is no fear in love. But perfect love drives out fear, because fear has to do with punishment. The one who fears is not made perfect in love.'

1 John 4:18-19 NIV

No-one on earth will ever accept you, forgive you, love you, develop you, provide for you, heal you or be there for you like God will. Deep down we all long to be known, held, looked after and loved intimately. A friend of mine recently said, 'I have always felt I had to carry myself. I was always there for everyone. But no one was ever there for me. And then I met Jesus'. Zephaniah 3:11 says God takes great delight in us. The literal translation of this is that He leaps, He twirls, He dances over us. Until we encounter the depths of that love, nothing will ever fill it. Human love can disappoint us, hurt us, betray us, abuse us and ignore us. God's love is perfect. All other love pales into comparison.

Relationship is critical as it helps us understand who God is. It helps replenish us and gives us the safety of living under the perfect care of this love. When we experience the truth of this, we increasingly trust who He is. When we *know* Him, we know who He is. When we really know He is who He says He is, nothing can shake our confidence in His name.

Just pause for a moment.

- What mostly informs your view of who God is? How well do you know the depths of who He is? How well do you know the fullness of who you are in Him? How does this impact on your view of what is possible?

- What distracts you from ongoing minute-by-minute daily communion with Him?
- What has the difference between God's love and human love been like for you?

As you reflect, spend some time praying about what you discover. Allow this to organically merge into a conversation with your Father. Allow time for silence and consciously allow the Holy Spirit to flow. Is there anything else He says?

The pattern to living it

In each chapter, we will explore the pattern that helps develop, strengthen and embed each strand. **The purpose of the pattern in the strand of relationship is to increase our inner sense of unshakeable authority.** It is how promise 2: His significance - our renewed identity is released and activated.

How to develop the 2nd strand of deepening relationship

'As for me, I will call upon God, And the Lord shall save me. Evening and morning and at noon I will pray, and cry aloud, And He shall hear my voice.'

Psalm 55:16-17 NKJV

This pattern has been broken down into the following three key loops:

1st loop: Search

Deepen your understanding of who God is - and who this makes you. Get into your bible and get into what it means. Consider all the other mediums of study and information available too. With the Holy Spirit's support, dedicate time and energy into learning about this incredible God we serve. Take to heart all that it says about who our God really is. Reflect deeply on what these truths say about you. Who you are to God. Why He made you. How He loves you. Nothing will help you fully appreciate and learn than reading The Book He effectively wrote Himself!

'I ask—ask the God of our Master, Jesus Christ, the God of glory—to make you intelligent and discerning in knowing him personally, your eyes focused and clear, so that you can see exactly what it is he is calling you to do, grasp the immensity of this glorious way of life he has for his followers, oh, the utter extravagance of his work in us who trust him—endless energy, boundless strength!'
Ephesians 1:18-19 MSG

2nd loop: Make time

This is about having a constant communion. Nothing deepens relationship more than spending time together. Prioritise making time to experience Him. This is when you really get to know someone. Don't rely on religious activity and don't rely on what you already know about Him. Make time to be with Him, on your own, when no one else is watching. These are the precious moments of the secret place. But it doesn't always have to be in some sacred, intensive, time-consuming way. It can also be developed in the minute-by-minute moments of life. When the pressure is on, nothing compares to the draw-down you can make from the deposits of time you have spent with Him in this way. This is irreplaceable.

'But you, when you pray, go into your room, and when you have shut your door, pray to your Father who is in the secret place; and your Father who sees in secret will reward you openly.'
Matthew 6:6 NKJV

3rd loop: Go to God first

Avoid the temptation of speaking first to well-meaning friends, or internalising things through inner dialogue with yourself. Make God your first port of call. Always. Wise counsel can be invaluable, but only after you have consulted with God first. Considered thought is essential, but only when aligned to God's perspective. Give of yourself and learn to receive from Him.

'In the morning, O LORD, You will hear my voice; In the morning I will prepare [a prayer and a sacrifice] for You and watch and wait [for You to speak to my heart]'
Psalm 5:3 AMP

Practical suggestions

As you engage with the Holy Spirit to weave these three loops into your life, your relationship with God will take you to new depths of love. With this comes a constant sense of being known, held and adored. As you experience pure love, you will start to become pure love. I describe this relationship as 'being in the light'. The more you experience it, the more this light radiates from within you.

To develop this strand, in the table below are suggestions you could practically work with. This is what can help you to develop the authentic gravitas you need to make impact. These could become useful tools. No doubt, you will have other ideas of your own that you can add over time.

Loop	Practical suggestions
1. Search.	• Study and if at first you struggle, persevere! - Ask people for advice about a good place to read in the Bible that may relate to what you need to know more about. Learning about the character of God

through the Psalms and the life and teaching of Jesus is always a good place to start.
- It may help to find a bible translation that works for you and uses language you can understand.
- Sometimes reading your bible alongside study guides and other Christian literature can help emphasise and highlight what's important.
- As you do this, specifically ask God to reveal more of Himself to you.
- Ask Him to show you who you are to Him.

- Ask the Holy Spirit to interpret, reveal and encourage you as you study.
  - Avoid trying to plough through as much text as possible, just so you have read it.
  - Take your time, consider the words, put yourself in the scenario, visualise it with your mind's eye, meditate on its meaning. Anything to make the resonance and perspective as clear as possible.
  - Whatever you are dealing with, study through the lens of: 'What does God want to reveal to me about this?'

- Proactively keep track of specific things you are learning.
  - These may be truths about God, about you or about His Kingdom message.
  - If you journal, include these insights.
  - As you do this, consciously think about any truths you are learning that directly apply to your life.
  - Write them down.
  - Learn key verses that inspire and encourage you.
  - Place key promises on post-its in prominent positions around you, so you make these reminders the first truth you revisit throughout the day.

2. Make time.	▪ Make ongoing conversation with God part of your day, either in your head (which He hears), or out loud.
	  - God wants to share every moment with you. Don't feel you have to keep anything back. Talk to Him about everything. Even when you are watching TV, in the company of others or attending a sports match, you can be interacting with Him. It's amazing what He will reveal in these moments. (He once even coached me in my backhand at tennis as we 'talked' whilst I was playing a game!)
	
	▪ If you know you are prone to wander and get caught up in life, make a plan to do intermittent 'time outs', where you consciously spend time with God.
	  - This could be when you grab a coffee or when you are moving from one place to another. It doesn't have to take long, or be formal.
	  - Make a point of having regular catch ups through-out the day.
	  - You may even need to start by setting up reminders in your calendar, just until you fall naturally into the habit.
	
	▪ For those special moments of time alone, put some thought into it beforehand. Get yourself in the mood for Holiness.
	  - Sometimes we need to 'wash off' the taints of the world, before we fully enter God's presence. Pray for anything that's clung to you that's not of Him, to fall away in Jesus's name.
	  - Consider the things that help elevate you spiritually and intentionally do them. (For me, certain worship songs or verses in the bible can instantly shift my headspace).

	- Think about what you can do to eliminate distractions. Turn off the phone and the TV. Wait until you know the kids are out, get a babysitter, or get them to sleep first!
3. Go to God first	▪ Before you even open your mouth, do a quick check: Have I gone to God with this yet? - If not, don't speak up, or allow a thought to fester until you do. Your soul will be quick, so try and nip it in the bud with this self-challenge, as early as possible. - If you are being pushed to commit to something that counts before you have gone to God, stall. Better to take a little longer than to have to retract at a later point. - If you receive news or experience something that puts you firmly back in the world or your soul, revisit your understanding of who God is. - Make revisiting who He is your first consideration and ask the Holy Spirit to reveal, 'what would God want to remind me of right now? What would He want to show me? What can I trust in?' Who does God want to be for me in this?' ▪ Give of yourself. If you want a dynamic relationship with God, this is about you opening up to Him. - Tell Him your heart's desires and share your deepest thoughts. Allow your defences to drop as you put your trust into this level of honesty. - If you find this level of vulnerability hard, ask the Holy Spirit to help remove any barriers you may be putting up. ▪ Listen. Be. Receive. - Allow the space for the Holy Spirit to move. Let Him have voice and energy within you.

- Avoid the one-way radio traffic of just constantly speaking at God.
- Just 'be with', rather than 'talking to'. With no agenda and no requests, simply enjoy the exquisite stillness of His company. Often, this may be in serene silence. In these moments, the Holy Spirit may want to comfort, remind, encourage, love, challenge, equip, warn, provoke, or whisper sweet nothings. The list goes on. Allow the opportunity to receive, dwell upon and swathe yourself in these wonderful blessings.
- Like any relationship, it's give and take. Don't make it all about you. What's also on God's mind? Make room for Him to impart what's also on His agenda.

The mirror

'Behold, I give you the authority to trample on serpents and scorpions, and over all the power of the enemy, and nothing shall by any means hurt you. Nevertheless do not rejoice in this, that the spirits are subject to you, but rather rejoice because your names are written in heaven.*

Luke 10:19-21 NKJV

Deepening our relationship is how we come to know who God really is – and the significance of who we are in Him. As we get to know and trust Him as our faithful Father, we realise we are a child of Almighty God. As we embrace this honour, our perception of ourselves starts to shift. We are changed by the security of knowing we are a child of the King. This gives us a royal countenance, as we carry God's presence. It is living in a deep vibrant relationship that provides it.

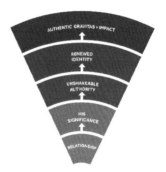

This is the Zoe wheel of life. The power of Christ in us. As we develop the strand of relationship, it enables us to live in His significance, releasing an inner provision of unshakeable authority, so we activate the promise of renewed identity. This makes a difference to our lives through the authentic gravitas in our countenance and the impact this carries.

Reflections

Before we move on, my encouragement is to take some time to review the tapestry of your life. Pray with and consciously invite the Holy Spirit to bring His insight into your awareness.

Consider the current pattern

- How deep is the understanding, honest ongoing, communication and trust in your relationship with God today?
- How significant do you feel in your day-to-day life, particularly when compared to the worlds lens of who you are?
- What is the level of unshakeable authority you apply in and over life's circumstances? Consider different situations.

- How embedded is this renewed identity within your inner psyche?
- Do you carry authentic gravitas and make impact?
- What wobbles you in this?
- What enables it's return?
- What are the largest canyons where such things are missing?
- Do you ever feel any of the following: a victim rather than a victor, pressured, weak, timid, overwhelmed or over your head, uncertain, alone, nervous, intimidated?
- Conversely how often do you feel strong, confident, courageous, assured, equipped?

Consider what you need to grow

- Reflect on promise 2 from part one. Of the examples of what His significance brings, what else do you need to develop?
- How would this help your life, others and the world?

Consider how to develop further

- How much time are you actually spending in the company of God, talking, praying, listening and responding? How special are you making your time together? How much intimate time do you experience getting to know God by just being with Him?
- How well do you know God's direct perspective on given situations? How much time have you spent checking, learning and deepening your knowing of His character, ways, perspective and instruction?
- How primary, potent and dynamic is your relationship with God? Have you been investing in seeking Him first? Have you been giving of yourself to Him? Have you been receptive to the move of the Holy Spirit, engaging with all He wants to impart to you? Is God the most exclusive relationship you give yourself to?

As you reflect, spend some time praying about what you discover. Allow this to organically merge into a conversation with your Father. Allow time for silence and consciously allow the Holy Spirit to flow. Is there anything else He says?

Stay connected, then review the suggested loops of activity you can take to help you grow in this area. Add any other activities that would work for you. Prayerfully consider these and then create a plan.

- What will you do, when and how?

- Visualise the impact

- Now get practising!

Recap

So far, we have practically explored how to live in all of Christ by considering:

- How to release His presence and activate our spiritual intimacy through the first strand of increased connection.
- How to release His significance and activate our renewed identity through the second strand of deepening relationship.

This relationship is how a royal countenance is released within us. As we increasingly deepen our perception of the significant permissions we have in Him, we become increasingly less deterred by what life throws our way. Our inner authority becomes branded within and blossoms until we can conquer any thought, any crisis and any situation in life. This leaves us in reverent awe and lights a fire in our hearts.

When you are ready, the pattern in the third strand shows you how to stoke the flame of this worship.

14

Developing a heart of worship
Adoration and gratitude.

How to release His perspective and activate our ability to clearly hear God.

'But a time is coming and is already here when the true worshippers will worship the Father in spirit [from the heart, the inner self] *and in truth; for the Father seeks such people to be His worshippers.'*
John 4:23 AMP

When we deepen our relationship, our understanding, communication and trust increases. When we learn the depths of who God really is and who we are in Him, our captivated hearts can't help but develop a heart of worship.

The Zoe life is only possible when we're focussed on God and worship is the vital state of heart that lifts our eyes off ourselves and onto Him. Jesus gave His life for us. We only have to gaze momentarily on this, to move towards this attitude of heart. Our praises start right there.

A heart of worship goes beyond sporadic appreciation and is constantly filled with a sense of God's unending goodness. This can't help but bring an ongoing flow of gratitude and adoration. It never switches off. The more we grasp the depths of His love, the beauty of His character and the bountiful supply of His grace, the more we will come to see the glory of God in everything. The deeper our relationship, the more there is to find and the more there is to praise.

Coming in so many different forms, worship is often most potent in the precious secret places when no one else is watching. When our heart is full of worship, somehow God pours yet more of himself into us, putting a spring in our step and a song in our heart.

The Lord is my strength and song, And He has become my salvation; He is my God, and I will praise Him; My father's God, and I will exalt Him.'
Exodus 15:2 NKJV

This breaks us from the many bonds that can hold us, lifting us to a whole different plane.

We may sing (whether literally or metaphorically through our lives) to God. But this is worship where our eyes are disconnected from anything that relates to us. Whatever we carry into the experience, at some point has to leave, for our gaze to be solely on Him.

If we ever leave worship in the same inner state we entered it, we haven't truly worshiped! By definition it leaves us changed within. How can it not do? Whole-hearted worship takes us into the very throne room of God, where we become connected to heaven itself. The throne room is joy. Even our limited grasp of John's prophetic imagery in the book of revelation creates a sense of God's resplendent glory, with angel upon angel singing in abandon. When elevated in this way, everything revealed comes through the filter of this joy. The glory of such moments are inexpressible. Nothing describes or compares to the unexplainable rapture flowing from our hearts when ascended to see life through heaven's perspective.

Jesus could have healed Lazarus before the fourth day, yet he rejoiced in how He was unable to. (John 11:15) In His intentional delay, He knew a greater miracle would be seen. His perspective gave him joy.

The provision is joy

In Psalm 16:11 David writes of the fullness of joy that comes from being with God. We are never closer to God than when connected to His throne room in abandoned worship. This is fullness of joy and no matter what our circumstances are, nothing can take this type of joy away. The deeper our worship goes, the fuller our joy becomes. This, is the outcome that takes us further into the Zoe life. Joy is our provision.

Whole-hearted worship brings fullness of joy. I'm not sure the English language can articulate the meaning of such joy. More than happiness, pleasure and satisfaction, joy from heaven is other-worldly. Exultation, rejoicing, exhilaration, elation, euphoria, radiance, delight; words that only capture a fraction of this state of heart. **This is ascended joy**.

The ascended joy God gives us has the power to invalidate any oppression our circumstances may bring. There is no earthly experience that can compare with the joy that God's joy brings. This is a joy that renders any impact from life's trials as nothing more than trivial distractions by contrast. When we experience such joy, we really do know that death truly has lost its sting. From crisis of health, through to struggling finances, whatever our circumstances are, the joy of the Lord really does have the strength to lift us beyond their grip of our souls. Regardless of our circumstances, such joy can be a way of being. We can learn to live in this place.

This is because wholehearted worship is our re-set button. Once our eyes are away from our own limited earthly lens, a different perspective can be shone. The starting point for wisdom is not the fear, uncertainty or heaviness we carry into the throne room. God's starting point is joy. This is His perspective - joy is His default setting. As our own perspective comes into alignment with His, He can then be the light on our path. Finally, we are cleared to tune into the mind of Christ and hear His whispers.

This is ascended joy; a joy that is different from happiness, delight or jubilation – no matter how amazing our experiences may be. Ascended joy lifts us to another realm of wonder entirely – a realm which is wholly unconnected to our earthly situations. Ascended joy is not dictated by the external influence of our experiences. It does not depend on our own emotions. **It depends on being in tune with the perspective of Jesus.**

Stop to reflect on your own life for a moment.

- How often do you live in this blissful ascended joy?
- Conversely how much time do you spend in either a mundane neutral state or toxic state of stress, discouragement, depression or sorrow?
- Do you yo-yo depending on how your day is going, or vary based on your circumstances? Do your emotions become a run-away train and start to run the show?
- What would your life look like if you could replace all those times of mundane life or uncertainty with a centred, calm of wonderous joy?

Worship is the strand we must deepen to release this provision.

The missing strands

If we don't make it all about God, it will always just be about us.

This is the catalytic strand that starts to take us beyond ourselves, to a spiritual reality that is beyond human comprehension. It brings a contentment like no other. The reality is that when we live life at the mercy of our circumstances, our thoughts and our feelings, such joy is often an elusive, intermittent experience, relegated to the occasional highs of life. Let's start by looking at three key reasons why we can't afford to miss this.

1. Because God's love, grace and mercy is extravagant. Our hearts should be the same.

'Jesus was at Bethany, a guest of Simon the Leper. While he was eating dinner, a woman came up carrying a bottle of very expensive perfume. Opening the bottle, she poured it on his head. Some of the guests became furious among themselves. "That's criminal! A sheer waste! This perfume could have been sold for well over a year's wages and handed out to the poor." They swelled up in anger, nearly bursting with indignation over her. But Jesus said, "Let her alone. Why are you giving her a hard time? She has just done something wonderfully significant for me.'

Mark 14:3-9 MSG

Jesus knew what was in this woman's heart. Utter adoration. He recognised and valued her extravagance. When we think about our own lives, how extravagantly do we worship Him today? As we are led to see more and more of God in our lives, it becomes impossible to limit our praise and adoration to a once or twice a week outpouring. We can't help but see His wonder and works in everything. From the petals of a blossoming red rose, through to the blood that washed us clean. We start to see Him everywhere, in everything. This demands a reply.

The natural response in our soul is to lift our hands and to bow before Him. Suddenly we lose all sense of space and time. The more we can bypass our mind, the deeper the worship erupting from our spirit. The presence and opinions of others disintegrate as we are connected to the mercy seat of God. When this happens, everything else falls away from our focus. We experience the closest thing to heaven that exists here on this earth. We are elevated to see things from God's point of view. It moves us out of our circumstances and into an eternal reality that changes everything. Down here on this earth, our thoughts can be so one-dimensional. This type of wholehearted worship lifts us beyond our own limited perspectives and we hear the whispers of heaven itself. We don't worship to 'get' any of this. We worship because we adore Him. As we do this, God responds and fills us with yet more of Himself. He smears us in His joy.

2. Because God's Glory is all around.

'Has God forgotten to be merciful? Has He in anger withheld his compassion? Then I thought, 'to this I will appeal: the years when the most High stretched out His right hand. I will remember the deeds of the Lord; yes I will remember your miracles of long ago. I will consider all your works and meditate on your mighty deeds.'
Psalm 77 9-12 NIV

Our lives today are so fast paced and we often move swiftly from one thing to the next. When we stop to think about things, we will ALWAYS find something that proclaims God's glory. But how often our busy, self-absorbed lives can miss it. Stop and think about all this for a second. Even when life is treating us well, how often do we actually stop to smell the roses, to recognise the great things, to dwell in them? How often are we expressively thankful for everything we have, from the breath in our lungs, right through to the breath of heaven's power in our lives?

The more we learn how to stop, dwell on, seek out and thank God for who He is, what He does and the impact He makes, the easier it will start to be to do this in every moment. We will naturally start to recognise more and more of His glory. As we do this, the greater our overall perspective will be. Not only Is It nourishment to our spirit now, it's amazing how this can sustain us through tougher times later. But even when we stop to do this, sometimes we have to consciously look for the silver lining.

'You will seek me and find me when you seek me with all your heart.'
Jeremiah 29:13 NIV

Sometimes we get overwhelmed, particularly when we are tired, pressured, or uncertain about things. Whilst some people are naturally more optimistic than others, for anyone, when we are locked within our own private world of thought, it's often not long before we have magnified something out of all proportion. At these times, we can get bogged down in an issue and miss all the hallmarks of God's intended benefit.

'Be alert and of sober mind. Your enemy the devil prowls around like a roaring lion looking for someone to devour'.
1 Peter 5:8 NIV

There are undoubtedly genuine times when we go through tough seasons of trials. The good in this can be so difficult to recognise, but even at such times, we can hold onto the certainty of God's character and purpose.

'And we know that God causes everything to work together for the good of those who love God and are called according to his purpose for them.'
Romans 8:28 NLT

This is not about putting on a 'positive mind-set veneer', where we try and will our way into feeling better, or where we try and feign what we show the world by being disingenuously upbeat or happy (people can spot a fraud from a mile off!).

The more we discipline ourselves to genuinely take stock, the more sunshine we will be storing in our tanks. If we think of the level of joy in our life as a bank account, the more deposits we make, the healthier it is. And the more we will radiate this to others. Remembering how incredible God is, recounting the amazing things

He has done in our lives and searching for the silver lining of hidden blessings, will always remind us of His magnificence. This is such valuable sustenance for the soul!

3. Because it is our witness.

'About midnight, Paul and Silas were praying (whilst imprisoned themselves) and singing hymns to God, and the other prisoners were listening to them.'
Acts 16:25 NIV

Despite dire circumstances, Paul and Silas worshipped. This selfless act of belief brought hope and conviction to all around. It must have been a choice. And how many of us would make the same one in the same circumstances?

When we walk through troubles, like never before, we are a key witness to others. Recognising the good things turns to appreciation, which leads to praise and ultimately to the joy of worship. The type of joy that wraps us in a warmth, security and glow we cannot describe - but a joy that others can see in us. This truly gives us something to sing about. This is when we most shine to those around us. We are magnetic as people recognise something special in us. They wonder how we bridge our difficulties with such peace, certainty and poise. People are baffled by our response to challenges. Stopping to praise God can actually help us to fulfil our greatest accountability. To go and actually make disciples.

> *'Now I want you to know, brothers and sisters, that what has happened to me has actually served to advance the gospel.'*
> *Philippians 1:12 AMP*

We need to recognise the power and goodness of God, so we can radiate, demonstrate and proclaim His glory to others around us. Our authentic countenance (how we are when no-one is watching and judging), is what carries this to others. If we are not consciously aware of the great things and, instead, are preoccupied with what's not working well, we miss massive opportunities; with joy comes the opportunity to shine His light.

Just pause for a moment.

- How frequently does the worship in your heart erupt from your life? How deep does the river of your gratitude run? When does this overflow? How much of your time do you spend humbled and lost in the wonder of reverent awe?
- How consciously do you stop, notice and value God's glory each day?
- What kind of example do you make? What would people say of the witness from your life? Would they see something in you they would want for themselves?

As you reflect, spend some time praying about what you discover. Allow this to organically merge into a conversation with your Father. Allow time for silence and consciously allow the Holy Spirit to flow. Is there anything else He says?

The pattern to living it

In each chapter, we will explore the pattern that helps develop, strengthen and embed each strand. **The purpose of the pattern in the strand of whole-hearted worship is to increase our inner sense of ascended joy.** This is how promise 3: His perspective - our ability to hear God is increasingly released and activated.

'Let my cry come right into your presence, GOD; provide me with the insight that comes only from your Word. Give my request your personal attention, rescue me on the terms of your promise. Let praise cascade off my lips; after all, you've taught me the truth about life! And let your promises ring from my tongue; every order you've given is right. Put your hand out and steady me since I've chosen to

live by your counsel. I'm homesick, GOD, for your salvation; I love it when you show yourself! Invigorate my soul so I can praise you well, use your decrees to put iron in my soul. And should I wander off like a lost sheep—seek me! I'll recognize the sound of your voice'.
Psalm 119:171-175 AMP

How to develop the 3rd strand: A heart of worship

This pattern has been broken down into the following three key loops:

1st loop: Notice what's good. Every day.

Consciously think it through. Get it in perspective. Remind yourself of everything you can be thankful for. Give yourself permission and space to get in touch with these things. Often the greatest threat to living in joy is not our response to crisis – this can often push us closer to God. It is living in an apathetic state where we neither notice or appreciate what we actually already have to be thankful for.

'And now, dear brothers and sisters, one final thing. Fix your thoughts on what is true, and honourable, and right, and pure, and lovely, and admirable. Think about things that are excellent and worthy of praise.'
Philippians 4:8 NLT

2nd loop: Share your gratitude and thanks

Honestly connect with the things you are thankful for. Talk to God about them - when you thank Him He listens! Then share them with others. The more conscious this becomes, the more your heart will connect and melt at the realisation of God's mighty hand. Integrate what you are thankful for, so you truly allow it to drop from your head, deep into your heart.

'Return home and tell how much God has done for you." So the man went away and told all over town how much Jesus had done for him.'
Luke 8:39 NIV

3rd loop: Open your heart - in all you do

Praise God in your own special way. There's no prescriptive method for this. It may be through singing, creating something, praying, giving, dancing or speaking out. Whatever is the most authentic, effective way for you to pour your heart into His; camp in that place. Let praise saturate your soul and give voice to His greatness. Focus entirely on God and elevate your praises into worship. As soon as you reach up in this way, your heart will start to be lifted. Your heaviness will be turned into strength, your apathy into vigour and as this happens you will be elevated beyond what holds you. This worship breaks down every barrier. It's the best form of warfare there is. When the Holy Spirit leads you into worship like this, the joy that erupts makes you untouchable by the taints of the world.

'Sing praise-songs to GOD. He's done it all!, Let the whole earth know what he's done! Raise the roof! Sing your hearts out, O Zion!, The Greatest lives among you: The Holy of Israel.'
Isaiah 12:6 MSG

Practical suggestions

As you engage with the Holy Spirit to weave these three loops into your life, your heart will shift. With this comes a constant awareness of God in everything. When this happens, gratitude will spontaneously erupt. You forget the natural world around you and, in that moment, you are purely present with the heavenlies. I describe this heart of worship as 'floating joy'. A Kingdom joy where nothing else matters.

To develop this strand, in the table below are examples of suggestions you could practically work with. This is what can help you to develop the ability to hear God's inspired revelation, so you can make wise choices. These could become useful tools. No doubt you will have other ideas of your own that you can add over time.

Loop	Practical suggestion
1. Notice	▪ Reflect on life and consciously think about what God has done, is doing and enabling for you. Make it personal. - Think about the big and the small (e.g. answered prayers, miraculous breakthroughs, unexpected provision, support through certain seasons. Recall how He's enabled you to be righteous, given you purpose, belonging, security, brought amazing experiences, enabled change etc.). - Turn this into a daily practice. Every day be honest about how you are and what you are grateful for. - Find a way of capturing these things when you notice them so you don't forget them (my friend has a gratitude notebook, another has a jar where she puts her thank you's on post-it notes). ▪ Reflect on what Jesus has done and who God is to you; what most leaves you in awe, wonder and adoration about His greatness? - Think from the heart. (e.g. He wants to know me, that his mercies are new every day, that He is goodness, all powerful, never changing and loves me with unfailing love). - As you do this, tune into anything you notice. As you connect in this way, often God will place an impression on your heart, or communicate something in response to your focus on Him.

	When you do this, you create a channel for hearing from Him. • If you are struggling, stick with it. Try additional angles: - Try taking yourself away from your current environment. Just a change of scenery, or even going from the inside to the outdoors can help. - Ask the Holy Spirit to step in and show you things you may not initially recognise yourself. - You can also review things that will be a reminder. Revisit any journals, photos, or memorabilia that capture a moment in time. Revisit any footage, films, articles, books, verses or clippings that capture God's goodness.
2. Share gratitude and thanks	• Savour the memories: this creates depth and the fullness of what you can be grateful for will emerge. - Visualise what you are thankful for in your mind's eye. - Re-live the memory in as much detail as you can. Indulge yourself with time to let these thoughts sink in. - If it helps, speak with people who shared the experience, who will be able to add even more positive colour to the memory. • Speak to God from your heart about why you are so thankful. Talk to Him about the impact of it, who you would be without it, what your future now means. Give Him your thanks. Give Him the glory. • Share your testimony with others. The more you externalise it, the more vivid it will become. Words have power. Not just to you, but to everyone else who hears them. They are a witness to your own

	soul and to the souls of others as well. The easiest way to share the gospel is to talk about what God enables in your life.
3. Open your heart	▪ Make it all about God. Tell Him what He means to you. Turn your gratitude into adoration. - Tell Him why you love Him. Be specific about what it is He does, continues to do, who He is. - Keep this as a constant attitude of heart. Every night, close your day expressing your heart towards Him. - Every morning, start your day doing the same. Do it whenever you see, hear or experience anything that stirs you. And also do it in the mundane. When you look for it, you can see God's glory everywhere. It only need take a few seconds. Make it a conscious part of your day. ▪ Ask the Holy Spirit to help you see God in everything and everyone. - Set your mind to be determined to worship God in everything you see, do, experience and give. ▪ Ask the Holy Spirit to intensify your worship. Make it extravagant. - Don't worry about your words. If you run out, or if you can't express the depths of your adoration, your spirit will soon take over. - This may be released by speaking tongues, through weeping, through hands lifted high, through dancing, through any manner of expression. Equally, it could also be in total silence. - Corporate worship can be wonderful, but prioritise time for private moments, so you can just let go with total abandon.

	- If you struggle with self-consciousness, even when alone, try turning out the lights. It may sound daft, but it may help you forget your awkwardness, so you can let go and release your unfiltered, deepest cries.
	- If you struggle and you just don't 'feel' like worshipping, ignore your soul and do it anyway. Seriously. Just start.
	- Allow yourself to receive from God
	- When reading the scriptures take time to dwell over the meaning and revel in what it says. The foremost way we ever hear from God is through the inspiration He brings when we unhurriedly read and dwell on His word.
	- Do whatever helps get you into God's presence the most. It may be reading certain verses, listening to certain songs, going for a brisk walk, starting to hum or praying fervent prayers.
	- Thank Him for whatever He seems to be giving back to you as you worship. This may be a general sense (such as His love, peace or security), or it may be specific information. (It's often only when our eyes are fully on Him, that we give the space for Him to be able to communicate back to us in this way.)

The mirror

'He answered, 'Love the Lord your God with all your heart and with all your soul and with all your strength and with all your mind'; and, 'Love your neighbour as yourself.'
Luke 10:27 NIV

As this way of life becomes the very air we breathe, we are pulled into a state of captivation. We become abandoned to God - mind, body, heart and soul - and it's this attitude of heart that takes our eyes off ourselves. Developing a heart of worship is what elevates us to the spiritual realm that changes all perspective. As we increasingly take our eyes away from ourselves and up to Him, an ascended lifestyle means we see things through heaven's filter. This brings unbridled joy and clears a channel so we are able to hear God's word, will and wisdom.

When our gaze is just fixed on Him, we can hear God's agenda. His agenda is freedom, light and love. The prospect of the righteous is joy. (Prov 10:28) It is living with a heart of worship that provides it.

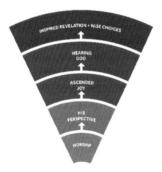

This is the Zoe wheel of life. The power of Christ in us. As we develop the strand of worship, it enables us to live in His perspective, releasing an inner provision of ascended joy, so we activate the promise of being able to clearly hear God. This makes a difference to our lives through the inspired revelation that enables us to make wise choices.

Reflections

Before we move on, my encouragement is to take some time to review the tapestry of your life. Pray with and consciously invite the Holy Spirit to bring His insight into your awareness.

Consider the current pattern

- Is your daily life a life of worship to God?
- Do you live in your circumstances, or in the elevated perspective of heaven's view about your circumstances?
- What is your level of daily ascended joy? Consider different situations.
- How clearly and frequently do you hear from God?
- How often do you receive inspired revelation from His word, will and wisdom, that enables wise choices?
- What triggers the passing of these experiences?
- What enables their return?
- What are the largest canyons where these things are missing?
- Do you ever feel any of the following: unhappiness, sorrow, pessimistic negativity, distant from God, bogged down, heavy hearted, unmoved, on auto-pilot or pre-occupied by what you don't have?
- Conversely how often do you feel elevated, weightless, energised, positive, hopeful, relaxed, captivated by God, mesmerised by His majesty, undone by His holiness?

Consider what you need to grow

- Reflect on promise 3 - His perspective, from part 1. Of the examples showing what His perspective brings, what else do you need to develop?
- How would this help your life, others or the world?

Consider how to develop further

- How frequently are you proactively considering all God is, has done and has given you every day?
- How much do you spontaneously allow your heart to overflow with thanks, sharing heartfelt gratitude with God and others around you?
- Have you embraced a lifestyle of daily worship, making it all about God, extravagantly worshipping Him in your heart and through your actions -even when you least feel like doing it?

As you reflect, spend some time praying about what you discover. Allow this to organically merge into a conversation with your Father. Allow time for silence and consciously allow the Holy Spirit to flow. Is there anything else He says?

Stay connected, then review the suggested loops of activity you can take to help you grow in this area. Add any other activities that would work for you. Prayerfully consider these and then create a plan.

- What will you do, when and how?

- Visualise the impact

- Now get practising!

Recap

So far, we have practically explored how to live in all of Christ by considering:

- How to release His presence and activate our spiritual intimacy through the first strand of increased connection.
- How to release His significance and activate our renewed identity through the second strand of deepening relationship.
- How to release His perspective and activate our ability to clearly hear God, through the third strand of whole-hearted worship.

This is how the promise of God's insight is increasingly released within us. Until then, we are often too absorbed by ourselves to make way for His leading to be revealed. We first need to achieve inner clearance. As we do, He becomes the lamp to our feet, which is always shone through the clearest beacon of His perspective. The starting point for wisdom is not the fear, uncertainty or heaviness we carry into the throne room. God's starting point is joy. This is His default setting. Once we experience this, the light can illuminate what God then wants to reveal. This is when we learn to increasingly hear His voice. Worship is the outpouring of a humbled heart in awe of a wondrous God. As this increasingly happens, our worship becomes a way of life. As this becomes a way of life, we learn to worship Him with our lives.

When you are ready, the pattern in the fourth strand of purposeful service will show you how.

15

The 4th strand

Purposeful service
Commitment to wholeheartedly apply ourselves for God.

How to release His nature and activate our accelerated change.

'Go to the lost, confused people right here in the neighbourhood. Tell them that the kingdom is here. Bring health to the sick. Raise the dead. Touch the untouchables. Kick out the demons. You have been treated generously, so live generously. Freely you have received. Freely give.'

Matthew 10:8 MSG

Worship elevates us to the ascended state of heaven's perspective. When we have seen God, there is only one way to respond - we abandon ourselves. As we do, our lives become our worship. From this captivated state of heart, we serve. This type of service is different from the things we decide to do from our own motivation or for our own sense of belonging, contribution or obligated duty. Blooming from the servant-hearted nature of Jesus within us, this is something the Holy Spirit quickens us to undertake - we only know we must. When born from this cosmic-to-earth unity, we will do anything - what we do to serve becomes irrelevant - just serving is what counts. This is purposeful service.

As we embrace this, the airwaves are cleared for us to increasingly be led by God. Either step-by-step, or with the dawning of a sudden revelation, He stirs our awareness of the vision He has for our lives. The nature of Jesus within us creates this servant-heart and this sense of service ultimately leads us to our purpose.

Purposeful service comes from within and takes us closer to the selfless character of Jesus. It's a reflection of the love we have for God, poured out by our deeds. We don't wholeheartedly serve in this way because it's expected, makes us look good, is 'our turn' or because we think we ought to. So, what is it that compels our sacrifice in this way? In one word – honour. The burning desire to serve our King is how we honour Jesus with our lives. This comes from our love, the fiercest motivation known to man. Love can make us do anything!

When we are surrendered, committed and hungry to fulfil our God-intended reason for being, our priority shifts from our own lives, to a bigger purpose.

The Zoe life brings a life of meaning. This comes from the fulfilment of why God made us - why we are here. This fundamental life question has three tiers to it:
- What day-to-day service are we here for? (to be Jesus in our world)
- What calling/ministry/mission are we here for? (to bring God's Kingdom to this world)
- What version of eternity are we here for? (to become the spotless bride of Christ)

The vision of our purpose may develop over time, but as we become clearer about this mandate, we align our focus, behaviours and commitments to what God wants us to do.

To get there, often God will take us on a journey. Where we start can be very different to where we end up. We start by seeing a need and filling it. I dare say Moses didn't know he'd end up leading the Israelites for forty-nine years when first compelled to protect their honour, by killing the Egyptian who was beating a Hebrew slave. (Exo 2:12) Something drew him to that scene. That something meant he was compelled to act.

Additionally, our overt gifts, opportunities and life experiences are often indicators towards our direction. We are to enjoy, savour and run with these. They make us who we are. Similarly, the passion, determination, energy and attention of things that just 'grab' us, can be other signals from God. What breaks His heart will often break ours too. We are to go where this energy takes us.

These are God's way of drawing us towards what He initially designed us for. The vision starts with a picture inside us, before it then becomes a reality through us.

As this happens, when we purposefully serve, something often just clicks into place. The conversation we have with the new neighbour we're befriending comes with ease. When we leave the intense office meeting we moved heaven and earth to get to, we recognise how vital our contribution was. The long hours serving at the food bank leaves us feeling energised instead of weary. Our purposeful service turns up the heat of our adoration further as our heart seems to ache from our proximity to God. We can't help but praise Him for the honour of serving this way. Oh that He even chooses to use us!

When we make ourselves available in this way, more of God is poured into who we are, which enables us to go on to do unimaginable things. The power inside us becomes far stronger than the pressure outside of us. As Tommy Tenney once said: 'Being a servant will take you to places your talent never could.' Nothing will accelerate our development into the character of Jesus more than when we do what He did. In whatever form it takes, either in the secular world or otherwise, we become more like Him when we purposefully serve. Nothing will stop such a force.

Purposeful service was the very power that propelled Jesus in all He accomplished. (John 5:34) Knowing why He came enabled him to fulfil it.

The provision is motivation

'Now I want you to know ,believers, that what has happened to me [this imprisonment that was meant to stop me] has actually served to advance [the spread of] the good news [regarding salvation].'
Philippians 1:12 AMP

In Philippians 1 we learn how Paul's chains advanced the gospel. What was it that gave him the staying power to suffer countless beatings, stoning's, imprisonment, shipwrecks and ultimately, to lose his life for his faith? In one word - purpose. Whilst not always called to suffer in such savage ways, the same principle applies to us. Purposeful service becomes our motivation – the driving force behind why we tenaciously press in to do what we do. In our darkest hours, biggest challenges and long narrow roads of diligent service, why we do what we do is the source of our perseverance.

Sometimes we face direct conflict and challenge. Sometimes we need to hold our commitment in the less glamorous, more mundane aspects of service - the days when we don't feel up to it, are frustrated with whether or not we are getting anywhere or simply think it's too hard / too boring / too risky. Fill in the gaps - we've probably all been there. When we know *why* we are there, in those moments where we question our very sanity, an invisible driving force picks us back up and propels us forward once again. **Purposeful service gives us motivation.**

The Oxford dictionary says the definition of motivation is the reason for acting in a particular manner. It is the desire or willingness to do something with enthusiasm.

This is the type of motivation that gave Noah the faith to build the ark, gave Esther the courage to risk her life for her people, gave Nehemiah the resource to re build the walls of Jerusalem and Mary the sacrificial heart to raise then watch Jesus die. The list is endless. With the type of motivation God provides, we really can persevere under trial. (Jam 1:12) We can show diligence to the very end. (Heb 6:11) We truly can glory in our sufferings – if we know why we are doing it. (Rom 5:3) When we do, this becomes our higher purpose and carries us to our ultimate destiny. This, is the outcome that takes us further into the Zoe life. Our purposeful service is the catalyst. Uncompromising motivation is the provision.

The strength of character we access through this galvanises a determination that leaves us knowing we simply can't not follow through with what's required, no matter how we may humanly want to quit! It will not let us let go, it will not allow us to stop, to compromise or to give in.

This is uncompromising motivation; a motivation that outstrips any impetus we can create from self-propelled determination – no matter how driven we are in our natural character. Uncompromising motivation has the power to withstand all opposition, hardship and difficulties, when its source stems from our maker and what we were born to do. It does not depend on our own convicting grit, inner reserve or strength of character. **It depends on the nature of Jesus we carry within.**

Stop to reflect on your own life for a moment.

- How often are you lifted by the unfaltering inner reserve that can only come from such uncompromising motivation? The times you know you just can't **not** do something – regardless of how much you want to avoid it for human reasons? How often do you find yourself applying yourself wholeheartedly with focus, relish and a fascination for what may come of it, regardless of the cost?

- Conversely, how often does your service stem from duty not desire? Do you find yourself doing things out of obligation, with boredom, weariness or even, with dread?
- What would your life look like if you could replace all those times of uncertainty with a driving force of pursuit propelled by uncompromising motivation?

Pursuing purposeful service is the strand we must deepen to release this provision.

The missing strands

If we don't know why we are here, we don't know where we are really going.

This is the strand that moves us from a quest for meaning into purposed action and is critical for us to find inner fulfilment in life. Let's start by looking at three key reasons why we can't afford to miss the loops of this strand:

1. Because we are here for a specific purpose.

'Go therefore and make disciples of all the nations, baptizing them in the name of the Father and of the Son and of the Holy Spirit, teaching them to observe all things that I have commanded you; and lo, I am with you always, even to the end of the age.'
Matthew 28:19-20 NKJV

This is our great commission. We've been given a job to do. When our focus, actions and commitments fully converge with why we were created, this is when we have the maximum power to reach and influence the world around us.

'But I have raised you up for this very purpose, that I might show you my power and that my name might be proclaimed in all the earth.'
Exodus 9:16 NIV

In Jeremiah 29:11, God tells us He knows the plans he has for us. We have all been created for something specific. God leads us to it. Often it relates to our own experiences and testimony, or sometimes to specific gifts God has given. Alternatively, it may be the thing you just get drawn towards. Bill Hybels wrote a brilliant book about this called 'Holy Discontent'. ^{Published by Zondervan 2007.} In it he speaks about the 'Popeye' moments we sometimes have, where we see something that just grabs our soul. Something that needs attention. Something that needs God. In that moment, we say the words of Popeye: 'That's all I can stands, and I can't stands it no more'. That's often when we know that what's on God's heart has been placed upon ours. But it's no good seeing the need, if we don't do something about addressing it.

'For as the body without the spirit is dead, so faith without works is dead also.'
James 2:26 NIV

Some people tell me that they are searching for this specific purpose. They describe how they know they are called, but don't know what to. Sometimes, it's just about starting somewhere. Just do something and see what happens then. If we focus on seeking God, not our purpose, our purpose will come to us.

'But seek first his kingdom and his righteousness, and all these things will be given to you as well.'
Matthew 6:33 NIV

We need to be open to serving God in everything we do. Everything we do, we do for Him. And every day He will lead us to something specific. Once we are obedient in the small things, clarity about the big things will come. God has to position our hearts and ready us for what He wants to reveal. Often, we will only ever be given one breadcrumb at a time. If we follow and honour each piece, it eventually takes us to the bigger picture of His plan. If we surrender to it, God will always get us to where He needs us to be. When our motive is purely about serving Him and not about serving our ego, we won't miss His will. If we have a heart to love God and a selfless desire to serve Him, He will reveal our purpose. He planned it at the beginning of time.

2. Because it humbles us.

'Jesus, knowing that the Father had given all things into His hands, and that He had come from God and was going to God, rose from supper and laid aside His garments, took a towel and girded Himself. After that, He poured water into a basin and began to wash the disciples' feet, and to wipe them with the towel with which He was girded. Then He came to Simon Peter. And Peter said to Him, "Lord, are You washing my feet?'
John 13:3-6 NKJV

Father God, who sent His son - becoming man, was about to make the ultimate sacrifice. He was about to lay down His life. And yet, here Jesus was, the night before that most brutal of ends, kneeling before the very people he had been leading.

'If I then, your Lord and Teacher, have washed your feet, you also ought to wash one another's feet. For I have given you an example, that you should do as I have done to you. Most assuredly, I say to you, a servant is not greater than his master; nor is he who is sent greater than he who sent him. If you know these things, blessed are you if you do them.'
John 14:13-17 NKJV

Wholehearted service will humble us. At times, we may wonder what on earth we are doing and why we are doing it. At others, we may find many comfortable and logical excuses that enable us to step away from what our part could be. Wholehearted service means sacrifice. When we engage with it, the chances are we may well be challenged, insulted, attacked, criticised and taken to the edges of ourselves. **We need to be, because it has to be about bringing glory to God, not to ourselves.** Often, this type of service will take extreme levels of commitment, perseverance, courage and determination. It has to, because we serve the Almighty God. His vision for our lives will far outweigh anything we could either imagine or accomplish ourselves. He wants us totally dependent on Him.

'But the greatest among you will be your servant. Whoever exalts himself shall be humbled; and whoever humbles himself shall be raised to honour.'
Matthew 23:11-12 NIV

I have often found that many wonderful people will actually serve their socks off. Often churches and organisations revolve around the few who are dedicated to the many. God sees this dedication. But even in this we can be humbled. If it ever becomes about what 'we are doing', rather than what God is asking us to do, or about 'what I can do', rather than about what God can do through me. Or if we dare to say, 'I suppose it's left to me, because no one else will do it'; at some point, this attitude of heart will be challenged. God will probably do whatever it takes to draw our attention back to Him being the author, the power and the focus. We will always eventually be humbled until we have truly made God King of it all.

'For it is [not your strength, but it is] [a]God who is effectively at work in you, both to will and to work [that is, strengthening, energizing, and creating in you the longing and the ability to fulfil your purpose] for His good pleasure.'

God may plant the initial vision, but through passion and exuberance, sometimes we then start to introduce our own wants, views and expectations. We imagine how it may pan out, what it needs to look like and the route to take. Before we know it, pride and ego can start to muddy the waters. Many may start the course, but God is looking for people who will stay with it, to serve His will, His instruction and His perfect plan.

'In their hearts, humans plan their course, but the LORD establishes their steps.'
Proverbs 16:9 NIV

When we let go of what we think is right, we are humbled under the mighty hand of a sovereign, all-knowing God. It has to be this way. We have to be surrendered. Without it, we will get in the way. This is the only way we can ever really serve God for His Glory and not our own. Just think about what Jesus sacrificed. Doesn't it demand our allegiance? Let us therefore get on with what He asked us to do. In our purpose and service, we play the biggest part we can. Our contribution becomes our action not our words. Jesus laid down his life for us. Let us lay down our own lives for him.

3. Because this brings inner fulfilment.

'Whoever finds their life will lose it, and whoever loses their life for my sake will find it.'
Matthew 10:39 NIV

Jesus knew what following purpose really meant. And when He breathed His last, saying 'It is finished', He knew what this enabled. Through His death and his resurrection, He enabled us to be made righteous and live in relationship with God Almighty. He lost his life so we could find ours. It's the perfect principle for us to follow. For when we lose our wants, desires, what we think is 'right' and bow before the wisdom of an all-knowing God, we gain the best life we could possibly imagine. The life that we were born for.

'It's in Christ that we find out who we are and what we are living for. Long before we first heard of Christ and got our hopes up, he had his eye on us, had designs on us for glorious living, part of the overall purpose he is working out in everything and everyone.'
Ephesians 1:11-12 MSG

The fulfilment we all desire is never truly reached, unless we find and do what it is we were made for. The desk I am writing on would be pretty pointless if it never got used for why it's been created. This is the alignment of all our God-given gifts, skills, experiences and character, with His divine purpose for us. Once Lance Wallnau said that according to his research, only 20% of Christians ever truly find this convergence. Yet it's our ultimate reason for being here. God is willing us on to find this. He has made us, counted the very hairs on our head, fashioned and shaped every fibre of our being. He has purposefully introduced every gene in our DNA. He's strategically positioned us around people, put us in jobs and given us experiences: all that will lead us to what He had planned from the beginning of time. He doesn't want any of that preparation to be wasted or any of that potential to be unrealised. This has all been done in accordance with His perfect plans.

'Now you [collectively] are Christ's body, and individually [you are] members of it [each with his own special purpose and function]'
1 Corinthians 12:27 AMP

God knows exactly what part of the body we are to be. All parts are critical. No purpose is any more or any less valuable in the Kingdom. However, if we don't bring our part, we let the rest of the body down. We've been equipped with just the right gifts for the job. It's essential we find and use them.

When we hear, submit and apply ourselves to purposeful service, it's a double blessing all round. We get to experience the greatest satisfaction. God gets the pleasure of seeing His incredible work take form in the world. Whether in secular work or otherwise, as He sees us applying ourselves to all He has in store, I can almost sense Him whispering to the angels in heaven; 'That's my boy. That's my girl. Just look at them now.'

Just pause for a moment.

- How clear is the vision of your purposeful service? How much passion does your heart have in serving this? How much of your God-given abilities do you effectively apply to this?
- What degree of sacrifice have you given to this?
- How much meaning do you take from how you serve at the moment? How much success, enjoyment and fulfilment do you have from the service you bring?

As you reflect, spend some time praying about what you discover. Allow this to organically merge into a conversation with your Father. Allow time for silence and consciously allow the Holy Spirit to flow. Is there anything else He says?

The pattern to living it

In each chapter, we will explore the pattern that helps develop, strengthen and embed each strand. **The pattern in the strand of purposeful service is to increase our inner sense of uncompromising motivation.** This is how promise 4: His nature – our accelerated change is released and activated.

How to develop the 4th strand – Purposeful service

'Therefore, I urge you, brothers and sisters, in view of God's mercy, to offer your bodies as a living sacrifice, holy and pleasing to God— this is your true and proper worship.'
Romans 12:1 NIV

This pattern has been broken down into the following three key loops:

1st loop: Make the commitment

Give God your commitment. Tell Him what you are committed to, then dedicate the time and energy into pursuing this. This may start in the most-humble way, as you simply serve wherever you see the need. Turn your intentions into actions. Do everything as service to the Lord. From looking after the children, to working on the checkout, right the way through to organising that fundraising event. This is not about doing things to earn your way into favour. There's nothing any of us can do to merit that. But it is about giving the best you can, out of a thankful heart that wants to honour Jesus.

'So, my son, throw yourself into this work for Christ.'
2 Timothy 2:1 MSG

2nd loop: Submit

As your service leads you to your purpose, a vision will emerge. These are the seeds God is sowing to get you started. Whilst we can plan the details of how, what and when, ultimately, it's God who must lead our steps. Without submitting, your will may interfere with God's. As the weight of your calling increases, it is essential you don't take on the burden that Jesus came to carry for you. Without submitting it all to God, it is impossible to hold such things lightly

Pray that the Holy Spirit will help you to lay down anything you may be holding onto that clouds what God may have planned. This may be your agenda, your desired outcomes and your wants. Or it may be your fears, doubts, your insecurities or your finances. Your hope has to be in God, not in the desired outcome of something. The joy that comes from releasing your own wants is worth the sacrifice. When you give something up for God, He fills in the space where it once was. The fullness you receive will encourage you to ever greater levels of surrender. (We will discuss this more in the 7th strand) Once you have started, keep on going. The freedom that comes from honouring God in this way will be so liberating, freeing you from the heaviness of what He has asked you to hold.

'Surrender yourself to the LORD, and wait patiently for him.'
Psalm 37:7 GWT

3rd loop: Prepare

As you put your intention into action, consider the things you can do that will help you to prepare for what lies ahead. What can you be doing to sharpen your knowledge, gifting, relationships, opportunities, experiences or development, right now?

In his book 'Outliers'[5]., Malcolm Gladwell states that his extensive research shows people at the top of their game have put in over 10,000 hours of practice. [5. Published by Penguin books 2008] Our practise is complimentary to relying on the power of the Holy Spirit to achieve the vision. This provision is God's part. Preparation is your part. It's about taking responsibility for how you can be getting ready for the future. And it's critical. The enemy will want to put seeds of doubt, discouragement and delay in your way. You need to be anchored by the strength of why this is worth it in the end. There may be times ahead when you feel lost in the middle of treacle, or under attack. Frustration, doubt, disappointment and difficulties can play havoc with your resilience. You have to be ready to counter such attacks. The clearer you can paint this picture, the more compelling your perseverance may be in times of difficulty.

'So prepare your minds for action, be completely sober [in spirit—steadfast, self-disciplined, spiritually and morally alert], fix your hope completely on the grace [of God] that is coming to you when Jesus Christ is revealed.'

1 Peter 1:13 AMP

Practical suggestions

As you engage with the Holy Spirit to weave these three loops into your life, your stride will change. You will find you run towards and embrace accountability. When this happens, a laser focus and fierce determination grips your soul. I describe this as a knowing feeling of 'being sent'. You know you are stewarding an ambassadorial undertaking for God's Kingdom. It might be scary, but it's also very exciting. This becomes our assignment.

To develop this strand, in the table below are examples of suggestions you could practically work with. This is what can help to develop the fruits of the spirit and your ability to act in the most appropriate way. These could become useful tools. No doubt you will have other ideas of your own that you can add over time.

Loops	Practical suggestions
1. Commit	• Get started – see a need and fill it. Beyond this, ask the Holy Spirit to lead you every day. - This may range from a sense to encourage a particular person, right the way through to providing the vision for a lifetime's ministry calling. Let God know you want to honour Him in all you do. Tell Him you are available for Him. - Ask Him to use you. - Ask Him to mould you.

	- Ask Him to open opportunities for you. - View every day as a new day to put yourself at His call. ▪ Make the commitment by putting all diligence into it. - Give yourself to every task, every person, every opportunity as you would if Jesus Himself was standing in front of you. - Be wholehearted in everything you do. If there are days you just don't feel like it, ask the Holy Spirit to lift you. - Ask to see the situation through God's eyes. - Ask for energy from heaven. - Ask for the character of Jesus to be alive in you as you serve. ▪ Pursue your commitment. - Practically consider what it will take. - Think about the people it affects. - Then agree a plan. This may include getting relevant permission, links, support and resources. Plan the timing and logistics of juggling other responsibilities so that you can turn the intention into a reality. If this is service that's above and beyond your normal routine, unless you discipline your schedule to carve out specific time, it's likely to stay as a well-meant intention. Words without action don't mean a thing in this world.
2. Submit	▪ Surrender your reactions to the service or calling: - Take a piece of paper and create 3 columns. At the top of one column write: my feelings. On the next: my thoughts. On the last one: my circumstances.

- Think about all the reservations, questions, challenges and internal reactions you notice you have when you think about how you feel led to serve.
- In the knowledge that God knows all and is able to do all, talk to him about these honest, unfiltered reactions.
- If any are negative, ask the Holy Spirit to help you surrender these things to God. Don't allow them to be an inhibitor. Pray for the faith to release these to Him.
- Ask the Holy Spirit to replace these negative reactions with faith-filled reactions.
- Write these faith-filled reactions down. Seek out verses that may help underpin these beliefs.
- One by one, as you feel a shift in your soul, cross off the feelings, thoughts and circumstances that may have held you back. This symbolises your surrender.
- Pray for the Holy Spirit to help you to fully release these to God.

- Surrender your version of it:
  - As you think about the service or calling, consider what you really want, how you want it and when you want it. Honestly. Tell God what this is.
  - Write it on a piece of paper.
  - Now think about the character of God. Ask the Holy Spirit to remind you about any verses, stories, experiences that show the faith you can place in Him. Dwell on the fullness of what this means in your current situation (e.g. He can be trusted, He will do things in perfect timing, He does know all things, He is infinite wisdom, He does know what's best for you. The list goes on).

	Think about these truths and fully embrace them. They confirm that God is over it all. - Now go back to the piece of paper. Ask the Holy Spirit to take away any hold you may have on it needing to be what, when and how you imagine. Ask Him to exchange these ideals for whatever God's perfect plan is. - When you feel ready, tear up the piece of paper and put it in the bin. This symbolises your surrender to it needing to be your way. (Whilst the vision may unfold exactly as you described, there is something powerful in acknowledging it ALL has to be God's plan, God's way.) - As you do this, pray and thank God He has put this burden in you. Then tell Him you are committed to doing it all His way for His Glory, not your way for your own.
3. Prepare	▪ Pray. Soak all of this in prayer. From conception to completion. - Ask God to equip you, lead you, protect you, to bring encouragement and to bring resources. - Ask Him to open and close the right or the wrong doors, to develop you and to influence others. - Ask Him to anoint the work, to bring fresh energy and creativity, to multiply your efforts and to add His power to the outcomes. - Pray big, audacious, imaginative prayers with expectation and anticipation. These are not one-off prayers. They are daily! - Step out each day with intention and excitement about what He will do. ▪ Consider what you can proactively do to be getting ready for any service, calling or purpose you sense may come in the future.

- Think about the knowledge, resources, skills, relationships and character you may need to call upon.
- Ask the Holy Spirit to lead you into developing these things.
- Practically find out what is available and start getting on with it ahead of time.

- Clarify, cement and protect the vision.
  - Find a way of bringing to life and capturing a compelling vision when it's fresh and new.
  - Visualise your sense of what the future may look like. Imagine yourself in that picture. Then think about the lives it will touch - the impact it will make.
  - Ask the Holy Spirit to illuminate the vision further. Don't play small; dream big.
  - Think deeply about WHY you are to do it. What would happen with or without it? How does it advance God's Kingdom? This may be something that happens over a period of time. You may need to keep on refining it as the Holy Spirit reveals more and more about it.
  - Keep this vision somewhere prominent. Keep reminding people of it. Build yourself up.
  - Keep thanking God for the vision and the provision He will release.
  - Bolster your faith through reading key verses, recall any prophecy you have been given and pray declarations of success.
  - Be careful who you tell, particularly when this is in its embryonic stages. Only share with people you know will encourage, support and offer wise counsel. Challenge can be useful, as long as the person giving it is aligned to the heart of what you are aiming for.

> - As you go, ensure you keep track of successes and celebrate. These become living signposts that indicate you are on God's path to success. Make sure you claim the ground that's been taken.

The mirror

Purposeful service is a wholehearted commitment that comes when we want to give ourselves in return for His love. Blossoming from the humility and servant-heart of Jesus' nature within us, it brings us uncompromising motivation. As we become more and more clear about what God is asking of us, our life takes on new meaning. As He reveals specific purpose, a desire is ignited in all our being to serve Him in it. This stimulates even more of a desire to be all we are meant to be. Pursuit of both our purpose and the way we need to change to fulfil it, accelerates our transformation into the image of Jesus.

With this determination, comes increasing awareness of our gaps. To fulfil our calling takes alignment with who we are made to be. It is this pursuit that accelerates our growth; God shapes us as we serve and this further elevates our sense of connection to Him. That's because when we find and fulfil our purpose, we are directly in line with God's eternal plan.

This is the Zoe wheel of life. The power of Christ in us. As we develop the strand of purposeful service, it enables us to live in His nature, releasing an inner provision of uncompromising motivation, so we activate the promise of accelerated change. This makes a difference to our lives through the fruits of the spirit that enable us to behave in the most appropriate manner.

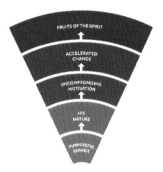

Reflections

Before we move on, my encouragement is to take some time to review the tapestry of your life in this strand. Pray with and consciously invite the Holy Spirit to bring His insight into your awareness.

Consider the current pattern

- How much meaning do you place in your current ways of serving? Is this something God has impressed upon you?
- Do you increasingly encompass the nature of Jesus, through a servant-heart?
- What is the degree of uncompromising motivation you have towards your purposeful service today?
- How much has your character grown or changed over recent times?
- What fruits of the spirit, previously out of reach, do you now manifest in tricky situations?
- What triggers the passing of these things?
- What enables their return?
- What are the largest canyons where motivation is missing?

- Do you ever feel any of the following: Overly-burdened, despondent, on the edge of quitting, bored, listless? Do you find yourself restless or temporarily seeking meaning from unhealthy things? How often do things seem pointless, frustrating or like a waste of your time? How often do you feel unfulfilled, unhealthily ambitious, or a poor comparison to what others may be doing?
- Conversely how often do you feel vibrant, fiercely determined, undeterred, like nothing will stop you? How frequently are you stirred and energised to address something, captivated by what could be improved?

Consider what you need to grow

- Reflect on promise 4 of part one. Of the examples of what His nature brings, what else do you need to develop?
- How would this help your life, others or the world?

Consider what you need to do to develop

- Are you inviting the Holy Spirit to lead your daily focus? Have you scoped, planned and started to wholeheartedly do what's been asked of you?
- Have you identified and truly surrendered anything that holds you back: your reactions, what you want, how you want it and when you want it? How surrendered is your heart really, in dealing with this situation the Lord's way, in His timing?
- Are you preparing as far as possible? How much prayer has gone into this? How are you sharpening your knowledge, gifting, opportunities and resources ahead of time? How deep does your vision and the reason why this is so critical still resonate with you and others? Are you recognising and celebrating what God is already doing?

As you reflect, spend some time praying about what you discover. Allow this to organically merge into a conversation with your Father. Allow time for silence and consciously allow the Holy Spirit to flow. Is there anything else He says?

Stay connected, then review the suggested loops of activity you can take to help you grow in this area. Add any other activities that would work for you. Prayerfully consider these and then create a plan.

- What will you do, when and how?

- Visualise the impact

- Now get practising!

Recap

So far, we have practically explored how to live in all of Christ by considering:

- How to release His presence and activate our spiritual intimacy through the first strand of increased connection.
- How to release His significance and activate our renewed identity through the second strand of deepening relationship.
- How to release His perspective and activate our ability to clearly hear God, through the third strand of whole-hearted worship.

- How to release His nature and activate our accelerated ability to change.

Purposeful service increasingly develops our character, as our focus moves from what we want, to what God wants of us. God's requests are rarely easy. In and of ourselves, we are always lacking in some way. The uncompromising motivation we're given enhances our desire to change into all we need to be to fulfil the calling. Coupled with our intentional focus, the Holy Spirit within accelerates our transformation, by freeing and moulding us into Jesus's image.

As this happens, we become more and more aware of our dependency and inability to fulfil this without Him. This leads us to an even deeper connection with the Holy Spirit as we realise we can only succeed if we truly partner with Him. As Smith Wigglesworth once famously said: 'You must come to see how wonderful you are in God and how helpless you are in yourself.'

When you are ready, the pattern in the fifth strand of partnership will show you how.

16

The 5th strand

Partnership
Learning to do things through the Holy Spirit's leading and power.

How to release His empowerment and activate our heightened ability.

'But you will receive power and ability when the Holy Spirit comes upon you; and you will be My witnesses [to tell people about Me] *both in Jerusalem and in all Judea, and Samaria, and even to the ends of the earth'.*

Acts 1:8 AMP

With a fire in our belly, the Zoe life is only possible through a Spirit-led life. We must learn how to partner with God. Without this we will fail. In the gospels, we read how the disciples were saved by Jesus, but time and again, despite being given a mandate, we saw their failure. They couldn't heal (Mat 17:16); they fell asleep when Jesus needed them most (Mat 26:40); they faltered (John 21:7); they lacked boldness (Mat 26:74); they all but gave up after the crucifixion. The promise Jesus made was that they would receive power, the same power that had filled Jesus Himself. In Acts 2:4, all were filled with the Holy Spirit and from that point on, everything changed. Healings, courage, focus and radical pursuit all led to an explosion of the early church. This same power is available to us - when we learn how to partner with Him.

'And He said to me, "My grace is sufficient for you, for My strength is made perfect in weakness." Therefore most gladly I will rather boast in my infirmities, that the power of Christ may rest upon me. Therefore I take pleasure in infirmities, in reproaches, in needs, in persecutions, in distresses, for Christ's sake. For when I am weak, then I am strong.'
2 Corinthians 12:9-10 NKJV

We are the vessel that brings God's power to earth. Partnership is the seesaw of this walk with God - working in combination with the Holy Spirit, so God can give us His empowerment.

We may pro-actively partner when the calmness of life invites the space for mindful consciousness. Alternatively, we may partner when the throws of crisis impale us towards it. But Spirit-led living can't be maintained unless this is a consistent focus.

I've always found that God constantly stretches the comfort zone of what I am capable of. This makes me dig deeper into my need for Him. I love that. It means that no request is ever too big. For if He has asked it, I know He needs to be the one to enable it. It takes all the pressure off, as it's not down to me, it's down to Him in me. All I have to do is make myself available and diligently prepare. He takes care of the rest.

At the moment, it is 'Strictly Come Dancing' season on TV. When the expert professional dancers work with the amateur apprentices, they are able to make even the worst dancers so much better. At first, the amateurs may look a bit stiff, awkward and uncoordinated. But over time with practice, mistakes, training, feedback and a few disappointing results under their belt, a shift starts to happen. With encouragement and the elevating support of their partner, over time, many become very, very good. If they persevere. As the weeks unfold, with training, they become fitter, trimmer and more and more connected to their expert partner. At times, their movements can be as fluid as if they are one. But, as soon as the amateur let's go of their partner, maybe to tap a few isolated steps, it becomes very clear who the professional is. Such is the effect of the Holy Spirit's partnership with us. He can multiply the impact of what we bring, helping to mould us into brilliance for the Kingdom. Although we undoubtedly develop in all we do through this process, as soon as we let Him go, on our own, we will never shine like we do with Him in the lead.

'Lean on, trust in, and be confident in the Lord with all your heart and mind and do not rely on your own insight or understanding.'
Proverbs 3:5 AMP

When we partner with the Holy Spirit, we hand over our control to be under God's governance. As this happens, our ability is heightened, as we are empowered to release all God has.

Jesus showed us through His disciples how partnership was essential. Peter is invited to walk on water – but soon found himself sinking. (Matt 14:30). He's asked if He knows Jesus – but denies him three times. (Mark 14:72) Only in the partnering power of the Holy Spirit was He able to achieve what was needed. Suddenly, not only can Peter stand up to the powers that be, (Acts 4:8) people are even healed by his shadow. (Acts 5:15) This is the confidence partnering with the Holy Spirit brings.

The provision is confidence

'Moses told the people. Fear not: stand still (firm, confident, undismayed) and see the salvation of the Lord which He will work for you today. For the Egyptians you have seen today you shall never see again.'
Exodus 14:13 AMP

It was God who heightened the ability of Moses, from enabling his speech, (Exo 4:12) through to anointing the staff he used. (Exo 7:20) Think about when he led the Israelites out of captivity in the Book of Exodus. The most direct route out of Egypt to the Promised Land was through Philistine. But the Philistines were at war. God knew that this would terrify the Israelites and that, in the face of that fear, many of them may flee back to the captivity they had been rescued from. So instead, God led them by the cloud and fire that hovered (the Holy Spirit), on the arduous and much longer journey through the wilderness. When the cloud moved or stopped, so did they -with much murmuring and complaining along the way. Can you imagine their confusion? To cap it all off, they then appear trapped, with the Red Sea on one side and Pharaoh's 600 approaching chariots hunting them down on the other. Despite the journey and the impending doom, despite their doubts, their fear and their anger at the seeming dead end they had been brought to, what did God do? He only then parted the Red Sea, enabling their safe passage and deliverance to the other side. He took them to a place where only His power (released through the outstretched staff of Moses), would do the job. It was a partnership. Moses led the people. God released the power.

Imagine the weight of the burden upon Moses's shoulders. What was it that enabled Him to stand the ground? In one word – confidence. He had been with God, experienced God, received His miracles, been led every step of the way and achieved everything through the power of His Spirit. He was confident in who his God actually was – and what would be enabled through His lead.

The closer our partnership with the Holy Spirit becomes, the more profound our impact will be. This is the confidence we place our trust in, so that when we are following His lead, we know we will succeed. This, is the outcome that takes us further into the Zoe life. Inner confidence is our provision. **Partnership brings inner confidence.**

The Oxford dictionary says that confidence is the feeling or belief that one can have faith in or rely on someone or something. When we are Spirit-led, we are assured, for our faith is in God not ourselves. When we trust this, our major interferences are eliminated. When our interferences are eliminated, God is free to do what is needed. This releases a heightened ability that multiplies anything we would be able to achieve on our own. When we are in line with His lead, our part in it -whatever He determines that should be, will flow.

This type of confidence is very different from the self-confidence we can have in our own capability. **This is restful confidence.** The type of confidence God provides has the power to overcome any hesitation, without trying. With restful confidence all worry and doubt are eliminated. This is a confidence that emboldens us with clarity, poise and assertiveness. It rests upon God within us. Even if in our own strength we are shaking, when the Holy Spirit brings His arms of certainty, we have the courage to follow His lead. As He empowers us, the full power of heaven is released into this world by what we do in that moment. When this happens we really do know that greater is He who is in us, than he who is in the world. (1 John 4:4) and that things happen through God's power not our own might and strength. (Zech 4:6) Regardless of the challenge before us, when we are Spirit-led, we will know accomplishment.

God is omniscient. He knows everything and as such, He knows where we need to go, how we need to get there, what we need to do and how we need to do it. Every decision, pathway and outcome He enables is perfect. **When we allow ourselves to be led through the Holy Spirit, we can live in the assurance that whatever happens, - it is perfect.** As such, when we are Spirit-led, we can let go of the outcome – often it is not how we imagine it to be anyway. This is the most liberated state to operate from.

For us to succeed, the outcome doesn't even matter – for the outcome will always be what God determines it should be. If we trust

God, we trust His wisdom – we trust the outcome. **This type of confidence brings us a deep rest that eliminates all burden**. (Matt 11:30) Taking the yoke of the Holy Spirit, this degree of rest can only come from knowing one thing: God has got it. All we need to do is camp in His Spirit and follow His lead.

This is restful confidence; a confidence that is superior to the inner belief we can have in our own powers, abilities, or capacities – no matter how established our track record, credibility or self-certainty is. Restful confidence eclipses the conscious self-application of our best, as it comes from a reliance on who is in us. It does not depend on our own competence or assertion. **It depends on our empowerment through Jesus.**

Stop to reflect on your own life for a moment.

- In situations that require much from you, how often do you live in the certainty of such deep restful confidence?
- Conversely, how much time do you spend feeling daunted, overly-burdened, overwhelmed, unsettled, unable or inadequate? Do you waver depending on your own level of confidence in yourself? Do you oscillate between resting in God's ability through you and the clamour of your own limitations?
- What would your life look like if you could replace all those times of uncertainty with a restful confidence that instead brings such stillness of heart, unfazed by either the outcome or the action required?

Partnership is the strand we must deepen to release this provision.

The missing strands

If we don't access God's power, we don't receive His promises.

This type of Spirit-led partnership lives or dies by the strength of this strand. The Zoe life is impossible without this empowerment. Despite this, it is often the most inconsistent strand in the tapestry of our lives. Let's start by looking at three key reasons why we can't afford for this strand to be missing:

1. Because we are incapable alone.

'So Jesus explained himself at length. "I'm telling you this straight. The Son can't independently do a thing, only what he sees the Father doing. What the Father does, the Son does. The Father loves the Son and includes him in everything he is doing'.
John 5:19-20 MSG

If Jesus Himself said he was utterly reliant on the Father, what does it say for the rest of us? This is precisely why the Holy Spirit lives in us. He is here to be the power source that shapes and leads us to eternity. Think about what Jesus endured, yet He lived a perfect life. Fully God, yet humbling himself to be born in a ruined shack. Experiencing the growing pains of youth and all that comes with it. Establishing a career from a standing start as an apprentice. Constant mocking and disbelief from siblings and friends alike. No great 'A' team to support Him when His time came. Constant aggression, suspicion and humiliation. Temptation from the devil himself. Elusive peace and quiet to recover from his grafting. People rarely ever looked out for His needs, but He was constantly there for everyone else. People expected miracle after miracle. Turning the other cheek when abused, diligently continuing when rejected, refusing to bow down when persecuted, only loving in return when He was invalidated. And in the end, so few truly believed in Him, supported Him or encouraged Him.

Is any of this starting to sound familiar? The chances are that if you have followed God's lead to serve and live His way, at some point you will come across such experiences. Just re-read the challenges

He faced and see how it may mirror your own challenges. Fulfilling our purpose is impossible without God's support.

All Jesus did was in the knowledge He would be betrayed, condemned, brutalised and would die the most barbaric of deaths. He looked straight into the pain of his mother's eyes and saw the twisted expressions of those who still threw yet more evil at Him. He descended into the pit of hell itself, carrying the burden of every sin past, present and future, separating Himself from the Father He had been with since before time began. All to save a bunch of people who were rotten to the core, many of whom denounced Him anyway. What must that level of sacrifice have been like? We will never know or understand the depths of it.

Even as the son of God, it was the Holy Spirit who enabled Jesus to do all he did. To live His life, to endure the challenges and to fulfil His calling, Jesus needed the Holy Spirit every day. And so do we. For without Him we do not have the resilience, ability or wisdom needed. We must always remember that God has walked our path before, therefore we need His lead in all things. Without it, we can so easily walk off in the wrong direction. God has a divine strategy we need to follow.

Think of Paul and Silas in Acts 16:6-10, when they were travelling through modern day Turkey. In verse 6 Luke says, *"They passed through the Phrygian and Galatian region, having been forbidden by the Holy Spirit to speak the word in Asia."* Here, we see the Holy Spirit at work in changing the plans of Paul and Silas. Then later, the Holy Spirit did not permit them to go to Bithynia. This was an historic moment in the history of the church. The Spirit turned the attention of Paul and his team to Europe instead. Throughout the Book of Acts, the pivotal directions taken are described as coming from the Spirit. God's strategy was Europe before Asia. Interestingly, within fifteen years, Peter took the gospel to Bithynia (1 Peter 1:1). God's timing is always perfect. Yet, how often do we think we know what is right in human wisdom? When the Holy Spirit leads, we know we are acting in God's time, for His purpose. He alone knows our when, what and how.

In the early days of my corporate business, my partner and I were invited to pitch for a piece of work in a major international corporation. We were both unsure about it, but when we arrived at the very impressive head office, we started to feel a little more upbeat. On paper, this was a perfect fit for the work we did. Then the strangest thing happened. During the conversations with the two people we were meeting, I noticed I had an uneasy feeling. I ignored it at first. Then, it was as if a blanket had been pulled over my mind. I found I just could not call on any of the information it was crucial for me to share. Every sentence seemed so forced, unnatural and heavy. In the natural, I am usually able to speak freely and convincingly. On this occasion, I instinctively knew this ability was being blocked. It was an occasion where, despite the gifting God had given me, He was not anointing my ability to use it. As a result, we did not go any further in our conversations. For reasons known to God, He was steering our direction elsewhere.

Even when our intentions are right, we need to be malleable to what God is leading. The Holy Spirit is that lead. If we listen. If we trust. If we obey. If we don't, we can easily get lost.

2. Because we turn it into 'works'.

'But He answered and said, "Every plant which My heavenly Father has not planted will be uprooted.'
Matthew 15:13 NKJV.

In this, Jesus was saying that for anything to survive and bear fruit, God has to be the author of it. I know first-hand how I have often moved into works. By this, I mean the times when I have used all my own strength and stepped out from under God's empowerment. I've relied on me, not on God. Often this has come from good intentions: passion, hunger to serve, adoration, seeing a need and just wanting to fill it. But the minute it turns into my willpower, or feels like I am pushing water uphill, or just not making headway; I know I have moved into 'works'. At other times - if I am honest with myself, it has been about looking good, being 'right', making an impression, following my own agenda or fulfilling something for myself.

The second it turns from being about God's glory to our own, we are in 'works'. The moment we are 'trying and forcing' something to come, we are in 'works' as the sovereign-self takes hold.

As an example, about two thirds of the way through writing my first manuscript, I suddenly seemed to hit a wall. No amount of effort, concentrated focus or wilful resilience could push through it. I must have spent hours in the frustrating cycle of writing, then deleting, rewriting and deleting again. I went around in circles and nothing seemed to be clicking into place. The only thing that removed that blockage was to stop, rest and reconnect with God and the Holy Spirit's guidance.

These 'walls' can come in so many different forms; being overly tired, the death of a loved one, or the times we are stewing from a hurt – these are just a few examples. These are the blocks that we simply cannot get past in a wholesome way through our own 'works'. God has made us dependent on Him for good reason. He wants relationship. And He wants us to do amazing things - things that bring His Kingdom to earth - things that we are incapable of doing in our own strength and ability. No amount of trying our very best will ever be enough to sustain it.

Jacob's bedroom is downstairs, below where my husband and I sleep. At times, I need to make the inevitable trips to see him during the night. But have you ever tried to navigate a familiar room in the dark? You think you know where the furniture is and where the door frame stands. In our familiarity, we can think we know where we are going and what needs to be done. But if we have our eyes closed or we are in darkness, the chances are, we will still bump into things.

Despite knowing this, sometimes we do unplug, either assuming we are fine or forgetting we are not. Often this is not through intended self-will, or our ego taking over. Ironically, the very motivation our purpose provides can be the blockage that prevents the Spirit leading us. Sometimes, it is purely because of the burning desire that we press in, push ourselves hard and gradually disconnect from the source that enables us.

If we ever find ourselves holding onto 'stuff, (fixing, striving or controlling) - even if driven by all the right reasons, when a heavy burden of weight falls, we know we have stepped into works. If we find our thoughts racing like a run-away express train, the chances are we have taken over the control.

'Come to me and I will give you rest—all of you who work so hard beneath a heavy yoke. Wear my yoke—for it fits perfectly—and let me teach you; for I am gentle and humble, and you shall find rest for your souls; for I give you only light burdens.'
Matthew 11:28 TLB

In the fields, when two oxen were paired together, a yoke was placed across the back of their necks. The combined strength enabled a greater pulling power. In this passage, it teaches us that if we put on the yoke of the Holy Spirit, we will receive all the strength of Jesus. We will not need to rely on our own works. We will not be burdened. If we ever feel we are, we need to go back to the first strand of connection and plug back into the Holy Spirit immediately. If you experience frustration from a lack of breakthrough, heaviness from the load or negative emotions such as jealousy or comparison, in that moment you have moved into works. You have turned it into what you are doing, not what God is doing through you. In this moment, you are not partnering with the Holy Spirit.

3. Because we live in a fallen world.

'Establish my footsteps in [the way of] Your word;. Do not let any human weakness have power over me [causing me to be separated from You].'

Psalm 119:133

Despite the miracles they saw, the default mind-set of the disciples was to see things how the world saw them. Isn't it interesting how when five thousand-plus hungry people needed feeding, their first reaction is 'where is the shop'? (Matt 14:15)

There are three key things that can overshadow our partnership with the Holy Spirit:

- The influence of the world around us (culture, upbringing, relationships, media, lack of 'true' knowledge and input)
- The influence of our own soul (mind: what we think, will: what we want and emotions: what we feel)
- The influence of the devil (deception, doubt, disappointment, demons)

We therefore have to be rigorously disciplined, to ensure our actions are not swayed in the wrong direction.

Our ability to partner and follow God's way is enabled when: 1. we are connected; 2. in deep relationship; 3. we worship; 4. we purposefully serve. But even when all the first 4 strands are strong; even if we are sold out and working towards a God-given vision; even if we have the most-sincere of intentions - without partnership, at some point, we will be compromised. We will make mistakes. We will misjudge, mishear and miss cues. We will eventually run out of energy, vision, ability and possibly even desire.

As humans, we can often be impatient. Of course, in the calmness of a centred state of mind, we can examine the truth. But life is rarely so static. Life is so busy, we often don't think we have time to stop and think, let alone time to stop, think and ensure what we are thinking or doing is right! So often we will move straight from decision needed, to decision made, from this has happened, to an automatic reaction or response. In seeking, knowing and following the Holy Spirit, we can access the right action, decision, path, ability and behaviour. To walk in the Spirit requires a preoccupation with the truth and we must be hypersensitive to anything that is in conflict with this. We need to give the Holy Spirit a chance to penetrate.

'Do not quench [subdue, or be unresponsive to the working and guidance of] the [Holy] Spirit.'
1 Thessalonians 5:19 AMP

This is not about what you want: it's about what God, through the Holy Spirit, wants to impart. In his book 'The Wonderful Spirit-Filled Life'[6,] Charles Stanley pens it perfectly; 'Holy Spirit talks to neutral hearts. By that I don't mean passive or indifferent hearts. God gave us the ability to dream dreams and make plans. By neutral, I mean being consumed with what pleases Holy Spirit, rather than working to convince Him'. [6. Published by Thomas Nelson 1992.] In this, Stanley is saying our attitude needs to be about what God wants to say, not what we want to hear.
God wants to save us from that unnecessary time, pain, waste, emotion, hardship and commotion. That's why our partnership with the Holy Spirit is so critical.

Just pause for a moment.

- How frequently does the Holy Spirit lead your daily thoughts and activities? How conscious is your partnership to His steer? What impact does His power in you have on your abilities?
- When does this partnership seem natural and intuitive? When does this partnership seem forced or false?
- When do the pressures of the world around you impact on your thoughts, feelings, decisions and behaviour? When have you felt hoodwinked or overtly driven into what this influence dictates,

above what the Holy Spirit may be leading? How often does God's steer even factor?

As you reflect, spend some time praying about what you discover. Allow this to organically merge into a conversation with your Father. Allow time for silence and consciously allow the Holy Spirit to flow. Is there anything else He says?

The pattern

In each chapter, we will explore the pattern that helps develop, strengthen and embed each strand. **The pattern in the strand of partnership is to increase our inner sense of restful confidence.** This is how promise 5: His empowerment - our heightened ability is increasingly released and activated.

How to develop the 5th strand of Partnership

'If any of you lacks wisdom [to guide him through a decision or circumstance], he is to ask of [our benevolent] God, who gives to everyone generously and without rebuke or blame, and it will be given to him. But he must ask [for wisdom] in faith, without doubting [God's willingness to help], for the one who doubts is like a billowing surge of the sea that is blown about and tossed by the wind'.
James 1:5 AMP

This pattern has been broken down into the following three key loops:

1st loop: Create rest
This is when the Holy Spirit leads you - so you need to be ready to tune in. If our starting point is striving, we may block out the spiritual channel needed. This is about creating the space and environment

for the Holy Spirit to lead you, by dialling down what your own mind, will and emotions may be trying to communicate. It may sound counterintuitive, but your starting point actually needs to be from a place of rest. Park your agenda, so you can receive from a neutral place. Do the things you need to do to stop the internal chitchat. If you practise, it will start to only take a matter of seconds. Be still and know He is God. (Psalm 46:10)

Such tranquillity can come when we are anywhere, regardless of the noise that may surround us. Rest has nothing to do with how busy we are, or our environment we are in. It is how stilled we are internally.

'And He said, "My Presence will go with you, and I will give you rest."
Exodus 33:14 NKJV

However, sometimes we have to go after this stillness with intentionality. In the evenings when Jacob is in bed, my husband and I will often talk about our day and generally just reconnect. It's hard to do that when the TV is blaring in the background. If you were planning an intimate dinner with someone special, the chances are you would consider the lighting and the ambience. You might prepare candles on the table and have the right kind of music playing. You would be attentive, show interest and possibly pay some authentic compliments. Maybe you would talk about meaningful things, enjoying one another's company and feel comfortable enough to just sit with the pauses and be together. The preparation, attention and joy of such an experience would make you want to do it again. If you would do all this for someone special, what can you do to give this thought to how you meet with your sovereign King?

2nd loop: Deepen your communion

This is when we learn how to just be with the Holy Spirit. The Holy Spirit knows the thoughts of God, so when we enter this deepest secret place, we are connected to the throne room itself. Through this we evolve from praying 'to', to 'praying with'. As we pray with The Holy Spirit, we are given the things of God. We start to hear, think and pray about God's thoughts, not our own. This prayer then turns into a dynamic two-way conversation and conversation then turns into the constant chitchat of a best friend we do everything with. It's raw, unfiltered, intimate and honest. Question, challenge and speak about what you receive. Notice when you feel in the flow of this, as you learn to recognise the sense of being connected in this deeper way – He is training you to recognise His steer. Conversations with the Holy Spirit and the sense of His presence can be as real as with the person sitting next to you. Whether out loud or in your head, whether in stillness or in activity, a constant flow of communion will help you increasingly recognise, understand and respond to God's leading.

'Let us go right in to God himself, with true hearts fully trusting him to receive us because we have been sprinkled with Christ's blood to make us clean and because our bodies have been washed with pure water'.

Hebrews 10:22 TLB

3rd loop: Trust God's lead
Trust the waiting, the discernment and the guidance you receive. Get used to pro-actively 'scanning' for what your spirit may be sensing. The Holy Spirit's lead can be a process. Be comfortable with not hearing immediately, but know that clarity will come. It may be that in the most unexpected moment the Holy Spirit reveals something to you. Wait with faith and anticipation, not with strain, worry and uncertainty. The devil will try and sow seeds of doubt like; 'This is never going to happen you know, He won't talk to you, it won't do any harm to do x, y, z'. Expect that. And totally discard the lies. Whilst we do sometimes experience spells where we just don't feel like we hear from God, this is often when He is stretching us to makes us press in more. Stick with it.

Consider most young children waiting for Christmas through Advent. They don't know what presents they may get, but they are excited and anticipate – they believe it will be brilliant. They wait with total faith and expectation. How lovely is it when your child looks at you, with total belief that those presents will be under the tree? But you don't just want to give your children the bare minimum. You want to delight them, spoil them, give them more than they had hoped for. This is the type of giving we are promised from our Father. Now that is something we should be excited about! Be prepared to wait for your gift.

'For this is God, Our God forever and ever; He will be our guide even until death.'

                    Psalm 48:14 AMP

Practical suggestions

As you engage with the Holy Spirit to weave these three loops into your life, an ease will start to flow in what you do. With this comes a strong, authentic personal presence. When this happens, you are actually emanating the confidence of God. I describe this as the feeling of just being 'in Him'. A good friend of mine calls it 'surfing the flow!' Coming from the Holy Spirit's empowerment in you, this is the most fluid, natural experience in the world. It is how we were born to live!

The purpose of developing the strand of partnership is to release the provision of restful confidence. This is what helps to develop our effectiveness and from it, our credibility.

The table below contains examples of suggestions you could practically work with. These could become useful tools. No doubt you will have other ideas of your own that you can add over time.

Loops	Practical suggestions
1. Create rest	▪ Check your level of faith. If you are struggling to find rest – or if it is wavering, reflect on what you trust in God. - What do you know of the true, loving character of God? - Reflect on His omniscience and what that really means – how does that apply to your life? - Fill your mind with these truths: meditate on them. - Proclaim them as statements of faith. - Thank God for being able to lean on those promises. This will help you to let go of your dependence of both yourself and the outcome. - As you do, ask the Holy Spirit to breathe the stillness into your soul that brings deep rest. ▪ Consider what might get in the way of you switching to neutral. - If it's things you don't want to forget, make a note of them. - If it's interference from what your soul is communicating, go back to loop 2 of strand 4: surrender them to God. - You have the potential to tune into the maker of our universe! What else may disturb or get in your way? Plan what can you practically do to remove or limit these disruptions. ▪ If you are really struggling, do the healthy things you do, that can relax and calm you.

	- Things like physical exercise, singing, being in nature, fasting, listening to soothing music. For me, worship songs that focus on Jesus (rather than the challenges of life) help elevate me to stillness of rest. - Return to the loops in strand one, to reconnect with His presence.
2. Deepen your communion	▪ Consciously spend time just being with God - After you have returned to the loops of strand one (connecting to His presence), allow yourself to just be with Him, without the need for conversation. You can do this anywhere – you don't need to be in the isolated quiet of a secluded place. Allow yourself to just be in this place of stillness with Him. Stay in this rest for as long as the moment holds. The more you do this, the more you will start to recognise a pull in your spirit – the times when He is intentionally drawing you to something of Himself. This may be so He can reveal a specific message or simply so you are aware of His closeness. **In this, He is training you to be sensitive to the deepest tremors of His presence.** It is worth the perseverance, as often our busy lives try and pull us away from this. This is when deep calls unto deep. (Psalm 42:7) - Whether internally or externally, when with others or not, whether in your native or your spiritual tongue, speak to Him. At first, this may feel strange, but it will eventually be something you can't do without. When something resonates, speak to Him. When something seems off, speak to Him. When you hear something on the news that disturbs,

delights, angers, heartens, speak to Him about it all.

- The more you do this, the more you will start to notice His response. Intentionally tune in and listen for it. This may come as a slight sense, a gentle nudge or a clear word. God reveals His messages through this. It might start with guidance on what you should pray for, be the illumination of a certain biblical word, or provide specific practical instructions. Intentional communion will gradually start to reveal more and more of what God wants to impart.

- Ask the Holy Spirit to reveal more as you engage in spiritually nourishing activities. Consciously do it all with Him.
  - Read the word, listen to sermons, praise God, pray, read Christian literature.
  - Purposefully include Him as you do these things. See it as shared activity. Repeat back to Him what you sense is being revealed. Challenge what it means and ask Him to challenge you back. In the gentlest way, He will. He loves a willing learner.
  - Write to Him. This might sound strange, and sometimes, (particularly if we are running a bit dry), it can be tricky to get started. But often when we start to write, another level of consciousness is tapped into. It's incredible how we can start off feeling we haven't much to say, yet end up writing pages. This will help you tap into what your spirit wants to commune about, rather than your mind.
  -

	▪ 'Scan your spirit'. Regularly and pro-actively tune into what your spirit is sensing. - During times when you know you are spiritually connected, consciously scan your body; do you notice any physiological sensations anywhere? - In silence, scan your senses, pay attention and notice anything at all you are spiritually seeing, hearing, feeling, smelling or tasting. These senses can be subtle so don't rush past them. - Ask the Holy Spirit to reveal their relevance.
3. Trust God's lead	▪ Trust Him. If a response, experience, revelation or direction doesn't appear, just trust it will - when it's meant to. - If you are unsettled by this (e.g. with doubts filling your mind, disappointment filling your heart, frustration filling your body), go back to loop 1 - your soul is not in neutral. - Sometimes when we do hear, God speaks to us about something else! It may relate to something we have not even yet thought about or raised with Him. If this happens, write it down with the date. If the Holy Spirit doesn't immediately bring interpretation, trust He will, in due time. Don't force it until He does. - Praise Him. This may seem like a strange thing to do at this time, but nothing will elevate you beyond the circumstances, the pressure, the desire for an answer more. It may be the very last thing you feel like doing. Ignore your emotions. Just tell them you are not going to be ambushed by them. Even if it starts through gritted teeth and a hard heart, if you

start recalling His goodness, His mercy, His wonder, the Holy Spirit will elevate your heaviness and turn it into joy. Before you know it, so many things you are thankful for will flood into consciousness. As this happens, the urgent demand of needing clarity now will just seem to fade away. This is the most liberating way of moving beyond any impatience.

- Trust His discernment.
  - Until you become extremely certain of even the faintest whispers, always weigh what you believe you have heard. It will always align with the Bible.
  - Even if it leaves you feeling nervous, unsure or a bit scared, there will be an underlying sense of calm. You will just know. If you have any other response, it's not from God. When it is, despite some human jitteriness, you will develop an increasing certainty.
  - You may need to validate it with other trustworthy Christians; talk it through and pray together.
  - If you are feeling strong emotions at the time of hearing direction, it's unlikely to be God; it's probably your soul's response. One way to discern this is to test yourself: if you really want what you think God has said, but it transpires it's not His will, would you be willing to sacrifice and let go of this, without resistance? Or do you find yourself 'willing' this to be the right answer? If, honestly you might feel disappointed, it may indicate your soul has taken over; seek further reassurance from Him.

- When it's validated, ask God to find ways to reassure, encourage and remind you of what His leadings are. It's incredible how many signposts He will provide.

- Trust His instructions.
  - Follow the lead you sense you have received, by praying for His power to heighten what you now do.
  - Avoid talking yourself out of what you sense the lead is. Human wisdom can get in the way of spiritual guidance.
  - Before you take any steps ensure you have pressed reset, as explained in Strand 1: Connection.
  - Ask the Holy Spirit to lift any burden or fear, so that you can let go of the outcome and rest in His ability in you.
  - As you take the action required, thank Him for who He is and what He has put within you. Remind yourself who is Lord of it all!
  - Repeat this after any action. Ensure the glory is centred on what He does through you, not what you do. Then make sure you give him the glory afterwards.

The mirror

As we learn to partner with the Holy Spirit, his empowerment moves us from what we can do in our own might, to what God can do working through us – He multiplies what is possible. These are the times when God anoints what we do. Whilst this potential is always in us, it's not always active. It is our trust in His partnership that provides the inner confidence we need. This is what releases a heightened ability that enhances our effectiveness and impact - when we converge God-inspired gifts with God-inspired opportunities. The anointing of God can achieve the unimaginable through us. All we have to do is learn to let Him.

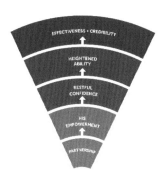

This is the Zoe wheel of life. The power of Christ in us. As we develop the strand of partnership, it enables us to live in His empowerment, releasing an inner provision of restful confidence, so we activate the promise of heightened ability. This makes a difference to our lives through our increased effectiveness creating credibility that enables us to influence our world.

Reflections

Before we move on, my encouragement is to take some time to review the tapestry of your life. Pray with and consciously invite the Holy Spirit to bring His insight into your awareness.

Consider the current pattern

- How frequently do you trust and follow the Holy Spirit, pro-actively partnering this way?
- How much of God's anointing empowerment are you seeing released in your life?
- When much is required, how much restful confidence do you apply to life's situations today? Consider different situations.
- How are your natural independent capabilities being multiplied to a heightened ability? What have you achieved that would be impossible through your own limited capability?
- How is your effectiveness and impact improved by His empowerment within?
- What wobbles you in this?
- What enables it's return?
- What are the largest canyons such things are missing?
- Do you ever feel any of the following: pressured, low, downtrodden, impatient, lost, stuck, frustrated, or like you are pushing water up hill?
- Conversely how often do you feel strong, confident, courageous, effective, assured, dynamic, assertive or powerful?

Consider what you need to grow

- Reflect on promise 5 from part 1. Of the examples of what His empowerment brings, what else do you need to develop?
- How would this help your life, others or the world?

Consider how to develop further

- How well are you quietening your soul, intentionally setting it to neutral and finding inner rest?

> - How pro-actively are you partnering with the Holy Spirit? How much time are you spending each day just being with the Holy Spirit about what is going on?
> - How patiently are you waiting on the leading of the Holy Spirit? Are you proactively scanning what your spirit is sensing? Are you sure you are operating in the will and power of God?

Stay connected, then review the suggested loops of activity you can take to help you grow in this area. Add any other activities that would work for you. Prayerfully consider these and then create a plan.

- What will you do, when and how?

- Visualise the impact

- Now get practising!

Recap

So far, we have practically explored how to live in all of Christ by considering:

- How to release His presence and activate our spiritual intimacy through the first strand of increased connection.

- How to release His significance and activate our renewed identity through the second strand of deepening relationship.
- How to release His perspective and activate our ability to clearly hear God, through the third strand of whole-hearted worship.
- How to release His nature and activate our accelerated ability to change.
- How to release His empowerment and activate our heightened ability.

Such partnership is how we increasingly develop our ability to live a Spirit-led life. As we do, we become increasingly emboldened to tackle whatever situation we find ourselves in. The restful confidence we place in this leaves us feeling totally secure in whatever our circumstances bring.

As this happens, our eyes are opened to the tangible realities of doing life the Spirit-led way. But often, God needs to prepare us for what He is yet to reveal and do through us. The level of supernatural power God releases in, through and around us is directly correlated to the character and wisdom we must have to handle it.

When you are ready, we'll learn how God equips us for this in the 6th strand of spiritual growth.

17

The 6th strand

Spiritual growth
Developed, shaped and refined as we mature into our full spiritual stature.

How to release His sovereign power and activate our supernatural might.

'Here's another way to put it: You're here to be light, bringing out the God-colours in the world. God is not a secret to be kept. We're going public with this, as public as a city on a hill. If I make you light-bearers, you don't think I'm going to hide you under a bucket, do you? I'm putting you on a light stand. Now that I've put you there on a hilltop, on a light stand—shine!'
Matthew 5:14-15 MSG

With God's empowerment anointing our natural ability, we see more and more of what is possible when we live in Him. **The more powerful we become, the more reverent we must become.** Without this humility, our own ego starts to soak up the glory, when all glory should go to Him. For God to trust us with more, He first ensures we are equipped – He will never release more than we are ready to handle. God equips us by maturing our understanding, spiritual gifts and our character. We should increase our comprehension of the spiritual realm. (2 Kings 6:17) We can earnestly seek the spiritual gifts that bring God's power to earth. (1 Cor 14:1) These are things we can all develop. But in His kindness, the spiritual growth God brings is also about the preparation we need to handle them – the character we require. In this, God matures us, creating the spiritual understanding, wisdom and resilience we will need for all God has in store.

God knows His intended destiny for us. He knows exactly where we are now in relation to that. He also knows the gap. All our development needs are different and the Holy Spirit is an expert in guiding us through the change needed - if we let Him. Over time, God can use every experience, every gifting and every opportunity to manoeuvre us forward towards that intended destination. As this happens, He uncovers more and more of the potential He has put within us. He has created us specifically and knows all we can be - and are yet to become. As a hunger develops within us to lean into more and more of Him, a desire is lit. A desire to press in deeper.

This takes intentional pursuit - beyond attending church, the home group or the purposeful service we bring. This takes our time. However, our time is often so pressed, so this is often where we compromise. We may press in when time allows, only to retreat when other pressures commands it. Alternatively, we may pursue it when the need compels it, only to retreat when the intensity of the situation abates, or when life just gets easier.

Whilst other things are prioritised, our self-imposed limitations of spiritual growth don't always relate to a lack of time afforded them: They relate to our lack of focus. Sermons, books, meetings, conferences can all provide much needed stimulation, input and a wealth of information. But without the deeper introspection of how all that applies to how we live our lives, ultimately, their impact is marginalised. Spiritual growth is not an increase of information, it is not reliant on how long we have been a Christian and it is not affected by how theologically qualified we become. Whilst those things are brilliant, spiritual growth is what it says. To grow –

spiritually: **To be ever- more equipped to operate in the spiritual realm.** Irrespective of how sincere our dedication and faith are, without this refinement, we will always limit what God can release.

This takes more than a casual co-operation. It takes guts. We can all grow when we are experiencing wonderful new gifting or witnessing the manifest miracles of God. But the deeper spiritual growth comes when we actively also pursue it, regardless of how painful it can be – the times when we have to push ourselves towards something that hurts. When we are in the gym working new muscles, it can be uncomfortable. If pushed to the limit, it can burn. Yet we know the regime is good for us in the long run. After the work out, we may even revel in the pain we feel, as we know it must have made an impact. And in the next gym battle, the muscle is always stronger, the pain is less. In the same way, deep spiritual growth can be painful. It can be hard work. It can mean sacrifice. It takes honest self-awareness, means diligent self-discipline and often means uncomfortable change. Our compensation (if we need one), is that in His love, God pours yet more of himself into us. We can persevere because this makes it worth it all.

'I am the true Vine, and My Father is the vinedresser. Every branch in Me that does not bear fruit, He takes away; and every branch that continues to bear fruit, He [repeatedly] prunes, so that it will bear more fruit [even richer and finer fruit]'.
John 15:1-2 AMP

This is where God intentionally stretches, draws us up higher and sometimes gives us 'tough love' to mould us to maturity. It's the kind of love that can sometimes seem to hurt - but is truly for our own good. Every experience, problem and challenge we encounter is specifically timed. It all has a divine purpose, so we can be – and achieve all God has destined for us. Whatever the stretch, we need to trust that we will need this growth for the blessings He has in store. When things are hard, this could intentionally be God's agenda!

In His mercy, God brings us chance after chance. He will use every circumstance He can to get our attention onto what He wants to show us through them. We either embrace and accelerate into all He has for us, or we live a marginalised, compromised version of the best God has planned. There is simply no get-out card or way of bypassing where we need to spiritually grow. For us to get where God is wanting to take us, we have to be prepared to do the work. This often means facing into things that need to grow or change.

There are two different realities we can live in. The first is a world of permanent ups and downs. This is a world where chains seem impossibly heavy, where restrictions have dominion and where change is imprisoned by an iron grip. In such a world, we are at the mercy of powers and principalities that strangle the liberation and possibility of movement, never mind finding breakthrough or victory. Its hallmarks are the torment of worry, stress, instability and fear. How often do we experience these emotions?

The second reality is a world where anything is possible, where an unlimited source of supreme power can influence any situation. This is a world in which atmosphere's, decisions, and culture are shifted by the highest power that exists – God's sovereign might. In such a world, there is both expectancy and distribution of God's will over any restriction known. This is the domain of the supernatural and its currency is called miracles.

Both realities co-exist, but which reality we see depends on our spiritual stature. We know we do not wage warfare as the world does (2 Corinthians 10:3). Through spiritual growth, God readies us for the type of battle He has in mind. He moves us from spiritual vulnerability to becoming spiritual warriors. This takes us from being a victim of our circumstances, to rewriting them. It takes us from spiritual lameness to taking spiritual ground. It takes us from human limitations, to being infinite powerhouses for the Kingdom.

God has, does and will bring His sovereign might to earth. It's our prayers that ensure it. But the frequency of events beyond limitation known to man, directly relates to our spiritual stature. **Our spiritual stature has nothing to do with how well trained we are, what special gifts we've been given, how well we can communicate or with any other natural abilities**. The newest spirit-filled Christian is as qualified as the oldest prophetic apostle. It directly relates to our spiritual eminence - which of the two worldly realities we most frequently live in. Which world we live in directs our prayers. Our prayers release God's supernatural power, in, through and around us.

The more we spiritually grow, the more we spiritually mature and the more we are therefore equipped to handle the spiritual realm. The more equipped we are to handle the spiritual realm, the more supernatural power we will see. The more supernatural power we see, the more our world is tangibly changed before our very eyes. The more we see, the more we believe. Spiritual growth is the most rapid way to increase our faith in what we expect God to do. **Spiritual growth increases our faith.**

The Oxford dictionary says that faith is complete trust in someone or something. However, there is a huge difference between having faith that God exists and having faith that He will do everything He says. His word – our precious Bible, is given so we can take Him at it.

My Mum is currently planning ahead of time and preparing her will. Like any covenant contract, once this is signed and sealed, it is legally binding. In the crucifixion and resurrection of Jesus, The Word was signed and sealed. Full stop. What He says goes – it is legally binding. So, whatever we bind or loosen in His name, it is done. (Matt 18:18) This leaves us no room for doubt.

As our spiritual growth leads to the exposure of ever greater outpourings from God, our expectations are increased. This is the faith we put our trust in, so that when we pray, we know it has been answered. This, is the outcome that takes us further into the Zoe life.

Faith is our provision

This type of faith is very different from the hopeful faith that one day - if it is His will, He will somehow – in His mercy, answer our desperate prayers. **This is an unrelenting faith. The type of faith that pays no attention to what is being seen, heard or experienced in the natural before us.** This unrelenting faith doesn't waver, even when all before us seems lost. This is a faith that asserts its potency above and not below. (Deut 28:13) A faith that will open or close every door required. (Rev 3:8) A faith that always knows the angel is already on its way. (Dan 10:12-13) A faith that excites us by the prospect of more than we can even dream (Eph 3:20). A faith that tells us NOTHING is too hard for Him (Jer 32:17). A faith that is never affected by the storms of life. (Eph 4:14)A faith that actively expects the Holy, omnipotent fire-power of God to be released. It does not depend on our own self-willed trust in Him. **It depends on the supernatural faith we receive through Jesus within.**

As we mature in this way, we are no longer confined by the limitations of what we see, hear, touch, feel and smell through our natural senses. We no longer dismiss this type of unrelenting expectancy as the fantasy of extremists. We no longer relegate the accountability to the few charismatic so-called anointed ones. We don't even need to psyche ourselves up to build the courage to step out. **Such belief becomes the place that we live from.**

Stop to reflect on your own life for a moment.

- How often do you pray with the total belief that a supernatural act of God will actually take place – in this world, not just at the end of time and not just in the next? How often do you proactively step out and command the release of His supernatural power?

- Conversely, how much time do you spend praying from a place of despair, feeling helpless, uncertain, daunted, or inadequate? How many situations have you walked on by, that with a supernatural act of God, would have changed the outcome - either in your life or the life of another?
- What would your life look like if you could replace all those times of uncertainty with an unrelenting faith that instead brings one hundred percent belief and the answer to prayer along with it?

Spiritual growth is the strand we must deepen to increasingly release this provision.

The missing strands

If we don't access God's power, we don't receive His promises.

This is the fundamental strand that moves us from glory to glory (2 Cor 3:18) as we are refined into readiness to command all of heaven's power here on earth. It brings a certainty like no other.

Let's start by looking at three key reasons why we can't afford for this strand to be missing:

1. Because we have a destiny.

'For we are God's (own) handiwork (his workmanship), recreated in Christ Jesus, (born anew) that we may do those good works which God predestined (planned beforehand) for us (taking paths which He prepared ahead of time), that we should walk in them (living the good life which He prearranged and made ready for us to live.'
Ephesians 2:10 AMP

God never designed us to play small. Since the beginning of time, He has had big plans - for all of us. Beth Moore once said, 'God is busy making you someone no one else has ever been.'

To fulfil the destiny God has planned takes spiritual maturity - in our knowledge, wisdom and character. **We limit our own destiny, if we limit our spiritual maturity.**

Left to our own devices, we will never step even close to that potential. Joyce Meyer explains it so well: 'God gives us a possibility, not a positively'. By this she means, that it's possible to fulfil our destiny, but not a certainty that we will see it happen. God will bring everything He needs to enable it, but we have to play our part too. God has put everything in us already, but we have to engage in the process necessary to turn it from an aspiration to a reality. To use us and trust us with His Holy fire, God has to develop us.

'But now, O LORD, You are our Father, We are the clay, and You our potter; And all of us are the work of Your hand.'
Isaiah 64:8 NKJV

As we are moulded by the potter's hands, we become more and more mature in our walk. As this happens, God will allow more and more situations to be used to shape, refine and develop our spiritual muscle. But He will never allow us to face things before we are ready. So, take heart, even if in the circumstance you feel overwhelmed. It wouldn't be happening, if God thought you didn't have the spiritual horsepower to move through it with Him. (1 Peter 1:5) He never gives us more heat than we can cope with and He holds us the entire time. If we allow Him to, God will keep on turning us, moulding us and developing us, until He starts to see Jesus within us. (Mal 3:3) With our intentional engagement, He can complete the work that our salvation once began. (Phil 1:6) This is our journey to holiness.

'But whenever someone turns to the Lord, the veil is taken away. For the Lord is the Spirit, and wherever the Spirit of the Lord is, there is

freedom. So all of us who have had that veil removed can see and reflect the glory of the Lord. And the Lord – who is the Spirit – makes us more and more like Him as we are changed into His glorious image'.

2 Corinthians 3:16-18 NLT

A few years back I had a vision - as clear as the things surrounding me in my office now. In it, I was sat under a tent, cosy and secure. The canvas represented the close proximity of God's protection and love. In it, I felt totally safe. Suddenly the canvas started to be pulled upwards away from me. As it was stretched, I noticed I didn't like the feeling, because the blanket of God's protection seemed to be getting further and further away. The canvas was being stretched so high, the top of the tent started to look out of reach. Then I noticed that I was being stretched too. Like a scene from Alice in Wonderland, I was getting bigger and bigger, until my head once again sat snugly underneath the roof of the canvas above me. An interpretation instantly came. In every circumstance, God is growing us. Sometimes He has to stretch the boundaries of our comfort zone, so that we will have the room to grow into what He has made us. If at times He feels further away, we are to trust it's because He is making way for this. God is constantly calling us higher and we are to proactively pursue this. As we do, we rise and start to stand taller in our true identity. When this happens, we take on new strength, courage, stature and ability. With that comes heightened credibility, influence and position. We are to notice these changes, recognise our growth and step into the fullness of what God will then do through us.

T.D Jakes once said: *'God has invested entirely too much in you for you to be comfortable in anything less than you were created for.'* To aid our spiritual growth, **God will often not reveal or bring into being what we are praying for, until we have grown into the stretch in faith this requires**. Think about it. I am never going to get Jacob a bigger bike if he has not shown me he can properly handle the smaller one he already has. When there are no answers, no signs, no support and no human indications of a way forward, we must trust God is using it to take us to a point of growing our faith into being able to handle what He will then provide. It will far outweigh what we could ever hope for.

Rembrandt once said, *'A picture is finished when it expresses the artist's intention'*. The Holy Spirit knows what that picture is. He knows exactly what we are destined for. He knows where He needs to get us from and to. This destiny is different for all of us. Some will be called as foot soldiers to faithfully release His supernatural power. Others will be called as warriors who run towards spiritual warfare, embracing the conflict. Wherever we lay on that spectrum, we are all called to fight – in one-way shape or form. Sent as lambs amongst wolves, we must be prepared- prepared to be as wise as serpents and innocent as doves. (Matt 10:16) To be equipped, we have to be undergirded by the knowledge, wisdom and character needed to handle it. When we partner with Him, The Holy Spirit gradually moves us through a process from blissful ignorance, naivety or denial, to awareness, conviction and change.

2.Because we are instructed to grow.

*'And be **continually renewed** in the spirit of your mind [having a fresh, untarnished mental and spiritual attitude]'.And put on the new self [the regenerated and renewed nature], created in God's image, [godlike] in the righteousness and holiness of the truth [living in a way that expresses to God your gratitude for your salvation].'*
Ephesians 4:23-24 AMP

God has already given us gifts. At conversion we were changed, but we are instructed to go on to mature into the image of Christ. Attending church once a week, doing 'good deeds' and praying sincerely every evening are great things to do. However, on their own, they will not radically challenge us to grow in the way we are intended to. We are actually instructed to reach the full measure of Christ! (Eph 4:13)

With the Holy Spirit's help, we can pursue this. We know God uses imperfect people - we only have to look at the disciples to see how true that is. We don't have to be perfect before we can get our sleeves rolled up. However, without our determination to 'grow up' and into all God has for us, we will forever remain spiritual infants. (Heb 5:14)

At conversion, this 'new self' is placed in us. (2 Cor 5:17) But it takes self-awareness and a decision to find it. Our 'old self' default thoughts, the feelings they create and the actions they result in will not always align automatically. It's why we need to be continually renewed. This takes time, awareness and process.

Kenneth E. Hagin explains it like this: 'The spirit of man is the part of man that is born again. It is the part of man that receives eternal life, which is the nature and life of God. It is the spirit of man that becomes a new creature in Christ Jesus. The soul is not the innermost being at all. It is not the soul that is born again. The saving of the soul is a process. How you can be led by the Spirit of God. Kenneth E Hagin. Published by faith library publications. 1978'

'Test and evaluate yourselves to see whether you are in the faith and living your lives as [committed] believers. Examine yourselves [not me]! Or do you not recognize this about yourselves [by an ongoing experience] that Jesus Christ is in you—unless indeed you fail the test and are rejected as counterfeit?'
2 Corinthians 13:5 AMP

But sometimes, it can be difficult for us to humanly see the deepest things within ourselves. Many of our thought patterns, character traits and resulting behaviour will stem back to deeply embedded circumstances that may relate to how we were raised, how we learned to adapt to this world, or may be part of our in-built DNA. Take heart:

'The word of God is alive and active, sharper than any double-edged sword. It cuts all the way through, to where soul and spirit meet, to

where joints and marrow come together. It judges the desires and thoughts of the heart'

Hebrews 4:12 GNB

The amplified bible adds that it 'exposes, sifts and analyses the deepest part of our nature'. With the Holy Spirit as our guide, we will come to an accurate level of awareness. We will then know what we need God's help to develop within us.

It's incredible how, over time, even without our conscious cooperation, the Holy Spirit matures us. Often, we don't realise how much has shifted, until we stop and really take stock. However, such growth is only accelerated when we consciously choose to engage with it. In addition to our character, this includes our growth in spiritual gifts such as healing and prophecy. Unless we pursue and start to step out, our spiritual status will always be limited.

You might not think you have the capability or strength to grow as you need to, but as you show God your faith, He will show you His faith in you. If you do what you can do, God will do the rest. But it must start with action and as you take this, God will guide you and never take his eyes off you. (Psalm 32:8) At times, you may wonder if it's all worth it, for it will take discipline, focus and effort. But God reassures us that if we faithfully follow His instructions, we will be rewarded. (Gal 6:9) With your commitment and God's support, you will get there.

3. Because we are God's chosen vessels.

'Behold, I am coming like a thief. Blessed is he who stays awake and who keeps his clothes [that is, stays spiritually ready for the Lord's return], so that he will not be naked—spiritually unprepared—and men will not see his shame.'

Revelation 16:15 AMP

The truth is that One day, Jesus will return and life as we now know it will end. In the parable Jesus told about the ten virgins, (Matt 25:1-4), He was effectively saying be ready for my return. Many go part of the way towards this, but we are to steward the responsibility, ensuring our lamps are full of oil (a symbol of the Holy Spirit). The growth we experience with the Holy Spirit is preparing us for the holiness our eternal life requires. But over and above ourselves, we also have a world around us to ready. This is our great commission. (Matt 28:19-20) On His return, Jesus will give to each of us according to what we have done. (Rev 22:12-13)

Knowing we are sorted with God, does not mean our purpose on this earth is complete. As discussed in the fourth strand, our purpose is about why we are here. We are here to be Jesus, so we can make disciples. This comes first through our prayers and then through what we do.

God has given us all the resources we need, both in our human gifts and in the supernatural power He is able to release through us. (Joel 2:28) Whenever we pray we have the power to call heaven down (Matt 18;18), but for it to happen, we so need to pray. Spiritual gifts are given for the benefit of others. (1 Cor 12:7) They are a fundamental part of our toolkit to help evangelize the world (Luke 24:48-49), Acts 4:29-31, 1 Cor 12:24-25) (For more information on such gifts see Rom 12, 1 Cor: 12, and Eph:4) But we do need to be prepared to use them.

If we don't steward what is available, we limit what God could otherwise be doing. The parable of the talents (Matt 25:14-30) tells us, this is His expectation. So, we serve, we partner with His Spirit and we call down His supernatural fire to earth.

Just pause for a moment.

- How frequently do you stop to reflect on your spiritual growth?

- How often do you consciously take stock of the thoughts, feelings or actions that cause you to falter? How often do you consciously engage to stretch your spiritual comfort zone? (This is not in relation to what you are doing – it's about how you are developing in the spirit.)
- What supernatural gifts have you sought, embraced and utilised? Do you know what supernatural power God can release through you to change situations?

As you reflect, spend some time praying about what you discover. Allow this to organically merge into a conversation with your Father. Allow time for silence and consciously allow the Holy Spirit to flow. Is there anything else He says?

The pattern

In each chapter, we will explore the pattern that helps develop, strengthen and embed each strand. **The pattern in the strand of spiritual growth is to increase our inner sense of unrelenting faith.** This is how promise 6: His sovereignty - our supernatural might is increasingly released and activated.

How to develop the 6th strand of spiritual growth

'(For my determined purpose is) that I may know Him (that I may progressively become more deeply and intimately acquainted with Him, preceding and recognising and understanding the wonders of His person more strongly and more clearly), and that I may in that same way come to know the power outflowing from His resurrection (which it exerts over believers, and that I may so share His sufferings as to be continually transformed (in spirit into His likeness even) to His death, (in hope) that if possible I may attain to the (spiritual and

moral) resurrection (that lifts me) out from among the dead (even while in the body).

Philippians 3:10-12 AMPC

This pattern has been broken down into the following three key loops:

1st loop: Seek spiritual nourishment

In this, you need to proactively make time to pray, seek, study, savour and saturate your life with the things that will help you to grow. Just as a sapling requires fertile soil, plenty of water and the radiance of sunshine, you need to dig deep into the things that cultivate your spiritual development. When you partner with the Holy Spirit on this, one-by-one, He will lead you to both situations that require it and the insight to understand it.

'Let the [spoken] word of Christ have its home within you [dwelling in your heart and mind—permeating every aspect of your being] as you teach [spiritual things] and admonish and train one another with all wisdom, singing psalms and hymns and spiritual songs with thankfulness in your hearts to God.'

Colossians 3:16 AMP

2nd loop: Personally review

This is about learning to consciously review your maturity in light of God's word and instructions. As you become more spiritually aware, the Holy Spirit will start to convict you about things you need to address, along with supernatural gifts you can receive and develop. The key is to adopt a mind-set that accepts this responsibility. Where are you in alignment? Where are you not? What needs to change? What needs to start? What needs to stop? This is about pro-actively examining yourself honestly, without expecting yourself to be perfect. We are all a work in progress.

'Search me, O God, and know my heart; test my thoughts. Point out anything you find in me that makes you sad, and lead me along the path of everlasting life.'

Psalm 139:23-24 TLB

3rd loop: Act upon it

Make a decision to act upon what you find and then engage with the Holy Spirit to help you do it. To actually move forward, it may be that you need to forgive something, repent about something, embrace something, eliminate something, believe for something, change something, start something, stop something or continue doing something. Take accountability for the fact that you need to own this. Then you need to actually do it. Keep pressing into God for His 'more', through prayer and practise with the spiritual gifts He gives. Seek them, request opportunities to use them and step out of your comfort zone to apply them.

'Whoever says he lives in Christ [that is, whoever says he has accepted Him as God and Saviour] ought [as a moral obligation] to walk and conduct himself just as He walked and conducted Himself.'

I John 2:6 NIV

Practical suggestions

As you engage with the Holy Spirit to weave these three loops into your life, your perspective and expectation of what God is capable of exponentially increases. In juxtaposition, there's also an irony that you will find the scale of His might ever more incomprehensible. Witnessing what God is capable of leaves you even more astonished at what He is capable of! I describe this as a feeling of 'reverential authority'. It's a sense of 'Oh my goodness. My Father is here. What IS He going to do?!'

To develop this strand, in the table below are examples of suggestions you could practically work with. This can help you increasingly release the power of God's supremacy, so you can take dominion in the world. These could become useful tools. No doubt you will have other ideas of your own that you can add over time.

Loops	Practical suggestions

1.
Seek spiritual nourishment
	• The number 1 will always be to spend time with God, reading the word, praying and worshipping. There is simply no shortcut to this.
	  - Regardless of how well you think you know God's word and voice, still spend time searching for new depths. It's a life-long process of discovery we will never get to the end of.
	  - Ask the Holy Spirit to breathe new depth, understanding and conviction into you.
	  - Invite His guidance about what you should focus on, what activities you should do and what resources you should dig into deeper.
	  - Ask God to enable new gifts of the Spirit within you.
	
	• Consider and take part in activities that will help you grow.
	  - Try to include a combination of things you do alone and with others. Things like prayer groups, fellowship meetings, fasting, service, giving in some way, spending time with people who are more spiritually advanced, getting close to a ministry you don't know much about.
	  - Ask the Holy Spirit to illuminate new spiritual depth as you do these things.

	▪ Seek out trusted resources that will help you grow, again combining individual and shared experiences. - Things like bible study, Christian books, sermons, films with Christian messages embedded, Christian radio, or (with caution) Christian TV. - Reflect on key principles and messages. Savour, dwell on, pray about and talk about what's being revealed with the Holy Spirit. - Consider everything through the reflective lens of what it means to how you live your life.
2. Review	▪ Keep a learning journal - Put 4 columns on a page. Write the following words, one statement in each of the columns: 1. What God's word says; 2. What I need to do or change (this will either be to start, stop, do more of, or do less of something); 3. Practical things I can actually do; 4. How well am I doing? - As you learn more about God's word, stop, reflect and answer questions 1-3 above. - Intermittently go back and review your progress addressing question 4. - Thank God for the specific changes He is making in you. ▪ Give space for the Holy Spirit to bring conviction into your heart. - Listen to the cues that indicate something you are thinking, feeling or doing needs addressing. This can be anything from a niggle or a bout of conscience, through to clear instructions to stop or start doing

	something. Take every thought captive (2 Cor 10:5) - If you find yourself facing the same thing over and over, God is trying to teach you something/get you to grow beyond something. Ask the Holy Spirit to show you what that something is. Instead of complaining or praying about the problem, ask the Holy Spirit to reveal and help you overcome the root cause. - Also pay attention to the whispers of encouragement that tell you where you are gifted and developing well. - Explicitly consider the gifts of the Spirit and the ones you feel led to pursue. - Keep a record of what it is, the date and repeat the learning journal process above. • Invite accountability. - Consider who your trusted Christian friends may be and invite 1 or 2 to help you develop. - Share your tendencies and the areas God is working on with you. Explain your plans and invite their suggestions. - Agree what you are going to do and then get them to provide ongoing feedback, encouragement, challenge and discipling. - Ask them to help hold you accountable to this progress. - Agree that you will go to them if you are struggling, need help to press reset, or need feedback from them.
3. Get going!	• Act upon what is revealed

- When God reveals an area of growth, it will always mean at least one of the following is needed:
  - ➢ Repentance for something you have been doing (either purposefully or inadvertently) that goes against His word or will.
  - ➢ Forgiveness of someone (which may include forgiving yourself).
  - ➢ A choice to change (this may be to stop, start, do more of, or do less of something).
  - ➢ A desire for more (supernatural gifts such as healing, prophecy, words of knowledge)
- Ask the Holy Spirit to help you action what is required.
- Ask the Holy Spirit to exchange your limited old way with whatever fruit of the spirit will enable you most. (Gal 5:22-23)
- If these steps are difficult to take in some way, consider who you can ask to support you and invite accountability as above.

- Prepare
  - Any growth and change starts with prayer. Pray for God to support, strengthen, encourage and guide you.
  - If the area of growth is an ongoing area of change, it may help to create a plan that's S.M.A.R.T:
    - ➢ **Specific**: what are you committing to address and tangibly going to do.
    - ➢ **Measurable**: what will success mean and feel like? How will you know you are making progress or have achieved this?

	<ul><li>➤ **Achievable**: are the specific steps in your plan achievable? Is there any additional support you require from other sources?</li><li>➤ **Relevant:** sense check that this plan will take you towards the direction you want to head in.</li><li>➤ **Timely**: What will you do by when? What timescales are involved?</li></ul>- Review the plan:<ul><li>➤ In light of your past/your track record to date/your experiences so far, what is the wisest course of action?</li><li>➤ In light of your current situation, what is the wisest course of action?</li><li>➤ In light of what you believe your future may hold, what is the wisest course of action?</li></ul> ▪ Step out. - As with all things, this starts with prayer. Ask God for divine appointments and opportunities. - Humble yourself and get your face on the floor, to call upon God for His more. Press in, fast, cry out and pursue. Refuse to budge until like Jacob, His blessings arrive. (Gen 32:26) - Ask God to give and anoint the spiritual gifts you need. (1 Cor 14) Earnestly make it your quest. (1 Cor 14:1) - Pro-actively pray on spiritual armour (Eph 6:10-18) and ask for ongoing protection – for you, your family and all around. - Pray for the peace, authority, perspective, motivation, confidence and supernatural faith of Jesus as you increasingly step out.

	- One of the best ways to spiritually grow is to intentionally stretch your comfort zone. See a need and meet it. You can do this by getting involved in things not yet encountered. - Purposefully get practising. Step out in faith and believe for the spiritual gifts you will need as you do. - Speak to others who are spiritually advanced in a gift, to gain insight, mentoring and encouragement. Or become a mentor yourself. The best way we ever learn is to help others learn! - If you start to feel burdened, weak, a sense of failure, disillusionment or like giving up, you may need to return to the loops of the earlier strands we've covered. - Expect the unexpected. We can't manipulate God's power. He's running the show. Bow to this.

The mirror

As the power of God increasingly touches what we apply ourselves to, we increasingly bow to who He is. From this place of reverence, the passion in our hearts grows – we hunger for more. This pursuit accelerates our spiritual growth, which equips us with the knowledge, wisdom and character needed for His supernatural power to increasingly be released. This leaves us rock solid and takes us to a courage where we will literally stake our very lives on. This is when we experience His miracles invading our world.

'For dominion belongs to the Lord and he rules over the nations'.
Psalm 22:28 NIV

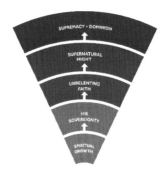

This is the Zoe wheel of life. The power of Christ in us. As we develop the strand of spiritual growth, it enables us to live in His sovereignty, releasing an inner provision of unrelenting faith, so we activate the promise of our supernatural might. This makes a difference to our lives through the supremacy of God taking dominion over the world around us.

Reflections

Before we move on, my encouragement is to take some time to review the tapestry of your life in this strand. Pray with and consciously invite the Holy Spirit to bring His insight into your awareness.

Consider the current pattern

- How frequently do you intentionally invest in developing your spiritual growth? What spiritual growth do you recognise in yourself?
- How much of God's sovereign power are you seeing released through your prayers and in life? Is this increasing?

- How unrelenting is the level of the supernatural faith you apply to life's situations today? Consider different examples.
- What manifestation of God's supernatural might have you personally released? (for example: words of knowledge or prophecy)
- How has God's supreme power enabled you to take dominion, through miracles and His sovereign hand at work in the world?
- What detracts your pursuit of such things?
- What encourages them?
- What are the largest canyons where such things are missing?
- Do you ever feel any of the following: limited, spiritual blockages, oppression or intimidation, powerless, spiritually out of depth/impotent/frightened, or at the mercy of the world?
- Conversely, do you ever feel equipped, enlarged, spiritually courageous, powerful, confident to navigate the spiritual realm?

Consider what you need to grow

- Reflect on promise 6 from part 1. Of the examples showing what His sovereignty brings, what else do you need to develop?
- How would this help your life, others or the world?

Consider how to develop further

- Above and beyond routine, how much have you proactively invested in the time, activities and resources that will help you spiritually grow?
- How frequently do you intentionally consider the specifics about what you need to address and develop to accelerate your spiritual growth?

> - How many times do you follow through with decisions and specific actions to address these areas? How much have you stretched your spiritual comfort zone?

As you reflect, spend some time praying about what you discover. Allow this to organically merge into a conversation with your Father. Allow time for silence and consciously allow the Holy Spirit to flow. Is there anything else He says?

Stay connected, then review the suggested loops of activity you can take to help you grow in this area. Add any other activities that would work for you. Prayerfully consider these and then create a plan.

- What will you do, when and how?

- Visualise the impact

- Now get practising!

Recap

So far, we have practically explored how to live in all of Christ by considering:

- How to release His presence and activate our spiritual intimacy through the first strand of increased connection.
- How to release His significance and activate our renewed identity through the second strand of deepening relationship.
- How to release His perspective and activate our ability to clearly hear God, through the third strand of whole-hearted worship.
- How to release His nature and activate our accelerated ability to change.
- How to release His empowerment and activate our heightened ability.
- How to release His sovereignty and activate our supernatural might.

As we grow spiritually, we are effectively taking any self-imposed brakes off what God wants to release in and through us. There is a direct correlation between the degree of supernatural abundance we experience and our maturity in being able to handle it. The maturing of our character and the development of spiritual gifts creates a channel for God's sovereign will to be released. We are brought to a place of readiness for all He has planned. This enables God to release His sovereign might, so we experience breakthrough, victory and blessing. Witnessing His power, deepens our faith and increases our expectations for more of God. The combination of our character, spiritual gifts and expectation releases yet more of His supernatural might, so we actively command and receive dominion. These miracles change our world in, through and around us.

It's experiencing this supernatural power that causes our ultimate surrender. We are humbled by His might. This is what causes us to fully yield every area of our lives to God. For when we experience the tangible manifestation of His almighty power, our reverence brings us to our knees.

When you are ready, we will consider this next in the 7th strand of obedience.

18

The 7th strand

Surrender
Yielding our whole life.

How to release His strength and activate our victory.

---

*'Walk in obedience to all that the Lord your God has commanded you,
so that you may live and prosper and prolong your days in the land
that you will possess.'*
                    Deuteronomy 5:33 NIV

*'And this is love: that we walk in accordance with His
commandments and are guided continually by His precepts. This is
the commandment, just as you have heard from the beginning, that
you should [always] walk in love.'*
                    2 John 1:6 AMP

When we reflect on the providence of God's hand on our lives, our
faith can't help but increase. The track record of history always
shines His greatness. As our trust in God increases, our self-imposed
grip on life decreases. Ironically, the more we understand how in
control God actually is, the free-er we become. This is what enables
us to increasingly submit all our thoughts, feelings and actions in line
with His will. When we yield, we trust.

Layer by layer, our outer shells are peeled away and we gradually learn to submit everything to His Lordship. When we come to realise how our lives are not our own, we learn to exult Him through lives that are utterly surrendered and reliant on His fathering. This means de-coupling from the independent agenda of what we want, imagine or hope for. In exchange for our own selfish desires, we place all our trust in God's will. The sanctified soul is when our own will is forced into submission to the Spirit. What we are asked to surrender will be different for all of us. The Holy Spirit knows what it will take to set us free. What I find difficult, you may not and vice versa.

We may be able to surrender when it's easy, when we have no choice, when we are brought to the end of ourselves or when we simply dare not obey. This yielding has to be in all things, not just the ones we find easier, or when we feel in the enlightened mood to persevere! The surrender God requires is a willing surrender that comes without regret. A surrender that comes from the state of heart that is simply bowed to His command – without question – without self-pity – without self-attention.

Jesus laid it out for us. He showed us perfect surrender. In sacrifice, He yielded His whole life and instructed us to do the same – our lives are not our own. (1 Cor 6:19) In every way He bent in submission to God's will, even though He did not have to (Matt 26:53). Despite His surrender requiring His life, not once did He doubt who God was. **Our surrender is not dependent on understanding, liking or wanting what God has planned**. It's simply trusting His wisdom.

This surrender comes in a multi layered quilt of depth - from the purpose of our life, right the way through to how we live each and every day. When we yield, we are saying; 'You are my all in all – have my all in all'. In this submission we run towards God's will and the Holy Spirit who enables it.

Yielding in this way does not come from moral obligation. It comes from a sold-out love for the King. A love that so captivates our hearts that all we want to do is honour Him. The love of God compels us. If this means sacrifice, we run towards it. If this means stretch, we embrace it. If this means pain, we endure it. A fully yielded life does not count the cost. All cost is counted as privilege.

'But those who wait on the LORD, Shall renew their strength; They shall mount up with wings like eagles, they shall run and not be weary, they shall walk and not faint.
'Isaiah 40:31 NKJV

In His mercy, it is God who gives us the very strength we need to press in. We need it. To overcome the force of our own soul-ish reactions to life, we need a power far greater than our own good intent. With an incredible irony, the more we sacrifice, the more strength He gives us. The more strength He gives us, the more we can sacrifice. God enables the very surrender He requests.

'For whoever desires to save his life will lose it, but whoever loses his life for My sake and the gospel's will save it. For what will it profit a man if he gains the whole world, and loses his own soul?'
Mark 8:35-36 NKJV

This is what brought the outer strength that enabled Samson to pull down the pillars of the Philistine temple. (Judges 16) This is the inner strength that enabled Daniel to walk into the lion's den. (Daniel 6) Both were prepared to surrender their lives. Samson lost his - Daniel didn't. **Surrender is not just being prepared to do what is required. It is also being prepared to surrender the outcome when we do.** This is only possible when our trust is in the wisdom of God's sovereign bigger plans. Surrender is step one. Fully yielding to whatever then happens is step two. Often, it's not what we expect! Often, we don't even know what our surrender will mean!
Brother Andrew once said: *'That's the excitement in obedience. Finding out later what God has in mind.'*

Our surrender today may not be our lives. It maybe we surrender our hurt. Fully yielding to this means that we can wrap our arms of forgiveness around the cause. And that if the cause only hurts us again, we surrender the hurt once again. It maybe we surrender the much wanted/needed job. Fully yielding means that even if we are facing impending bankruptcy, we can still let it go – even when the tempting offer comes back on the table. It maybe we surrender the long-held ambition we have given our life to. And if that means starting all over again from scratch, we can do that with gladness.

With total surrender, it doesn't matter. This type of surrender is not about us. It's simply about yielding to whatever God asks of us. No questions asked. **We don't surrender in the hope of what we get in exchange. We surrender because our hearts simply what to obey our incredible God.** This obedience is often a magnetic attraction to God's hundred-fold favour. (Gen 26:12)

John 8:36 tells us that who the son sets free is free indeed. Our surrender brings our freedom. This freedom means we no longer hold onto offense, pain, hurt, doubt, fear or anxiety. We become free from the weight, toll and history of our lives. But there is a cost to this freedom. The cost is our will. (Luke 9:23) In exchange for our lives, we gain our lives. (Matt 16:25) All burden is replaced and all striving ceases. (Psalm 46:10) Giving over all our being, we utterly yield to God's surpassing lead.

What is it that enables this exchange? In one word – love.

Whatever we sacrifice, God more than replaces. As we surrender, He lavishes us with the indescribable weight of His glory – he showers us with His love. Nothing can compare to the density of this presence – the majesty of His smile – the warmth of His feathers. Like a cloak of grace - we feel the tangibility of the royal robes He tenderly places across our shoulders. When, at the very edge of ourselves, we bow and honour all He asks, He delights in us. Pouring yet more of Himself into us, the sacred infilling of His very being is beyond compare. In the epicentre of this privileged anointing, our hearts are sealed. In its magnitude and eminence, our wholeness is complete. From this place of fulfilment, to freely surrender, is all we want to do. Surrender is no longer a sacrifice. It becomes a way of being. This is our provision. The provision is wholeness. **Surrender brings wholeness.**

The Oxford dictionary says the definition of wholeness is the state of forming a complete and harmonious whole; unity. The wholeness God brings leaves us in perfect balance: mind, will, emotions and spirit, carrying the power to eliminate any distress, any impact and any emptiness. **Whatever our sacrifice, wrapped in His glory, we gladly give it.** When we obey in this way, our surrender means there is literally nothing that separates us. Such is the sense of completion this brings, the fulfilment replaces any solace or inferior contentment we would other-wise experience.

This is far beyond the inner satisfaction of being content with your lot in life. This is **contented wholeness;** a wholeness that is different from the wholeness we may get from any other connection – no matter how earth-shatteringly blissful it may be. This is because such contended wholeness can only ever come when we are fully joined to our maker. No amount of searching, other-worldly state or mystical enlightenment will ever compare. Remaining in this state does not depend on our own inner zen-like capacities. **It depends on living in the strength of Jesus.** This is what gives us the courage, self-control and ability to surrender.

Stop to reflect on your own life for a moment.

- How often do you live in the strength of Jesus needed to enable a life totally yielded to whatever surrender is needed?
- Conversely how much time do you spend living with restlessness, unfulfillment, searching, spiritual pining or blockage?
- What would your life look like if you could replace all those times of uncertainty with a permanent state of contented wholeness?

Surrender is the strand we must increase to release this provision.

As Kathryn Kuhlman once said: *'God does not ask for golden vessels. He does not ask for silver vessels. God asks for yielded vessels. Those who will submit their will to the will of the Father. And the greatest human attainment in all the world, is for a life to be so surrendered to Him that the name of God Almighty will be glorified through that life.'*

The missing strands

When we limit our 'yes', we limit God's too.

This is the life-changing strand that moves us into the fullness of life that completes us. Yet it can be our last, firmest stronghold. Let's start by looking at three key reasons why we can't afford for this strand to be missing:

1. Because our soul is strong.

'I do not understand what I do. For what I want to do, I do not do, but what I hate I do.'
Romans 7:15 NIV

In this, Paul was saying that even though he knew what was right, at times, the pull of his soul (his mind, will and emotions) just seemed to gate-crash those intentions. As we think about our own lives, the same is often true.

When the obedience of our surrender tugs at what our soul cries (our mind, will and emotions), it can be very hard. The volume of this cry can vary from the smallest desire, right the way through to a raging compulsion. It can relate to any manner of motives - fear, uncertainty, self-preservation, ego, pride, insecurity and doubt, to name just a few. Unless, that is, we access the power of the Holy Spirit within us, to bring the strength that's needed. If we allow Him to, the Holy Spirit will always provide the power we need to overcome these default settings.

Watchman Nee became a Christian in Mainland China in 1920. In 1952 he was imprisoned for his faith and remained so until his death in 1972. His was a surrendered life. He once wrote: 'Holy Spirit has one goal in all His disciplining work: to break and dismantle the outer man, so the inner man can break forth'. Once the outer man is broken, the inner man is released and the Spirit is able to function'. The breaking of the outer man and the release of the Spirit. Published by Living stream ministry 1997.

This is our key to surrender. To surrender means we need to obey – in everything. But often our reaction to circumstances drowns out what the spirit needs to follow. It is the limitations of our outer man - our soul (mind, will and emotions), that prevent the surrender we intend.

Often, we don't consciously set out to disobey God. Our response initially may be to deny the lead we sense. We may try and ignore it. Or we may procrastinate. However, delayed surrender is really disobedience. We may just become distracted from doing it, but how many times do we make a deal about when we will do something, only to find that with the passing of time, it somehow never seems to happen?

Alternatively, deception may creep in. This could be through doubting whether or not we have heard right; whether or not it really matters; whether or not God's really going to come through or whether or not we are up to the task. These are thoughts of fear. They never come from God. The trouble is that the more we pass over honouring even the little things, the more our spiritual senses can be blocked. Before we know it, our perspective can shift beyond all recognition of the lead we have received. Alternatively, our motive inaccurately filters what we think God's will may be. The pull of our soul can be so very, very strong.

The other way our soul can really hurt us is when we become impatient. In the past, I have lost count of the times I have prayed 'When God when?' Joyce Meyer once said *'Patience is not the ability to wait. It's how we behave when we are waiting'!*

Impatience is dangerous. It's when we are most likely to step out in our own might. When we do, we step out from under the Holy Spirit's governance. This form of disobedience isn't about not doing what we have been led to. It's doing what we haven't been led to.

When we can't make sense of what is going on, we don't need to try. Instead of striving to figure things out, when we go to the God who already has, everything falls into place. This means trusting that when we don't have all the answers, when we haven't yet sensed God's lead and when things are seemingly at odds, He is still in control. Instead, how do our own anxieties, problem solving and impetuous actions try and take over? **Ultimately our obedience is often not a problem when His will is explicitly clear – the challenge is when it is not.**

As soon as we take over, we've become disconnected and this is when we are in the greatest danger of missing it. Not by overt wilful defiance, but through the inner wrestle of our souls taking over the show. When our souls are back in charge, so is the worry, the burden and the stress of life.

2. Because it costs us.

'And being in agony [deeply distressed and anguished; almost to the point of death], He prayed more intently; and His sweat became like drops of blood, falling down on the ground.'
Luke 22:44 AMP

Jesus showed us how surrender costs. He paid with His own life. He knew what he was about to suffer and the night before his crucifixion, he was on his knees in agony at the thought of what lay ahead. Yet despite this, we know he obeyed.

'And He withdrew from them about a stone's throw, and knelt down and prayed, saying: 'Father, if You are willing, remove this cup [of divine wrath] from Me; yet not My will, but [always] Yours be done.'
Luke 22:41-42 AMP

Sometimes our surrender will cost us. As the Holy Spirit leads us on, we leave more and more of our old lives behind to follow Him. This can mean sacrifice, inconvenience, isolation, discomfort and sometimes pain. This is when we can really feel set apart. But God is so gracious and kind to us. Because there is a cost, Holy Spirit always prompts this awareness beforehand. He doesn't want to hoodwink us into obedience. God wants us to say yes, knowing the cost. With every big thing I have ever surrendered, the Holy Spirit has always shown me the implications beforehand. It's as if God really wants to make sure we know what we are agreeing to. Obedience is only obedience when it comes from a fully yielded heart. God will never trick us or trap us into action. Those are the tactics of the enemy.

'Enter by the narrow gate; for wide is the gate and broad is the way that leads to destruction, and there are many who go in by it. Because[j] narrow is the gate and difficult is the way which leads to life, and there are few who find it'.
Matthew 7:13-14 NKJV

As Jesus grips our heart, we reach a point where the only thing that matters is what He says. The burden, depression, grief, unfulfillment and loss we experience when we don't do as we are led is far greater than anything we set aside to follow. We may not experience it at first, but with the passing of time we will. When we don't surrender, we will come to see the consequence of our actions unfold. These may be in lost opportunities to bring God's Kingdom to earth, disconnection in the unity and closeness with Him, or the jeopardy of what it means to our long-term state of mind. It's never worth what we compromise.

'What then shall we say to all these things? If God is for us, who can be [successful] against us? He who did not spare [even] His own Son, but gave Him up for us all, how will He not also, along with Him, graciously give us all things?'
Romans 8:31-32 AMP

Surrender doesn't mean plain sailing. In fact, it can actually mean many hurdles. These obstacles will test whether we have the tenacity and faith to keep going regardless. These obstacles often cost us – through opposition. If we are waylaid by this opposition, we take our focus off what we are actually meant to be doing. Opposition can come in different forms. It may be opposition from our own souls as just discussed, but it can also be opposition from the people we have around us. People who don't understand, support or get what the Holy Spirit is saying. Even well-meaning friends can have this effect.

I remember when Jacob had just been born. Despite the circumstances, the Holy Spirit was elevating me to a place of strength. His instructions were simple. I should keep my eyes entirely on God and not even glance in any other direction. Some lovely friends were leaving me empathetic messages which I just couldn't afford to listen to, for their well-intended sympathy momentarily caused me to indulge my human emotions of fear. My instructions were clear: 'Don't listen to anything that speaks to your soul. Listen only to what fuels your spirit.'

The other form of opposition we know we can expect is from the devil. By following the Holy Spirit, you are directly bringing God's plan into being. That is the biggest possible threat to the enemy. He will use any tactic possible to prevent the Kingdom from growing. It is not personal; his aim is to prevent any part of God's Kingdom from reclaiming territory in this world. So, if you are being obedient, know that anything and everything will be thrown to try and create obstacles to your progress. These can be spiritual or very practical. But we have good news:

'Then Jesus came to them and said, "All authority in heaven and on earth has been given to me.'
Matthew 28:18 NIV

Jesus has ALL authority. The enemy doesn't have control. It's our reaction to him that does. We don't need to run scared, but we do need to run strong. It's the Holy Spirit that gives us that strength. Our strength is the strength of Jesus. Surrender is our warfare strategy.

3. Because we will never know lasting contentment without it.

The deep, contented wholeness surrender brings is matchless. In its void, we spend our lives searching, filling and removing things from our life, in an attempt to find the illusive contentment it provides. In comparison to the real thing, any temporary satisfaction we ever gain is only ever an illusion.

- We search for purpose – but even our chosen career, the long-awaited qualification, our dedicated service or even our life's calling does not complete our meaning.
- We fill our lives with things – children, material assets, hobbies, holidays, events – but even what's most sacred eventually loses its once-magnetic pull.
- We remove the things that seem to detract from our inner wholeness – the wrong friends, unhealthy food or drink, the burn-out schedule – but their withdrawal is eventually only replaced with something else to fill the void they leave.
- We yearn for answers or ways to be mindfully content – but the good practices or initial enlightenment is short lived as soon as the next tornado hits.

- Even when we do feel nothing is missing in life, there is always something that eventually brings us the discomfort, pain, restlessness or dissatisfaction that prevents such a deep inner sense of completion.

All avenues to wholeness will eventually leave us wanting more – so we search more, do more, buy more, become more, fill more. That is, until we experience the utopian wholeness that can only ever come from our majestic Lord Almighty. Even this is only ever maintained when we give everything away to live in it. Our surrender becomes our reward.

Once the contented wholeness of a life fully yielded is embraced, we eventually get to the point where we can't exist without it.

Just pause for a moment.

- How difficult do you find it to let go of things (unhelpful thoughts, negative feelings, your own wants and desires, how you think it should be?) How often have you gladly surrendered something that would once have been difficult to let go of?
- What level of sacrifice have you bowed to, even knowing the cost? What opposition have you experienced?
- What 'things' have you gained momentary wholeness from, that have ebbed away over time?

As you reflect, spend some time praying about what you discover. Allow this to organically merge into a conversation with your Father. Allow time for silence and consciously allow the Holy Spirit to flow. Is there anything else He says?

The pattern

In each chapter, we will explore the pattern that helps develop, strengthen and embed each strand. **The pattern in the strand of**

surrender is to increase our inner strength. This is what gives us the courage, self-control and ability to surrender and is how promise 7: His strength - our victory, is increasingly released and activated.

How to develop this 7th strand of surrender

'Therefore do not cast away your confidence, which has great reward. For you have need of endurance, so that after you have done the will of God, you may receive the promise.'
Hebrews 10:36-37 NKJV

This pattern has been broken down into the following three key loops:

1st loop: Prepare

This is about getting the right mind-set, protection and support in place. It's this preparation that enables us to surrender any situation, full of the Holy Spirit's enabling strength. It's like anything: if we prepare well, we will do well. All too often, we blindly walk from one situation to another, easily becoming disheartened if things don't go as planned. Remember that surrender is warfare. The enemy will try any tactic to prevent it. So, like any battle, our spiritual muscle needs to be ready for the fight.

'Be prepared. You're up against far more than you can handle on your own. Take all the help you can get. Every weapon God has issued'.
Ephesians 6: 13 MSG

2nd loop: Practice

Nothing is forced upon us. The choice to surrender is left with us. Some things can really seem to count whilst on the surface, others may seem to be less important. Yet how often do we sing that Jesus is Lord? Is He? Is He really? In everything? This is about using as many of life's opportunities as possible to turn obedience into a natural everyday way of responding. I have sometimes found myself pressing into God for the big, life-changing decisions, whilst the day to day things can slip due to busyness, familiarity and the often-automatic nature of living. However, if we start by yielding to the easier things first, the bigger things will eventually not seem as difficult to surrender. If we stop to notice the impact of our obedience and become more conscious of God's power, it will encourage us.

To develop in this, we need to invite the Holy Spirit to help us review, address and change the things that hold us back from letting go. We need to make it an active, conscious, continual process. Don't just wait for the big booming voice from heaven telling you to put your last month's bonus into the offering. Seek out the ongoing daily ways you need to surrender. There are so many layers to this and with each one, your soul is gradually aligned to your spirit.

'The things which you have learned and received and heard and seen in me, practice these things [in daily life], and the God [who is the source] of peace and well-being will be with you.'
Philippians 4:9 AMP

3rd loop: Praise

When we praise God for all He is doing, we are celebrating and elevating His glory. This can become the very strength in our veins. We can praise Him with our thanks, with testimony and with a fully yielded life. When we turn our surrender into praise, it keeps our eyes off ourselves and focusses them on God. It keeps our surrender from being about what we are giving up, to who we give it up for. When we truly understand that God has given us everything we have, we avoid becoming prideful about it. There's no doubt about it: God is a good, good father, who brings us favour right from the beginning. But the more our deeds bow under His Lordship, the more favour we experience. It is the most humbling thing and many times we cry how we are not worthy. Let's never take anything He does for granted.

'Blessed and worthy of praise be the God and Father of our Lord Jesus Christ, who has blessed us with every spiritual blessing in the heavenly realms in Christ.'
Ephesians 1:3 AMP

Practical suggestions

As you engage with the Holy Spirit to weave these three loops into your life, the more you will hold everything in this natural world lightly. That even includes your purpose. Mortal life takes on the perspective of a fractional part of an eternal existence. The best way I can describe this is to say 'I bow. I surrender. I bow'.

To develop this strand, in the table below are examples of suggestions you could practically work with. This will help you develop ultimate fulfilment and can't help but attract God's favour. These could become useful tools. No doubt you will have other ideas of your own that you can add over time.

Loop	Practical suggestions
1. Prepare	▪ Prepare your mind-set. - Ask God to father you through this. - Think about why it is worth surrendering to God. Consider the cost if you don't, the impact if you do. - Go back to your responses to loop 2 of strand 2 - Relationship, to reflect on your understanding of who God is. What does His character mean to you?

- Go back to loop 1 of strand 3 – worship, to remind yourself of why you want to follow Him.
- Go back to loops 1-3 of strand 4 – purposeful service, if you find there are things holding you back.
- If you still struggle to surrender something, ask the Holy Spirit to reveal the reason it's hard. Ask His help to remove those barriers. Don't give up. Some things take time and process.

- Prepare your protection.
  - Re-read Ephesians 6: 10-18 and pray for this armour to be effective. Visualise yourself stood before Jesus wearing it. Ask Jesus to anoint your protection.
  - Determine not to become disheartened ahead of time. Challenge and opposition will come, so decide the faith that will fill you before it happens.
  - Re-read key promises and verses God has given you. Re-read biblical stories that have a similarity to your situation.
  - Write up/learn/pin up faith building verses, so you will be prominently reminded of them.
  - Pray with God before, during and after all activity, claiming the same protection and power.

- Prepare your support.
  - Think about who you could ask to pray for you.
  - Consider any other practical support that would help you and make arrangements for this.
  - Before you do anything go back to loops 1-3 of strand 1 - connection. Invite a refilling, decide upon and be specific about the support you need from the Holy Spirit. Tell Him where you feel

	weak, unsure or unable and ask Him to replace those insecurities with His empowerment. - If you still feel uncertain go back to the steps in strand 5 - partnership.
2. Practice.	▪ Just get started! - Follow the small nudges you get. (for example: pick up the item of clothing that fell off its hanger in the store as someone accidentally brushed it off, ask that person who you find a bit annoying round for coffee, honour the speed limit when driving). Then move into more challenging things. - Ask God to pour more of Himself into you as you let go. - Savour how it feels and bask in the freedom and beauty of what God pours into you as you surrender. - Reflect on the impact to you and others. What then happens that could never happen without this surrender - what does it enable? - Thank God for the privilege of His power enabling it within you. - Ask the Holy Spirit to reveal more opportunities for you to surrender. The more you do, the less scary the prospect is. The more you will naturally recognise what you need to hand over to His Lordship. - If you are struggling with this whole notion of surrender, start with something small. Think of something that matters to you that you will commit to giving up. Even if it is initially only for a set period of time. Fasting in some way can be a good starter. - Ask the Holy Spirit to take away any bond this thing has on you and for strength to release it to God.

- Ask the Holy Spirit to exchange what you are surrendering for more of God in its place.

- Make surrender a conscious practice
  - Whenever something feels inappropriately negative in any way (with toxic emotions being the indicator), ask the Holy Spirit to reveal what He is trying to show you need to let go of. He will gently and compassionately reveal the areas where you need to surrender your thoughts, emotions and actions to His lead.
  - If there is something specific you are struggling to let go of (often deep desires or painful emotions can be the hardest), return to the 2nd loop of strand 4 – purposeful service. Apply the same suggestions to the specific stronghold.

- Review how you are doing
  - Ask the Holy Spirit to show you where you did and didn't follow His lead.
  - Talk to Him about those times: what happened?
  - Repent where you didn't yield to Him.
  - Reflect to consider whether there is a recurring pattern. If there is, ask the Holy Spirit to reveal the root cause (for example: you may be reacting to fear, selfishness or holding onto the emotional reaction to things).
  - Ask the Holy Spirit to take those inhibitors away. Consciously picture yourself handing those things to Him. Lay them at the foot of the cross and in your minds eye, allow Jesus to pick them up.
  - Ask for a refill of guidance and strength tomorrow.
  - Review how well you did at the end of each day.
  - If you feel low in motivation towards this, go back to the steps in strand 6 - spiritual growth.

3.
Praise
	▪ Through thanks:
	  - Thank God for His glory and what He is enabling through you.
	  - Think about and praise Him for the special favour He is bestowing.
	  - Declare His power and ongoing authority over the situation.
	  - Go back to the loops in strand 3 - worship.
	
	▪ Through testimony:
	  - Update your story. Consider everything God is doing through you. Think about how He is moulding and using you. Think about where you came from. Think about the differences. Identify the specific things only God could do.
	  - Consider how you would explain this to people if you got the chance. If it helps, write it down.
	  - Ask the Holy Spirit to open up and nudge you into the right opportunities to then share this testimony.
	
	▪ Through yielding your whole life.
	  - Praise Him through your life. Make the commitment that your life is not your own. Tell God how you want to exult Him in everything. Ask Him for purity to become your beacon. Actively seek the holiness that yielding everything brings.
	  - Offer Him your life and as you do, ask for His purifying blood to wash you clean. Still yourself in His presence. Ask the Holy Spirit to reveal any areas of your life that you may not yet have yielded. This may not happen immediately and will be a gradual unveiling – one thing at a time. When you read your bible, when you are doing daily life, when you spend time with Him, He will speak.

	- Ask the Holy Spirit to lead you in how to give those things up. Listen for His steer – He will ensure you hear His lead as long as you consciously tune in. - If appropriate, return to loop 2 of strand 6 - spiritual Growth. - Thank Him for the privilege.

The mirror

As we increasingly surrender, God pours Himself into us. This gives us the strength we need to let go of things that have often long-held us captive. As we submit these things to His Lordship, we remove any barrier between us and God. Surrender enables all of God to freely work through us as He wills, as we live in Christ's strength not our own.

Such is the umbilical bond this creates, we are cloaked in the glory of God. This indescribable covering brings with it a covering like no other. This is how we win. For in this place, we are left wanting for nothing else in life. And in the process, we never feel more alive!

This is the Zoe wheel of life. The power of Christ in us. As we develop the strand of surrender, it enables us to live in His strength, releasing an inner provision of contented wholeness, so we activate the promise of victory. This makes a difference to our lives through the ultimate fulfilment we are blessed with and the favour God pours into our lives.

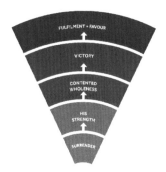

Reflections

Before we move on, my encouragement is to take some time to review the tapestry of your life in this strand. Pray with and consciously invite the Holy Spirit to bring His insight into your awareness.

Consider the current pattern
<ul><li>How frequently do you consciously surrender your thoughts, feelings and actions, bending them into submission of God's will?</li><li>As you surrender things, how conscious are you of His infilling strength?</li><li>How consistent is the level of contented wholeness in spirit, body and soul (mind-will and emotions) in your life? Consider different situations.</li><li>How much victory have you gained over the thoughts, emotions, actions that have held you back in the past?</li><li>Do you live in the circumstances of your life or take dominion over their challenging grip?</li><li>What wobbles you in all this?</li><li>What stabilises you in all this?</li></ul>

- What are the largest canyons where these things are missing?
- How often do you experience heavy emotions? For example: feeling offended, self-pity, restlessness, addiction of some kind, jealousy.
- Conversely, how often do you experience lightness, freedom and a sense of liberation?

Consider what you need to grow

- Reflect on promise 7 from part 1. Of the examples showing what His sovereignty brings, what else do you need to develop?
- How would this help your life, others or the world?

Consider how to develop further

- Do you stop to prepare before surrendering or do you just wade in? Are you clear on why it's worth it? Have you protected yourself in the prayers, the word and armour of God? Have you considered the practicalities and support of others? Have you consciously operated in the power of the Holy Spirit instead of your own might?
- Do you purposefully honour God by being obedient in the small nudges as well as the big ones? Do you stop to notice the impact your yielding makes? Do you consciously stop to review how frequently you are obedient? How far has your level of surrender stretched you? Has your surrender cost you?
- How frequently do you praise God for the strength He brings you to let things go? Does this flow into spontaneous worship? Are you clear about what He has done? How often do you share this testimony with others?

As you reflect, spend some time praying about what you discover. Allow this to organically merge into a conversation with your Father. Allow time for silence and consciously allow the Holy Spirit to flow. Is there anything else He says?

Stay connected, then review the suggested loops of activity you can take to help you grow in this area. Add any other activities that would work for you. Prayerfully consider these and then create a plan.

- What will you do, when and how?

- Visualise the impact

- Now get practising!

Recap

So far, we have practically explored how to live in all of Christ by considering:

- How to release His presence and activate our spiritual intimacy through the first strand of increased connection.
- How to release His significance and activate our renewed identity through the second strand of deepening relationship.
- How to release His perspective and activate our ability to clearly hear God, through the third strand of whole-hearted worship.

- How to release His nature and activate our accelerated ability to change.
- How to release His empowerment and activate our heightened ability.
- How to release His sovereignty and activate our supernatural might.
- How to release His strength and activate our victory.

It is surrender that enables us to live life to the full. As we fully yield our whole lives, we gladly exchange more of ourselves for more of God. Our delight to let go is enabled by the strength He pours through us. This umbilical union bring us the sweetest contented wholeness and this fulfilment becomes our victory. Our obedience is a magnet for God's favour, as His overwhelming blessings are lavished upon us.

This becomes our way of living – and is the final key strand that enables the Zoe life.

Part three

The impact of the Zoe life

'You are the light of [Christ to] *the world. A city set on a hill cannot be hidden, nor does anyone light a lamp and put it under a basket, but on a lampstand, and it gives light to all who are in the house. Let your light shine before men in such a way that they may see your good deeds and moral excellence, and* [recognize and honour and] *glorify your Father who is in heaven.'*
Matthew 5:14-16 AMP

19

The reality of Zoe life

'In Him was life [and the power to bestow life], and the life was the Light of men.'

John 1:4 AMP

At the start of this book, if I had told you that you could have the best day of your life - every day - would you have believed it? The truth is, that when we learn to lead the Zoe life, that's exactly what our reality can become. When we intentionality engage with each of the seven strands, God overwhelms us with His support to ensure this. The aspects of Jesus within us bring the provision we need to release the promise of His word. From this place flows abundance. Abundance in:

1. The constant refilling of the Holy Spirit within us. In His presence we receive peace that abides. The intimacy of this leaves us experiencing love beyond measure, so we operate from knowing we are protected. When habits, busyness and emotion try to overwhelm us, it is this covering that draws us closely back to the giver of life.

2. The depths of a relationship with God that surpasses anything known to man. In the significance of who He is - and who we are in Him, we build inner authority that is unshakeable. The result of this renewed identity gives us an authentic gravitas that carries the presence of God and makes impact. When we wrestle with feeling 'less than', it is this conviction that gives us the courage we need.

3. A heart that overflows in adoration, gratitude and worship. With eyes lifted to the throne room, God's perspective floods within to fill us with joy. This ascended lens clears the way for us to hear God. We receive His inspired revelation, which enables us to make wise choices. When we strive to figure things out, getting self-absorbed or lost in the process, it is this clearance that enables us to find our way back to the stability of truth.

4. A meaningful purpose as we whole-heartedly serve. His nature within propels us towards the desire to pursue our destiny. Then He motivates the conscious choice to be changed into who we need to be to fulfil it. The Holy Spirit uses this uncompromising focus to accelerate our change, so the fruits of the spirit gradually replace our old faulty ways. This enables us to positively change outcomes by behaving in the most appropriate way. When our hot buttons trigger our old unhelpful ways, it is this maturity that re-aligns our responses to who we really are.

5. Partnership that enables us to be led by the Spirit. Working in unity, His empowerment is released which replaces grinding effort with natural flow. This brings us a confidence that rests on His ability, not our own. As God multiplies what we could ever achieve without His anointing, we experience a heightened ability, which increases our effectiveness and enhances our credibility. When we ache to be more, it is this uplift that draws out more than we ever dreamed we had in us.

6. Spiritual growth that develops the hidden depths of our potential. The maturing of our understanding, our character and the development of spiritual gifts creates a channel for His sovereign will to be released. Witnessing His supreme power deepens our faith and increases our expectations for more of God. The combination of our character, spiritual gifts and expectation releases yet more of His supernatural might, so we actively command and receive dominion. When we long for more of God, it is this power that resets all parameters. As we say in Yorkshire – when God's in the house, all bets are off!

7. Surrender that enables us to live life to the full. As we fully yield our whole lives, we gladly exchange more of ourselves for more of God. Our delight to let go is enabled by the strength He pours through us. This umbilical union brings us the sweetest contented wholeness and this fulfilment becomes our victory. Our obedience is a magnet for God's favour. When we want to see change, break-through or deliverance, it is this blessing that sets us free.

Adopting the Zoe wheel of life enables it.

In all situations, with all people, at all times, we can be equipped to handle anything, become anything, achieve anything and receive anything. This is the Zoe way of life.

The application

As we engage in these activities, the Holy Spirit will take us through the development of each strand in different ways, sequences and durations. Every one of our journeys will be different and the learning in each is never done. It is a living, ongoing creation. Each strand will always complement the next, so, as each develops more dimension, the additional texture will actually enhance the rest.

As an example, the more I partner with the Holy Spirit, the more I get to experience God's incredible ways, so the more I have in my heart to worship. The more I worship, the closer I want to remain, so, the more I plug into that daily connection.

But it is not until all the strands have developed the density required that we will start to see the full picture of our intended life's tapestry emerging. This is when we learn to fluidly move between all the different parts of the Zoe wheel. The more we invest in this, the closer we are to God's intended plan for our lives.

As we mature, the conscious activities we've followed start to move from a process we engage with, to a natural automatic way of being. Gradually we move from knowing what to do, to just being it. As this happens, we become fluid, intuitively moving gracefully between the different parts on the Zoe wheel of life.

To illustrate this, consider the three examples below:

1. You're in a situation where sometime fairly soon you need to make a critical decision. This isn't a moral dilemma - it is a very

practical one. However, you're conscious that the decision you make may have lasting consequences. You previously sensed God's advice about the first step, which you're just about to take. But you're already second guessing what may happen thereafter, wanting to be prepared. Now the complexity is causing you to doubt whether this first step is indeed the right one. Having prayed, done your research and considered all the options, you still feel no clearer about what to do. The more you think about it, the more unclear the right way forward seems to be. In some respects, its impossible to know what is right, as you try and project ahead to how different scenarios may or may not play out. Lost inside your own private world, your thoughts have moved from helpful considerations, to energy sapping and increasingly burdensome. You become conscious you feel heavy.

With this realisation, you know you need to reconnect with the Holy Spirit and tune in to His lead - but with all these thoughts, it seems difficult to peel yourself away from your own desire to reach a conclusion. Knowing you will only carry on going around in circles, you force yourself to focus on Jesus and start to talk with Him. In the kindest way, you sense the Holy Spirit's message – that you are holding onto your own idea of how things could pan out, instead of trusting what that is to Him. He helps you see this is why you've been thinking of different scenarios – not because you really need to know what to do this very day – but because you are trying to engineer the outcome you most desire. You know He's asking you to let go of this and to follow Him one step at a time. You're reminded that He will make your path straight and His omniscience is perfect. This truth enables you to let go of your grasp and as you do, a lightness returns. The Holy Spirit cloaks you in His presence. Where moments earlier you felt heavy and oppressed, you now feel joyous and at peace. Where before you were anxious, now you find yourself singing with tranquillity.

The decision is still not made, but you are filled with faith that in perfect timing, it will be revealed. It will be revealed because your focus is no longer locked internally – it's locked into Him. This frees you and you celebrate how God's stretched you to achieve this. Suddenly the outcome and the decision that once felt all-encompassing now feels undaunting. You know God knows the plan – and that's good enough for you. Filled with a renewed sense of perspective, your awareness of God's protection returns. You know you're His child and that He has your best interests at heart. A few days later, a knowing sense seems to come from no-where. With it falls a sureness and a peace. You know God has spoken and without any striving, the next step falls perfectly into place. Who knows what the one after that will be? You are content to just wait and see.

Can you recognise the strands of connection, relationship, worship, surrender, spiritual growth and partnership working together?

Take another common scenario:

2. You've hit a brick wall in a relationship with someone you work with. Both passionate about what you are doing, different views on how to make progress are increasingly apparent. After what seems like an age, things are deteriorating and conflict seems inevitable. You know you need a break-through, but all you can feel is increasing agitation and frustration. Recognising this, you pray for patience, kindness and self-control. These fruits of the spirit seem to be wrestling with your natural desire to entertain how you feel. You talk to God about how strong these reactions seem to be. You feel justified; some harsh words have been said to you. These feel unfair as all you want to do is make a difference. As you share this with God, you feel His presence drawing you close. You still yourself for a moment and take a deep breath. You know you need to speak to the person who you've been at logger-heads with. Speaking a simple prayer, in conversation with God, you sense His whisper. In kindness not

condemnation, your spirit becomes convicted, as you realise you have been holding onto the need to blame this person for something. For a moment, those old emotions of feeling like its justified return - after all that's happened, you feel you're entitled to point the finger. But in His grace, the Holy Spirit reminds you that vengeance belongs to the Lord. This penetrates your soul and you spontaneously ask Him for forgiveness. With it comes a lightness and joy as you are freed from the grip of a toxic internal feeling of anger and hurt. As the nature of Jesus's love fills your heart, you realise you have been looking for an excuse to hide behind. This work is so important and after you pray, you decide the best course of action is an honest face to face conversation. When the conversation comes, you ask for the Holy Spirit's guidance. His influence in your heart and on your tongue enables you to speak clearly without aggression or blame. His presence seems to shift the atmosphere and a calmness spreads. A constructive conversation is enabled, which ultimately leaves you with a contentment that progress was made. You're filled with a glow. The glow is God.

Can you recognise the strands of connection, partnership, spiritual growth and purposeful service working together in harmony?

Finally, reflect on this last example:

3. You're nervous. You've been asked to do something that seems perfectly acceptable on paper. The only problem is that deep within, you know it is not what God wants you to do. With others putting pressure on you, the temptation to go with it seems huge. You fast, pray and listen closely. The knowing sense does not budge, but how can you take a stand, knowing everyone else will disagree? You feel so isolated and more-than a little intimidated, so praying for courage, you ask God for the strength to see it through. The time comes for you to make your case and whilst no-one else shares your view, amazingly, you don't feel alone. You know God is with you. As you sense His reassurance,

your countenance shifts – you're His child, you're an heir; you have authority. In a humble yet assertive way, you share your view, landing it in a dignified manner. When the inevitable disagreements come, your composure remains, enabling you to speak with conviction and boldness.

Can you recognise the strands of relationship, partnership, surrender and connection working together in harmony?

What enables this type of quick, natural call down is regular exercise of all the strands. If only one strand is developed, our spiritual muscle will be weaker in the other areas. Each is a critical strategy for warfare.

As you grow and become more of who God intends you to be, this will rub off on everything and everyone around you. Think about when you have been to the beach and walked barefoot in the sand. Afterwards, the sand clings to anything it touches. It seems to get everywhere. Wherever you go, little particles will be left behind and weeks after, you will still find little traces. It's so hard to shake off and it gets into those really hard to reach places. Such is our effect, when we have walked closely hand-in-hand with the Holy Spirit. Long after you have disappeared, a little trace of heaven will still be left behind, often in places you are not even aware of.

20

This is God's 'more'

'God's not finished. He's waiting around to be gracious to you. He's gathering strength to show mercy to you. God takes the time to do everything right—everything. Those who wait around for him are the lucky ones.'

Isaiah 30:18 MSG

God is the artisan who, in you, has designed a unique piece. He commissioned the tapestry of your life and He can enable you to become it.

When we learn to lean into God, we receive a power that is far greater and deeper than anything we can create in ourselves. As we do, everything around us shifts. Whilst our engagement will enable us to receive this blessing, it is not us that creates it. It is God's grace that does. **It is not by what we 'do', it is by what we make ourselves open to receive that creates this opportunity.** As God's anointing falls on, in and through us, we experience the blessing of His promises flowing in abundance. This affects how we see God, ourselves and others in the world around us. It then influences how we interact with God, with ourselves and with others. As God changes us, we become different. This is the difference that needs to shine.

I once had a vision that showed a mountain with a huge blazing bonfire on its top. Fire was raging from it like a beacon in the darkness. Then, as the image widened to take in a more panoramic view, it became clear that beacons were being lit on every mountain top around it. In fact, as far as the eye could see, beacon after beacon began to rage brightly into the sky. Each was an encouragement to the next. Across continents and across the globe, these beacons were burning with furious power. They brought hope to the people in the plains below - a light in their darkness. They brought warmth to the wintry inverted coldness of the valley bottom. They brought strength to the isolated struggle to survive.

'The people who were sitting (living) in (spiritual) darkness have seen a great light, and for those who were sitting (living) in the land and shadow of (spiritual and moral) death, upon them a light has dawned.'
Matt 4:16 AMP

We are to be these beacons in the world. It is our light that needs to burn so brightly. We illuminate a route to a different future. We magnetically draw people to the promise that comes from this light. The promise of God. It is the Zoe life that enables us to do this. The strands we weave into our lives are what release God's power. This is God's 'more'.

'But indeed for this purpose I have raised you up, that I may show My power in you, and that My name may be declared in all the earth'.
Exodus 9:16 NIV

Whilst we benefit greatly, the more of the Zoe life we experience, the more we realise the fundamental purpose of it is not actually about us at all. It's about what God can do through us.

None of us lives for himself [for his own benefit, but for the Lord], and none of us dies for himself [but for the Lord]. If we live, we live for the Lord, and if we die, we die for the Lord. So then, whether we live or die, we are the Lord's.
Romans 14:7-8 AMP

The 'more' of connection – love and protection

'The church is Christ's body, in which He speaks and acts, by which He fills everything with his presence.'
Ephesians 1:23 MSG

Connection immediately takes us from a reliance on our own limitations. When we allow ourselves to be vulnerable in this way, we undo the lock to enable true intimacy with God. This humility then starts to influence how we interact with other people. As God softens our hearts, the walls of self-defence start to fall in our other relationships too. We start to let people in. Not on a friendly 'saying the right thing' level, but on a deep, 'stuff that's really going on' level. We start to become more 'present' when we are with people.

Have you ever arrived at church after a stressful morning, a few choice words and a raging headache as a result? Only to immediately make a chameleon-like change the minute you set foot through the threshold of the building? Unless we instantly press reset, this change will be what I call our 'Sunday face' - the veneer of what we should say and do. It is our mask. When it is on, it blocks genuine, authentic connection with anyone else. Conversation will never get below the superficial level of polite exchange.

This is not the connection that Jesus showed us. He embraced the down and outs, the dodgy dealers and the disciples who were from all walks of life. When Jesus connected, he brought all of who he was. He was real. He came up close and personal. He laid hands on those who others wouldn't go near. He embraced people who had been shunned by society. He did personal life with the waifs and strays. There was no blockage, wall or distance in His connection with others. As a result, people were magnetically drawn to Him.

How often do you find yourself under the same family-roof, with barely a snippet of deeper conversation beyond your day-to-day transactional exchanges: 'What do you want for tea?' 'Are you home on Friday night as I have a tennis match?' 'How's it gone today? – 'Oh it was fine'. The danger is that the longer we leave it to truly connect, the harder it can sometimes feel to get beneath the surface. It's the same in our relationship with God.

As we start to learn to connect every day, this becomes easier and easier to do. As we lower the walls of closed off self-sufficiency, the intimacy in all our relationships can evolve into a nurturing, inviting, safe-haven. The more we let down our barriers, the more others will do the same. We start to walk the openness that Jesus showed us was so important.

'Let mutual love continue. Do not neglect to show hospitality to strangers for by doing that some have entertained angels without knowing it.'

Hebrews 13:1 NIV

When we are open enough to reach out and connect with others, we bring more encouragement than we can know. We effectively say, 'I see you. You matter.' As we build the courage to reveal our own vulnerabilities with others, just as it creates intimacy with God, it creates intimacy with them. We are effectively saying, 'I am putting my trust in you'. We are showing them that we honour them. Believe me, some people have never known this honour. For some, all their lives they have heard anger, threat or dismissal. They have been told they are not good enough, not worthy enough, not talented enough or not special enough. As we connect in this way, we effectively say 'you are worth it'. And when people then respond by lowering their own walls of self-sufficiency, revealing their own vulnerabilities, there is no greater privilege. It is then that God's love can flow.

The 'more' of relationship – gravitas and impact

'Blessed [with spiritual security] is the man who believes and trusts in and relies on the LORD, And whose hope and confident expectation is the LORD'.

Jeremiah 17:7 AMP

Intimacy makes us hunger for a deeper relationship; to get to know and be with someone more and more. When we realise we are at one with the divine order of things, it's no longer about us being enough. It's about who God is in us. This becomes the marker of who we are.

As we become clearer and more confident of who we really are in Him, we start to become more and more authentic with God, with ourselves and with other people.

Have you ever met someone you were just drawn to and, for some reason, you just felt able to speak openly with? These are the earthy, grounded people, who seem to have nothing to prove and accept you as you are. That's because they know who they are. People know the real deal! And if it's false, it never fools anyone. Wearing our 'outside the house mask', saying the right Christian things, trying to portray false happiness - none of it shines a light. People either think we are weird, or see the same old things in our lives as in their own world.

We need to infect an atmosphere without saying a word! And that's impossible, unless we are genuine. If we are not fully rooted in our identity and at one in our own skin, we can just come across as false. We don't have to be perfect. But we do have to be real. Beth Moore once said: *'People are not looking for you to have it together all the time. They are looking at what happens to you when you don't.'*

When the barometer is reset from how much we are, to how much God is in and through us, it brings a total shift in our perspective and with it, our identity. We know we are adopted as the sons of God. (Rom 8:15-16) When this finally rests deep in our soul, we realise our true self-worth. It is only when this happens that so many insecurity gremlins finally lose their grip. It is not about how successful we are. It is not about how much money we earn. It is not about how the world values us. It is about who we are in God. This is the only anchor that will ever truly take us to our real identity.

As this happens, we start to lose our fear of man, the need to please and the self-consciousness that makes us doubt ourselves. When we know who we are, we become strong enough to just be who we are. When we truly know how God sees us, what other people think seems so unimportant. When we really feel God's love, we start to love ourselves.

It doesn't end with how we start to see ourselves. When we come from this place of inner strength, how we approach other people changes too. It is amazing how different our behaviour becomes when we have nothing to prove. We lose our defensive edge, our 'right' to have our say and our knee-jerk reactions to personal insult. It becomes far less important to 'win' and 'not look foolish'. If we are misunderstood, judged by others or harshly criticised, we will remain the same. Our love for others is totally unaltered. Where before we may have been offended or hurt, it becomes easier to speak through the eyes of love and compassion. All the time. We start to be able to reach people where before, our own behaviours would have dismissed, discredited or disregarded them. When we experience God's love, we see love where before we may have judged, seen frustration or dislike. As we start to walk in this attitude, it will change everything we see around us. Instead of alienating people, we will draw them to us. This is when we are most able to love our neighbour as ourselves. (Matt 22:36-40)

The 'more' of worship – revelation and wise choices

'And let the beauty of the LORD our God be upon us, And establish the work of our hands for us; Yes, establish the work of our hands'.
Psalm 90:17 NKJV

One of the enemy's most successful techniques is to keep us focussed on ourselves. Worry, busyness, conflict can soon become the norm we just live with.

If you imagine a hot air balloon, the Holy Spirit wants to blow His warming breath into the canvas of our lives, to fill us with His energy and give us flight. But the heavy sand bags carrying our worldly focus hold us down. Whilst they are attached to the basket, we cannot get lift-off, but, as we start to worship, one by one, those weighty constraints can be cut away. As this happens, the balloon starts to rise. All those tensions fall to the ground. We are lighter. We are freer. As we gain flight, this lightness effortlessly lifts us beyond the immediacy of what's going on around us. We are free to raise our eyes above, without the weight of the world. As the balloon gracefully rises to the heavens, we start to see things from an elevated perspective. The song of gratitude in our hearts causes us to worship.

'Blessed are the pure in heart, for they will see God.'
Matthew 5:8 NIV

As this happens, we are connected to God. God is love. We see love. We feel it. We become it. Have you ever experienced a wonderful time of worship, when afterwards, you just want to hug everyone else around you? That's the love God has poured into you, pouring out to others. **Pure love brings spiritual sight.**

When we are lifted in the hot air balloon, beyond the limitations of what we understand through human eyes, we actually become aware of what heaven needs us to know. It's amazing how different our response will be to our circumstances with this perspective. Instead of fearing, we say 'bring it on'; instead of panicking we rest; instead of rushing headlong into something we may regret, with temperance, we wait.

As we learn to get our eyes off ourselves and onto God, we exhibit a steadfast approach to life. We no longer get easily distracted, side-lined or lost. When we stop running around in circles with our own lives, it gives us the capacity to tune into greater things of the Kingdom. That may relate to something God wants to show us. It may also relate to what other people are going through. When it's not all about us, there's room for it to also be about others and other things. This is when God may speak to us to give insight, a message or request for action. **Pure love brings spiritual hearing.** This always enables the wisest choices.

As we hear more through our spiritual ears, our level of discernment usually increases with it. It's this ability to tune into things, often unseen, that in turn, also helps us to hear people in a different way too.

Some people are naturally more empathetic than others, but when we are living this way, our radar changes. Our patience changes. Our ability to actually stop and give people the respect of actually being properly listened to can be radically different. This is one of the most powerful ways we can represent Jesus in this world: To give people the time to actually be heard. When people feel known, valued and accepted, it literally melts hardened, hurt and distant hearts.

All of this moves us into servanthood. We feel compelled to be God's hands and feet. Our life shifts from being about ourselves, to being about what God wants through us. Jesus showed the Father. We are to show Jesus. A life of worship creates the channel for God to reveal His deepest secrets. When we use this to bless others, we become His extended arm in the world around us.

The 'more' of purposeful service – fruits of the spirit

'I am convinced and confident of this very thing, that He who has begun a good work in you will [continue to] perfect and complete it until the day of Christ Jesus [the time of His return]'.
Philippians 1:6 AMP

Jesus is our King. But He also showed us how to live with a servant's heart. When we are open to hearing from God and hungry to be his hands and feet, He will provide an outlet for that. Whether it is by being a stay-at-home parent, or through running a worldwide ministry; God uses willing vessels. This wholehearted service brings us purpose.

The purpose God brings us is like a diamond on the horizon. We know it's unique, it sparkles with many different colours, it is expensive and will be costly. It may look out of reach and beyond anything we could create, but we are so drawn to its beauty against the stark landscape, that we have to pursue it with everything we have.

The nearer we move towards this, the more we see the things in ourselves that may hold us back from reaching it. This is when the Holy Spirit reveals where our behaviour is carnally driven. We see more and more of what we think and do that is not befitting of where we are heading - of who we are becoming. This brings a reason to want to change and the motivation it takes to make those changes. We seek change. It's no longer about what 'we should and shouldn't do as Christians. We want to be moulded.

We can all be sweetness itself when we want to be. When life is good; when we are enjoying ourselves with who we are with; when we are somewhere people may be watching us; when we put on the right face publicly, but say something else behind closed doors.

I often say to leaders that their people are watching their every move. Their mood, their language, who they stop and speak to, what time they leave the workplace, what they eat. You name it; it's all being logged. They are in a position of prominence. They stand out, but they often underestimate their impact. The same can be said for Christians. People will watch to see if our words and actions match up.

We cannot possibly keep up our best through willpower or a best intention to be 'nice'. At some point, there will always be things that trigger the wrong reaction. Our purpose gives us a motive to want to change. It becomes why we actively pursue developing the character of God. The character of God gives us the right reaction.

As we live a Spirit-led life, the changes we need to make no longer come from willpower or our best intentions. Changes are released by the power of God in us. As this happens, the fruit of the spirit starts to manifest in our lives. We start to engage with people in a very different way. When we see, hear and respond to people through the filter of the fruit of the spirit, the whole dynamic will change. Frustration turns to patience; compulsiveness to say or 'do' turns to self-control; giving up and quitting on someone turns to loyalty and faithfulness; offense turns to grace and gentleness; anger turns to love; disappointment and loss will turn into joy; turmoil will turn into rest and peace; hurt, dents to our pride and striking back will turn to forgiveness and kindness; self-indulgence will turn to temperate goodness.

'When we were controlled by our old nature, sinful desires were at work within us, and the law aroused these evil desires that produced a harvest of sinful deeds, resulting in death. But now we have been released from the law, for we died to it and are no longer captive to its power. Now we can serve God, not in the old way of obeying the letter of the law, but in the new way of living in the Spirit.'
Romans 7:5-6 NLT

As these changes start to become what people experience in us, they will notice something different. They will be attracted to the light of Jesus in us like a moth to a flame. Our lives will start to reveal Christ, regardless of how we are being squeezed, for our mind-set has shifted. We are no longer here for ourselves.

We don't make disciples through 'telling'. We make them by 'being'. By being Jesus in today's world.
This is our warfare. As we learn to walk in the opposite spirit to the one the enemy tries to trap us into, we are bending those forces into submission. We start to rule the circumstances around us. Not by changing them but by changing our reaction to them. Where we may have come into conflict before, we influence positively. Where we may have run scared before, we assertively walk forwards. Where we may have 'reacted' before, we are ushered into heaven's response.

When people see something authentic in how we live our lives, its attractive. They want it too. With Spirit-led abilities such as connection, building relationships, clearly hearing God and our desire to be His hands and feet, we are filled with a capacity to come alongside in just the way that Jesus did. He transforms our lives as we start to be equipped to help others do the same. When this happens, we are like Teflon to the enemy, and as he realises nothing will stick to us, he loses his grip on our soul.

The 'more' of partnership – effectiveness and credibility

'The Spirit of the Lord is on me, because he has anointed me   to proclaim good news to the poor. He has sent me to proclaim freedom for the prisoners   and recovery of sight for the blind, to set the oppressed free, to proclaim the year of the Lord's favour.'
Luke 4:18-19 NIV

The only way we maintain change is when we submit to the Holy Spirit's governance. We increasingly notice how we fail so frequently without Him. The things that we previously never really noticed about ourselves become more of a concern. We are led into pursuing holiness. Issues of the flesh take on second priority as we are compelled to serve God's commission in our lives. The enormity of it may scare us. In so doing, it makes us even more humbled by our dependency on God to achieve it. It is this that propels us ever more to partner with the God who is fuelling it all. As we learn to let go and let God steer us, we start to access the power only God can release in us. When we line up with what God is wanting of us, God's empowerment is released. As we bring everything we can, God brings everything He is. The result is that we experience heightened ability. What we touch can flow with abundance and favour.

We are so acutely aware that this is not us; it is God through us. This seems to ignite an even deeper passion for what God can do. We watch with amazement as we see what God is enabling. This heightened ability is not given for our own indulgent ego - it is always for the benefit of others. Interestingly, if we don't recognise God's role, in His grace, this heightened ability may still run for a period. But, eventually, something will happen that redirects us to the author of the greatness we are experiencing.

'The Spirit of the Lord God is upon me, because the Lord has anointed me to preach good tidings to the poor: He has sent me to heal the broken hearted, To proclaim liberty to the captives, And the opening of the prison to those who are bound.'
                                                      Isaiah 61:1 NKJV

When we recognise God's mighty hand, intuitively, we want to reach out to others around us, to bring them encouragement too. We are seeing the manifest power of God with our own eyes. We are stirred. And we cannot help but talk about it with others too. We are so compelled by the wonder of what God is doing through us, that we long for others to catch hold of this possibility too. This is when our courage can be boosted to boiling point. Where before we may have worried about offending others, concerned about what they would think of us, or secretive about our walk of faith, now we want to shout it from the rooftops. At first, with overenthusiasm, we can be spectacularly insensitive about how we do this. But as we mature, we learn how to couple the courage with the calm guidance of the Holy Spirit's steer, to land the clarion call as God intends.

The bible says we are to make disciples of the nations. (Matt 28:19-20) This isn't the job of the pastor/minister/leader. We are the ones who need to do what Jesus and his disciples did - to go into the world. Yet many of us don't truly take accountability for this. More than leading someone to salvation, it's coming alongside, mentoring and actively supporting the development of others in their spiritual perspectives, thinking and behaviour. It's more than just getting people over the line. It's about proactively bringing Kingdom principles down to earth; living the Kingdom way ourselves. And, in so doing, encouraging others to come up higher too. Not in a judgmental way - in an edifying, encouraging way.

We know what it is like to see the Holy hand of God and to feel so far from its standard. But we also know that God accepted us just the way we were. We know that at conversion we were made new; but that we need to walk through a process to become the fullness of that new person. (2 Cor 5:17)

When we partner with the Holy Spirit, we start to see others through that same lens. This is not about feeling spiritually elite. In fact, it is the opposite of that. Instead of seeing who others are now, we see how God sees them; who they already are to God. This takes away our focus from the sin in their lives. It means we can see them for who they can become. Instead of condemning who they are now, we love them into who God made them to actually be.

We can accept, love, encourage, build up and strengthen people around us, with an overflow of God's influence. God will supercharge our level of faithfulness, compassion and mentoring capability if we allow Him to.

As this happens, we pour more and more of ourselves into helping others to walk the walk we have taken. Whenever we see a life less lived, we ache for what's missing; the possibility of what God could do within that life. So, we pursue conversation, opportunity and friendship to come alongside from a genuine place of support.

One of the key things my business partner and I often find ourselves saying to senior executives is: 'No-one else is coming'. Often wrestling with ambiguity, complexity and huge change, even senior leaders sometimes seem to want someone to come rescue them. That person never comes. Likewise, we often see things in our world that need heaven's influence. So, we may criticise, we may pray, we may endure, when what we need to do is step up. This is our accountability.

To have voice, we need credibility. Heightened ability can bring this. But to have voice, we also need to strategically look for the opportunities to use the authority we have been given. It's not about 'fitting in'. But it is about coming alongside in a way that carries Kingdom culture. Sometimes it may mean going against the tide, sometimes it may mean saying the unsaid, sometimes it may simply mean being prepared to serve. Either way, it takes boldness and a preparedness to step into the space. We won't see the limitless heightened ability available unless we make ourselves ready for this. So, a fundamental prerequisite is that we all take the accountability we each need to take. What would happen in the world if every Christian, everywhere, intentionally made this reach?

The 'more' of spiritual growth – supremacy and dominion

'I use God's mighty weapons, not those made by men, to knock down the devil's strongholds.'

When we step up, God shows up through us. As we get ever more tuned into His lead, we will flow into the anointing He wants to bestow on, in and through us. Our natural and supernatural gifts are deployed wherever we are, whether it is in a secular or spiritual environment. The by-product of this is that the world sees different outcomes. They see what we would be unable to achieve in and of ourselves. When the world sees the outcome of God's sovereignty, by association, this elevates our credibility in the eyes of the world; it promotes us into the position of influencing those around us.

Witnessing the hand of God in this way makes us yearn for more. The more we see, the more we realise there is to see. This hunger drives us into the pursuit of truth and experience like never before. This is God preparing us for the fullness of the supernatural power He can release. He is getting us ready for what He will do. This growth is about the understanding we will need, the faith we will need, the character we will need and it is about the spiritual resilience we will need. He is crafting the heart of a warrior. When we burn inside for this stretch, spiritual growth is accelerated within.

As this happens, our sense of might increases. In the knowledge it all comes from God, we step into a *knowing* of what we carry. The more success we get under our spiritual belts, the more God will lead us into being the charging warriors of ever more spiritually demanding situations. He will not allow more than we are ready for. However, He will constantly be stretching our spiritual comfort levels. This brings experience. It brings track record. It brings the reality of God's faithfulness to the forefront of our awareness. It makes us dig ever deeper into Him.

As we mature, we become a role model for others who are younger in their spiritual maturity. We use our history, our own mistakes and what God has taught us, to inspire and help others to grow. We build up the faith of others and encourage their own pursuit to want more of God. In turn, we then see miracles in their growth, which encourages us all the more in return.

'Therefore I say to you, whatever things you ask when you pray, believe that you receive them, and you will have them.'
Mark 11:24 NKJV

All of this makes us increasingly bold. We have a testimony to share. We start to intentionally carry these messages into the arenas of life that previously would have seemed too dangerous. When we have seen such Godly might, we develop an acute awareness of the supremacy of His Kingdom. This gives us the ability to stand unwaveringly against the toughest opposition; be that from people, spiritual forces or circumstances. Whether overtly or covertly, we intentionally become proactive about sowing these seeds. Whether it is joining the local PTA to influence policy and decisions in our schools, or starting a charity to help underprivileged adolescents, our Godly ambitions start to infiltrate the world around us. We press in for God's 'more', we travail for anything less. Our hearts-cry beats ever-louder for His Kingdom come.

The 'more' of surrender – fulfilment and favour

'For whoever finds me finds life, And obtains favour from the LORD'.
Proverbs 8:35 NKJV

Once we experience the reality of supernatural power on earth, we are ruined forever. We bow in reverence to the Almighty Holy God. Our lives can never be the same. We want to give away to others, everything God has given to us. We yield all we are, which makes us untouchable to the enemy. This is when God has free reign through our spirit to make His impact in the world.

As our own lives showcase His power, we get our opening. But power must be controlled. Which is why God takes us to a place of total surrender before He will unleash His full might on, in and through us.

I remember many times in my earlier days where I would be so full of passion for God, that I would innocently but quite recklessly get very carried away in my enthusiasm, either through what I communicated or what I did. As we develop our obedience, the degree of our spiritual sensitivity will grow. Whereas before our passion may have caused us to rush in, now we calmly operate with a laser-like focus. Never too soon. Never too early. Our ability to hear the most-subtle of cues means that when we move, it is precisely how God needs us to. This means our impact with people will be far more effective. We will say or do just the right thing at just the right time. Whilst often this is in the natural, what we are really talking about is spiritual warfare. But spiritual warfare takes spiritual maturity. This maturity is about having power under control. When we develop it, we inherit the earth! (Matt 5:5)

'Now this is the confidence that we have in Him, that if we ask anything according to His will, He hears us. And if we know that He hears us, whatever we ask, we know that we have the petitions that we have asked of Him.'
1 John 5:14-17 NKJV

This is the favour awaiting us, when we surrender, obey and do it God's way. When this knowledge becomes our reality, our spiritual alertness is on a constant high. We see, sense and are spiritually led to the need all around us. So, we pursue those opportunities. This starts by praying fervent specific prayers of breakthrough. We seem to strut across the very war room of heaven itself, joining in the strategic assault of an enemy on the run.

'You have made them to be a Kingdom and priests to serve our God and they will reign on earth'.
Revelation 5:10 NIV

One of the hallmarks of God's favour is the anointing on those prayers. The more of God's unmerited grace and favour we see, the more we are drawn to ever more vigorous prayer. The more of God's power we see, the more audacious our requests become. God is bigger than we can possibly comprehend. He wants us to pray big prayers.

As we are elevated into Heaven's war room, our intercession takes on a different energy, potency and power. This is when our prayer moves from reactive requests. It moves to another level; a proactive and assertive pursuit to reclaim Kingdom territory. We press in, we burn for what we are led to pray for, we persevere and we get radically bold and ever more specific. We pray from a place of total expectancy. Our level of faith rises to unprecedented levels because we are praying with an unprecedented God. 1 Thessalonians 5:17 becomes a reality, not an aspiration. We pray without ceasing.

As this happens, heaven binds what must cease and loosens what must begin on earth. (Matt 18:18) We pull down strongholds and eliminate the enemy's influence. These warrior prayers precede our human involvement. Then we march.

We strategically and intentionally pioneer the change we want to see. Whether that's through the healthy atmosphere we create at the school tea morning, or through the promotion that makes us head of the organisation we want to influence. The sense of anointing in these moments often feels so tangible it's as if we know God is walking before us.

God elevates us into positions and spheres of influence for a reason. It is only God who can fix the brokenness of how our world works. We are His foot soldiers. When we are anchored in our God-given mandate of dominion, we can directly start to take control of the systems around us. For we will see what God sees. We will know what God directs. We will be enabled to carry that into being. The fire of God breathes life, hope and victory into all we touch, so we are able to start to change the very systems and culture we operate within. This creates followers; people who are magnetically drawn towards what 'the Kingdom way' enables. This creates legacy. It creates an open doorway from heaven to earth. It's when heaven's Kingdom actually comes to earth.

'For the LORD God is a sun and shield; The LORD bestows grace and favour and honour; No good thing will He withhold from those who walk uprightly.'
Psalm 84:11 AMP

Sometimes the fullness of all this can only be seen with the benefit of hindsight. The perspective we gain when we look back and see all the fingerprints of God stirs us yet again. And on our pursuit continues. Our pursuit of the favour God is waiting to release upon this world. This is God's 'more'.

Reflections

The ripple effect of God's 'more' shines a torch on the potential power of our lives. When we live the Zoe life, we change our world around us.

- Consider the impact your life currently has on the world around you. What else could God's 'more' achieve through you?
- Re-consider the reflections you had in part one and part two. Return to your plans. In the context of the difference your life could make, is there anything else you now want to include in your plan of action?
- What is the 'more' of God you now want to pursue?

21

As we close

'True wisdom and real power belong to God; from Him we learn how to live, and also what to live for'.
Job 12:13 MSG

Sometimes you need to step away and go back to something, to fully recognise the change that has taken place over time. Often, we evolve, grow and mature without quite recognising, valuing or updating our sense of who we have become. People can experience this when they leave a job for another, when they move house or when they encounter some form of crisis. Only on reflection or returning is there often the full realisation of how big the shift has been.

We recently spent Christmas where we used to live. On a trip down memory lane, our family returned for a short visit to the Northern Highlands of Scotland. This is the land where God first broke and re-built me. On my return, despite the time gap, I felt as if I knew every contour of the mountains surrounding me. In those hills, I spent countless hours in the presence of God searching, wrestling, enjoying, grieving and thanking Him. As I look back on my own life now, with the benefit of hindsight, I can see the golden weave of what Holy Spirit relentlessly purposed to do. I will always be learning, growing and changing - that's what makes this journey so exciting. But noticing the difference from then to now, during this recent trip, was overwhelming.

With every tree, rock and corner, memories of the secret times I shared with God came flooding back. The doubts, the losses, the yearning, the questions, the encouragement, the challenges, the victories; every thought filled my mind. As this happened, I seemed to re-live every emotion. Over and over, I kept whispering, 'how did you do it Lord? How did you manage to change me from that to this?' Not through ego, pride or self-adulation, for, if anything, I see more clearly than ever how far I have yet to go. But through reverence and gratitude, with a head bowed down in wonder about why a God so wondrous even chooses to do such a thing. I kept saying over and over, 'why did you do it, why did you stick with me'? The words in Psalm 8 seemed so poignant as I marvelled at God's fingerprints:

'What is man that You are mindful of him, And the son of [earthborn] man that You care for him? Yet You have made him a little lower than God, And You have crowned him with glory and honour. You made him to have dominion over the works of Your hands; You have put all things under his feet.'

Psalm 8:4-6 AMP

On Boxing Day morning I needed some private time with God and in the midst of gale force winds and a hail-filled sky, I found myself battling the elements on a storm-struck beach in Dornoch. It was such a metaphorical reminder of many of the times I had spent with Him in that wonderful but often desolately lonely place. At one point, the wind became so fierce, I hunkered down behind a rock on the beach to wait for the gale to abate. As I did, I immediately felt a relief from the elements and was mesmerised by the swirling of the clouds before me. As I looked out onto the horizon, a snowstorm arrived. It was as if I could see the very fingers of God stretching down from the sky, descending upon the slate grey sea and the mountains beyond. When I stepped back out onto the beach, it had turned completely white. In that moment, I sensed God answer my question; 'Why did you do it? How did you stick with me? 'Purity', came the response. 'Because I see you as whiter than snow. A spotless bride in white is emerging. You are mine for eternity.'

This is what it is all about. For all of us. Through God's grace we have been chosen. Through the blood of Jesus we are made righteous. And through the nurturing hands of the Holy Spirit, we are being shaped in readiness for who we are meant to become.

Looking back now, I wouldn't be able to bear living life the way I used to. So, whilst at times it has been tough; whilst on some occasions I have wanted to give up and give in to what seems easiest; whilst sometimes I just could not see the end or the purpose in things, I thank the Lord that in His mercy and grace, He didn't let me go.

God wants us to take Him at His word. The Holy Spirit living within us, enables us to receive every one of His promises. It is each promise that takes us into our precious Zoe life. The *alive* sort of life. An exceptional life of absolute fullness - the sort of life only God could imagine. It is God's intended plan and it is available to everyone.

God is right there with you now as you read these pages. Whether you walk with Him this way or not, He is willing you on to step into and embrace the most amazing, liberating, rewarding life possible.

I pray that in the pages of this book you may be inspired towards pursuing it. The Zoe wheel of life.

'It is finished'

...One year later, with key treatments complete, the cancer that once threatened life is now in remission. The physical impact will pass; my body will be restored; the curly locks will grow back again and I'm sure I will add a few pounds on the scales. But there's so much more than the healing that I walk away from this assignment with.

Thanks to the unceasing fervent prayers of so many, God's empowering grace covered me. Whilst at times it was physically tough, there's one thing I'll remember the most - and ironically, it's not the cancer. It's who God proved himself to be – through the trial, not just at the end of it.

I'm so thankful for that purpose. Through it I received the privilege of experiencing God's promises in vibrant abundance. Refined through the fire, I know His grace is sufficient in my weakness, I've experienced the joy of the Lord as my strength, I've received the peace that surpasses all understanding and not once did any promise return void.

With the frequent changes, critical crossroad decisions and periods of confusion along the way, living everything I believe was challenged to the very core. Through the process I dug deeper than I ever knew was possible. But God was true, as time and again He exchanged fear for faith, pain for protection and discouragement for determination. How was that possible?

By pouring all He is into me; His presence, His significance, His perspective, His nature, His empowerment, His sovereignty and His strength. This is what set me free - free from the crippling grip of the word we all know as cancer. Free to live the Zoe life He always intended.

Before this journey, I had always (very naively) thought that once cancer was gone, it was the happy end of the story. But as we've found along the way, with a disease of this nature, the medics speak about remission, not cure. Only once passed the ten-year mark, is the cancer considered to be gone. Ten years is a long time to be waiting for those words, particularly given the statistics on breast cancer re-occurrence or spread. I can understand how the fear from this could feel all consuming.

Whilst the main tumour has now gone, active individual cancer cells were found through-out the mastectomy tissue removed. Undetectable by scans, these were the unknown silent traces left. It was not the news we expected. What did that physical evidence mean? Could the disease already spread? Did it leave me feeling unsure? Had it rocked my spiritual faith? Questions that could not be avoided.

My beliefs have never been a blind faith or some psychologically induced, glass half-full optimism. I believe what I believe for a reason. I've lived it, known it and seen the tangible manifestation of its truth over and over again. Had this rocked my beliefs? Not one bit. God is God and I know Him, unchanging, everlasting.

But in the uncertainty of the not knowing, was this faith enough? - enough to stop the potential nagging worry, haunting doubts and precarious uncertainty? Pressing into these questions, a deeper treasure was revealed - the knowing realisation that I don't need to hear a Doctor say, 'it is gone', to live everyday with contentment, joy and a rested confident heart. The proximity of Jesus within and around me is my answer. He is who enables me to live everyday with an abandoned heart that's simply bursting with life – whatever.

Victory has nothing to do with being officially told I am cured and cancer free. It's all to do with how close I am to my King. The vibrant tranquillity of mind He fills me with every single day is more precious than any words from a Doctor. So, no waiting is needed for that formal 'cure' to be proclaimed; Zoe life doesn't start when we get to hear those words. My abundant Zoe life is now, in the beauty and dawning of every single day.

Despite the circumstances, pain and trials along the way, every day truly was the abundant Zoe life God gave me the hope of on New Years Day. Through-out it all, God was everything I'd ever dared to believe He was... and more besides... Every promise, every hope and every word He's ever said is true. In the immortal words of Jesus in John 19:30: 'it is finished'. This is the Zoe life.

'They will have no fear of bad news; their hearts are steadfast, trusting in the Lord. Their hearts are secure, they will have no fear; in the end they will look in triumph on their foes.'
Psalm 112:7-8 NIV

Coming soon

The promise

... and how to sustain it.